Supernatural
DREAMS *and* VISIONS

Supernatural
DREAMS and VISIONS

Bible Prophecy for the Future Revealed

by

Carmen Benson

with

FOREWORD

by

Dr. Ray Charles Jarman

PLAINFIELD, NEW JERSEY

Contents

Note—All Scripture references are from the Amplified Bible published by The Zondervan Publishing House (unless otherwise designated)

Foreword

by

Dr. Ray Charles Jarman

Carmen Benson has been my secretary for more than 20 years, and a dear and valued friend since 1945. She played an important role in my receiving the Lord Jesus Christ as personal Saviour after fifty-two years a modernist minister.

Several months before the new birth experience which so radically transformed my life, Carmen was the recipient of three very remarkable dreams. Not being a person given to dreams or visions, she was at a loss to know how to interpret them.

One thing was certain—the dreams had come from God. But what did they mean? What was the divine message hidden within them?

Carmen sought the explanation from books, and then from a dream-analyst. Both sources proved no more effective as dream-interpreters than were the soothsayers, astrologers, magicians and wise men of Biblical times.

Finally God Himself gave her the interpretation. As a result, she was instantly brought out of years of entanglement in metaphysics, Oriental religious philosophies, and esoteric and occult teachings. She was born again in Christ Jesus! Immediately the Holy Spirit began to open the scriptures to her, and to teach her the Word of God.

Always an earnest student, Carmen plunged into an intense and devoted study of the Bible. She delighted herself in the law of the Lord. Soon she was pointing out to me the false interpretations put upon the scriptures by the various mental science groups.

After my own eyes were opened, and I too had become a Bible-believing Christian, we co-authored a book, *The Grace and the*

Glory of God. It was published in 1968 and has since gone into numerous reprintings.

Because the Lord used dreams to reach and to teach her, Carmen took a particular interest in the dreams and visions recorded in the Bible. She was amazed to discover the importance God placed upon this means of communication with man. The revelations imparted through dreams and visions were astonishing!

Before long Carmen became aware that the Holy Spirit was directing her to make an exhaustive study of the subject. She began to write the material for *Supernatural Dreams and Visions.* As each section was completed, she read it to me for suggestions and criticism.

I was fascinated by the gripping narratives, and greatly inspired by every chapter. "This must be published!" I told her. "Everyone who reads it will be as thrilled as I am! I've learned a lot just listening to it. Now I want to study it more carefully with my Bible in hand."

Who among us does not wonder what the future holds? We know that God has disclosed "things to come" in His Word, especially in Daniel and Revelation. But because of the symbolism and mystery that enshrouds these books, most of us need help in understanding them.

Carmen's chapter on Daniel—"Secrets Hidden in Dreams"— and the one on Revelation telling "How It All Will End"—give a detailed and clear explanation that even the youngest Christian can comprehend. Yet the most mature saint will find new and rich treasures in these chapters.

As the final typing of the manuscript was being finished, God gave me a special confirmation regarding its publication . . .

It happened during a prayer meeting of Spirit-filled Christians. I had been thinking about Carmen's book and our ministry together through the printed word. Silently I inquired of the Lord, "Are my plans concerning circulation of her new book what You want me to do?"

At that moment a scientist stood to his feet and said, "God has given me a prophecy for one person in this room. I do not know who that person is, but this is the message:

'What you are doing is right, and you shall be blessed. The

one you are working with, I am blessing. And that one shall be a blessing to My people.' "

This was my answer! I knew the prophecy was for me. I wanted to shout out loud, "Thank You, Lord, thank You!" Here was definite word from God that His divine blessing was upon the book. I could hardly wait to tell Carmen!

And now both of us are waiting for you to read *Supernatural Dreams and Visions,* and to confirm for yourself God's promise that it will be a blessing to His people.

Introduction

If your telephone were to ring right now . . . and when you picked it up, the voice on the other end of the line said:

"This is God. I would like to come over and visit with you. May I?" . . . what would your answer be?

Perhaps you might reply with some kind of excuse. "I'm awfully sorry, dear God, but I already have other plans. Unfortunately, there are these things I just have to do. You know that I believe in You. I go to church, and I pray, and I give money for Your work. It isn't that I don't *want* to hear what You have to say. I wish I weren't so busy, but . . . well, can You come some other time?"

Suppose the voice of God continued to speak, reminding you that He has many things of great value to teach you—eternal truths to impart, exciting stories of past visits He has made that will instruct and help you in the present, and enlighten you about the future. Would you still turn Him down?

You may be thinking, "Of course not! I would be overjoyed if God would come to my house and sit down for a personal visit with me. I would put everything aside for an opportunity like that!"

Would you? . . .

God longs to call on you personally, to converse with you directly, to give you the rich privilege of learning more about Him. You don't even have to wait for Him to contact you on the phone. He has already provided a wonderful way in which to visit you. That way is through His Word.

Actually, the Bible tells us of seven ways in which God visits man:

1. by coming Himself
2. by sending Jesus Christ
3. by sending the Holy Spirit
4. by sending angels
5. by prophets
6. by dreams and visions
7. by His Word

In this book God is going to visit us through His Word, and tell us about other visits from Him through dreams and visions. And before He leaves, we are going to make a surprising discovery. We shall find that we have also been visited by the Lord Jesus Christ, by the Holy Spirit, and by angels and prophets as well! . . .

Someone who claimed to be a Christian once said to me, "I don't believe in dreams and visions."

My reply was quick and to the point. "Then you don't believe in the Bible, for it is full of them!"

From Genesis to Revelation God used this means of communicating with people. And what a fascinating way to communicate! The dreams and visions related in scripture teach us a great deal about how God works in the affairs of human beings. Not only do they make absorbing reading, but the scope of Bible teaching covered in a thorough study of them is astounding!

Those to whom these dreams and visions were given are most interesting people. You will enjoy becoming better acquainted with them as we take this method of delving into their private lives. Some of them are prominent Bible characters, others not so well-known. A few are kings, others servants. Some are prophets, and some just ordinary men—both good and bad. One is a woman.

Before we meet the first personality, we should define the word "dream" and the word "vision," and if possible clarify the distinction between them. This is difficult to do, even when we examine the root meanings of the Hebrew and Greek words used in the Biblical vocabulary. The border line between dream and vision is not easily determined.

Generally speaking, however, A DREAM IS A MENTAL PIC-

TURE WHICH COMES DURING SLEEP. It is made up of a series of images, thoughts, or emotions which seem real to the one who is dreaming. Dreams are believed to come from that part of the mind called the subconscious. On occasion they may be impressed upon the mind by a Superconsciousness, even by the Lord Himself.

A VISION CONSISTS OF SOMETHING SEEN OTHER- WISE THAN BY ORDINARY SIGHT. The person beholding it may be awake or asleep. Bible visions were directly revealed by God to a prophet or "seer" under varied circumstances, and for a particular purpose. The visionaries were men of action and out- standing intelligence; but not all of the dreamers could be so described.

Sometimes a vision is closely connected with a dream-state. God linked them together when He declared: "If there is a prophet among you, I the Lord make Myself known to him in a VISION, and speak to him in a DREAM" (Num. 12:6).

The inter-relationship between dreams and visions is similarly illustrated by this passage: "For God does reveal His will. He speaks not only once, but more than once, even though men do not regard it.

"One may hear God's voice in a DREAM, in a VISION of the night, when deep sleep falls on men, while slumbering upon the bed;

"Then He opens the ears of men, and seals their instruc- tion . . ." (Job 33:14-16).

How has the Lord made Himself known in visions, and *what has He spoken* in dreams? When He has opened the ears of men, *what kind of instruction* has He sealed upon their minds . . . ?

CHAPTER ONE

Beginning With A Spectacular

We first encounter the word "vision" in Genesis, the book of beginnings—and this opening vision is indeed a spectacular one.

The year is about 2000 B.C. The person to whom the vision came was none other than the illustrious patriarch Abraham, the ancestor of the Hebrew nation, and the father of the faithful.

Abraham

The Lord first called Abram when he was living in the prosperous Sumerian city, Ur of the Chaldees. Previous to this call, his family were idolaters. The call was repeated after Abram moved to Haran with his father *Terah,* his brother *Nahor,* his wife *Sarai,* and his nephew *Lot.* Haran was a flourishing metropolis in northern Syria, about six hundred miles northwest of Ur.

At this time God made a pledge to seventy-five year old Abram. If he would leave his country, his relatives, and his father's house, and go into a land which the Lord would show him, God would make of him a great nation. His name would be made great, he would be blessed, and in him all the families of the earth would be blessed.

Abram believed the Lord. He gathered his family, a throng of servants, and all his material possessions—which were considerable—and departed from Haran. Journeying southward some five hundred miles, they came to the land of Canaan. Here at a place called Shechem, about thirty miles north of Jerusalem, the Lord appeared to Abram. Apparently it was a visible manifestation.

God spoke a single brief sentence, but it contained a definite and significant promise. He said to Abram: *"I will give this land to your descendants"* (Gen. 12:7).

Because of the visitation, it was here that Abram built his first altar to the Lord. And because of the promise, Abram's descendants—the Arabs and the Jews—have fought over possession of that land to this day.

Soon afterward there was a famine in Canaan. Abram's family went down into Egypt to sojourn. Although Sarai was past sixty-five years of age, she was still a very beautiful woman. The Egyptians took her into Pharaoh's palace, with a view to adding her to his harem.

Abram had not told them she was his wife, fearing that if he did, they would kill him. He said she was his sister. This was not exactly a lie, for Sarai was his half-sister. But God intervened by sending plagues upon Pharaoh's house, causing them to release her.

After the family returned to Canaan, there followed Abram's separation from Lot, and later the nephew's capture by four kings from the region of Mesopotamia. In order to rescue him, Abram was forced to go to war with those kings, all of whom he successfully defeated. On his way home Abram received the blessing of Melchizedek, king of Salem and priest of the most high God.

It is at this point in Abram's life that God begins to unfold the first vision recorded in the scriptures. It is a momentous one.

"After these things the word of the Lord came to Abram in a VISION, saying, Fear not, Abram; I am your shield, your abundant compensation, and your reward shall be exceedingly great" (Gen. 15:1).

Abram is troubled over having made such powerful enemies during his battles with the pagan kings. Therefore, the Lord tells him not to be afraid, that He Himself will be his protection, and his reward will be great. Abram questions what the Lord can give him since he is childless, approximately eighty years old by now, and has made his steward Eliezer his heir.

But in the vision God assures Abram that he shall have a son of his own. Through him will rise the future nation. The Lord repeats a former promise saying that Abram's seed will be as numerous as the stars in heaven, and that he will be given the land of Canaan as an inheritance.

Abram believes God, but he asks a natural question: "By what sign or pledge will I know that I shall inherit it?" (Gen. 15:8).

God then confirms His promise of the inheritance of the land by a solemn ceremony . . .

Abram is directed to make the usual preparations observed when two parties are about to make an important covenant or alliance. Certain animals and birds used in sacrifice are slain, and the bodies of the former divided in two parts. (Hence the expression to "cut" a covenant.) The two parties then pass between the parts, meet in the middle, and take an oath of agreement. This signifies that if they are false to the covenant, they merit a similar fate to that of the slain animals.

Abram prepares his sacrifice—a heifer, a she-goat, a ram, a turtledove, and a pigeon. He divides the animals, but not the birds. When fowls swoop down upon the carcasses, he drives them away.

Then the Bible says: "When the sun was setting, *a deep sleep* overcame Abram . . ." (Gen. 15:12).

As the vision continues, Abram is given a glimpse into the future of his descendants, covering a period of many centuries. The Lord tells him that his seed will become sojourners and servants in a land not their own, and be afflicted by that nation for four hundred years. At the end of that time God will punish their enslavers, and Abram's descendants will come out with great substance. The promise is also made that he himself will die peacefully in a good old age.

Now comes that part of the covenant where the two parties pass between the divided animals, meet midway, and take their oath.

"When the sun had gone down and a (thick) darkness had come on, lo, a smoking oven and a flaming torch passed between those pieces" (Gen. 15:17).

This is the way in which God gives evidence that He is passing between the cut animals. The smoking oven and the flaming torch are visible emblems of His presence. Nothing could more effectively certify the security and immutability of His promise.

Thus the ratification of the covenant takes place. It is confirmed by a sanction that is irrevocable. God guarantees inheritance of the land and the multiplying of Abram's seed. Abram's obligation is continued trust, patience, and obedience.

And so the first highly significant vision, with all its import and scope, came to an end. Before this particular occasion the Lord had appeared several times to Abram and spoken with him. He was to appear to him a number of times afterward—and once even to eat with him in the company of two angels. But this is the only time the Lord ever came to Abraham in a vision!

Why do you suppose God chose such a method of communication in this single instance?

No doubt the reason was this . . .

A vision was the best way to entirely isolate Abram's mind from earthly scenes. In the sleep-like condition which overcame him, his senses were dormant but his mind awake to spiritual impressions. He was in a wholly yielded state where God alone could be seen and heard. Everything else was excluded. In this manner the establishing and the ratifying of the covenant, as well as the prophecy of Abraham's seed for the next several centuries, was vividly and indelibly stamped upon his consciousness.

Abimelech

The first *dream* in scripture is recounted in Genesis 20:3-7.

At this time we are still concerned with the life of Abraham, who is presently ninety-nine years old. Because Sarai had remained barren despite God's promise, she had given her maid *Hagar* to Abram, and the Egyptian bondwoman had borne *Ishmael*. The lad is now thirteen years of age.

The Lord again appeared to Abram, changing his name to Abraham. He enlarged the original covenant to include the everlasting promise: "I will be a God to you and to your posterity after you" (Gen. 17:7). As a sign of the covenant, the rite of circumcision was instituted. God promised that in one year Sarai, whose name He changed to Sarah, would bear a son to be called *Isaac*.

Shortly afterward there occurred the destruction of Sodom and Gomorrah by fire and brimstone rained down out of heaven.

Following this, Abraham left that country on a journey south. They came to the city of Gerar, near Gaza in the Negev foothills of the Judean mountains. Gerar was a city of early Philistine settlers. It is the king of Gerar who has the first dream recorded in the Bible.

He is called Abimelech, though that may not have been his real name. Probably it was the official title of the kings of that city, as Pharaoh was the title of rulers in Egypt. Abimelech exercised his royal prerogative by sending for Sarah and taking her into his court. Both she and Abraham had said they were brother and sister, the same story they had given in Egypt more than twenty years before.

Apparently Sarah had lost none of her beauty, and she certainly must have looked a great deal younger than her eighty-nine years. History was repeating itself, and God again intervened to save Sarah. This time He did not use plagues; He used a dream.

"But God came to Abimelech in a DREAM by night, and said, Behold, you are a dead man, because of the woman whom you have taken (as your own); for she is a man's wife" (Gen. 20:3).

This is quite a shocking statement for a king to hear, even in a dream. He had not known that Sarah was a married woman, but he knew that the penalty for adultery was death, according to laws then in force in the ancient Near East, as seen in the later code of Hammurabi.

"But Abimelech had not come near her. So he said, Lord, will you slay a people who are just and innocent?

"Did not the man tell me, She is my sister? And she said, He is my brother. In integrity of heart and innocency of hands I have done this" (Gen. 20:4, 5).

Abimelech points out that his people have not been guilty of any sin. And he rightly protests his own innocence and the integrity of his heart. The king appears to be a man of virtue and a true worshiper of God. He was not consciously violating any of his own rules of morality.

"Then God said to him in the DREAM, Yes, I know you did

this in the integrity of your heart, for it was I who kept you back and spared you from sinning against Me. Therefore I did not give you occasion to touch her.

"So now restore to the man his wife; for he is a prophet. He will pray for you, and you shall live. But if you do not restore her (to him), know that you shall surely die—you, and all that are yours" (Gen. 20:6, 7).

As soon as Abimelech arises the next morning, he calls all his servants and tells them about his dream. They are very much afraid of the consequences that might be brought on their kingdom. When the monarch calls in Abraham, the latter tries to defend his position and the arrangement he and his wife had made to conceal the truth. Abimelech responds in the most generous fashion.

"Then Abimelech took sheep and oxen, and male and female slaves, and gave them to Abraham, and restored to him Sarah his wife.

"And Abimelech said, Behold, my land is before you; dwell where it pleases you" (Gen. 20:14, 15).

The king tells Sarah that he has given her "brother" a thousand pieces of silver as compensation for all that has occurred, and to vindicate her honor in the eyes of those who are with them.

The episode closes with these two verses: "So Abraham prayed to God; and God healed Abimelech and his wife, and his female slaves, and they bore children.

"For the Lord had closed fast the wombs of all in Abimelech's household, because of Sarah, Abraham's wife" (Gen. 20:17, 18) .

Jacob at Bethel

The next personality we meet is Abraham's grandson, Jacob. He is the one who has the second and third dreams related in the scriptures.

Jacob, the son of Isaac, is another of the Biblical patriarchs. His name was later changed to *Israel,* after he wrestled with God and prevailed. He is known as the father of the chosen people. His sons became the heads of the twelve tribes of the children of Israel.

At the time of his first dream, Jacob is not yet married. The year is a little after 1900 B.C. Jacob is on his way to Haran to take a wife from among the daughters of his uncle Laban. It is interesting to note, through a careful study of the scripture, that when he makes this journey, Jacob is not the young man in his twenties that most people picture him. He is seventy-seven years old, and still a bachelor. But when we consider the longer life span in those days, we can see that he is actually in his prime, for he lives to be one hundred forty-seven.

Jacob has already had some rather colorful experiences. He was born clutching the heel of his elder twin *Esau,* and these two brothers continued the strife that began when they were in the womb together.

Esau, a rugged person covered with red hair, is an outdoor man—wild and restless. He cares only for the pleasure of the moment, and is without any lofty spiritual aspirations. Jacob, on the other hand, is a quiet man of domestic habits. He is the favorite of his mother *Rebekah,* while the father *Isaac* is partial to Esau.

In the book of Hebrews Esau is called a "profane person," which means a despiser of sacred things, an irreligious man. Jacob is quite the opposite. He believes in and seeks after his father's God, holding spiritual things in reverence.

Nevertheless, his character is marred by some baser elements. The trait of craftiness was plainly evidenced when he obtained his brother's *birthright* by taking advantage of Esau's hunger. The birthright included a double portion of the inheritance, headship of the family, priestly rights, and heirship to the covenant privileges. Esau valued these things so lightly that he willingly sold his birthright for a mess of pottage—a bowl of vegetable stew!

In addition, Esau proved by his marriages that he was indifferent to his parents' wishes and uninterested in the divine covenant. Both Abraham and Isaac strongly condemned marriage with Canaanites, who were outside the covenant of promise. Yet Esau married two heathen wives. This caused his parents much unhappiness.

Years later, when the brothers were in their late seventies, Jacob exhibited great deceitfulness. With his mother's help, he tricked

Isaac into giving him the *blessing* that by custom belonged to the firstborn. By means of a clever masquerade, Jacob beguiled his aged and partially blind father into believing he was Esau. Isaac then bestowed the blessing upon Jacob.

This act legally and irrevocably confirmed the birthright. Also it included the father's personal blessing and prophecy. Jacob thereby officially became the bearer of God's promise and the inheritor of Canaan. Esau received the less fertile region, which became known as Edom.

Although Esau was indeed unworthy of his spiritual heritage, Jacob's method of procuring the blessing was also unworthy. However, we must remember that God chose Jacob over Esau before they were born. The Lord told Rebekah that the elder twin in her womb would serve the younger. In so doing, God set aside the natural order and specified that the blessing be given to the one of His choice.

Esau's hatred of Jacob became violent after the stolen blessing. He determined to kill his brother. Rebekah told Jacob that he must flee from Esau's anger. She convinced Isaac that Jacob should be sent to Haran to seek a wife. Thus it is that we find him starting out on this particular journey . . .

At the end of the first day's traveling, Jacob arrives in the hill country near Bethel, the place where his grandfather Abraham had built his second altar.

"He came to a certain place, and stayed there overnight, because the sun was set. Taking one of the stones of the place, he put it under his head and lay down there to sleep" (Gen. 28:11).

Shepherds are used to sleeping out in the open, so this is no hardship for Jacob. Since a stone is his pillow, he probably folds his clothing to soften and cover it.

"And he DREAMED that there was a ladder set up on the earth, and the top of it reached to heaven. And the angels of God were ascending and descending on it!" (Gen. 28:12).

What a sight this is—a stairway extending beyond the stars, and angelic beings going up from the earth and coming down from heaven!

"And behold, the Lord stood over and beside him and said,

I am the Lord, the God of Abraham your father (forefather) and the God of Isaac. I will give to you and to your descendants the land on which you are lying" (Gen. 28:13).

We are not given a description of the Lord as He appears to Jacob, but through future dreams and visions, we will learn what He looks like from others who are privileged to see Him.

The purpose of this divine manifestation is to *confirm the Abrahamic covenant directly to Jacob from God Himself.* It had previously been committed to him by his father Isaac. Doubtless this vision of a ladder uniting earth with heaven is also to assure Jacob that, although he is in distress and fleeing for his life, he is yet the object of God's love and care. In the future he is to discover that all that happens to him is a part of the working out of the divine providence.

In John 1:51 Jesus alludes to this section of scripture . . .

He is conversing with Nathanael, whom the Saviour calls "an Israelite without guile"—in other words, a true descendant of Jacob, but without the deceit of his forefather. Nathanael marvels at the fact that Jesus knew him and saw him by the Spirit before He saw him with His physical eyes. Such a manifestation of divine knowledge convinces Nathanael that Jesus is the Son of God, the King of Israel.

Christ replies that he will see much stronger evidence than this. "Then He said to him, I assure you, most solemnly I tell you all, you shall see heaven opened up, and the angels of God ascending and descending upon the Son of man!"

This is the first prophecy to be spoken by Jesus. In it He predicts that Nathanael will see greater things—which he did, over the three-year period of Christ's earthly ministry. He witnessed many of Christ's miracles, His resurrection appearances, and His ascension. But when the prophecy is completely fulfilled in the hereafter, *everyone* will literally behold the Son of Man as the link between heaven and earth. Every eye will see Him when He comes with all His holy angels, in power and great glory. For Christ is the ladder that reaches from earth to heaven.

The prophecy which God gives to Jacob in his dream at Bethel promises that his seed will be as the dust of the earth, and that in them all the families of the earth will be blessed. The Lord goes on to say:

"Behold, I am with you, and will keep you (watch over you with care, take notice of you) wherever you may go. And I will bring you back to this land. I will not leave you until I have done all of which I have told you" (Gen. 28:15).

When Jacob awakes, he exclaims, "Surely the Lord is in this place; and I knew it not . . . This is none other than the house of God, and this is the gate of heaven." It is God's house because God was there, and the gate of heaven because he saw the ladder reaching up to heaven itself.

To Jacob, this was no mere dream. It was a profound spiritual experience.

As an interesting sidelight, this particular section of scripture is mentioned by one of Abraham Lincoln's biographers . . .

The President was telling a group of friends about a recent dream he had. In it he saw his own body lying in state in the White House. Lincoln said that after he awoke from the dream, he took his Bible—and strangely enough, it fell open to this 28th chapter of Genesis! He read the account of Jacob's wonderful dream. Then he turned to other passages. But he seemed to find reference to a dream or a vision wherever he looked.

"*If we believe the Bible,*" commented the President of the United States to his friends, "*we must accept the fact that, in the old days, God and His angels came to men in their sleep and made themselves known in dreams.*"

And, of course, God was still doing this in Abraham Lincoln's own day—for this conversation took place just before the President was assassinated! . . .

Jacob commemorates his dream by setting up the stone on which he had rested his head, and pouring a libation of oil over it. This is to mark the place where, for him, God was known to be present. Then he makes a solemn vow. In return for the Lord's protecting care, he promises that he will serve Him and give a tithe of all that he is to possess.

It was Jacob who established the idea of consistently tithing one's income, which became a religious principle in Judaism. However, the first example of *paying* a tithe was Abraham. He gave to Melchizedek a tenth of the spoils he had taken in his battle with the kings. But this was done simply because of a custom among ancient nations of giving a tenth of the spoils of war to the object of their worship. Abraham recognized in Melchizedek a priest of the true God, and so he gave him a tithe of the booty.

Jacob at Haran

Fourteen years later Jacob is to have another dream . . .

The intervening years have been spent in Haran working for his uncle Laban. This branch of Abraham's family remained in Haran after the patriarch migrated to Canaan. Abraham sent back to his home country to obtain a wife for his son Isaac. The girl who was chosen was *Rebekah,* Laban's sister. Laban played a prominent role in giving permission for her marriage to Isaac. When the time came for Isaac's son Jacob to select a wife, he too was sent back to Haran and his kindred.

Laban was related to Jacob in three ways. He was his uncle on his mother's side, his second cousin on his father's side, and he became his father-in-law twice over! Not that Jacob *intended* to marry more than one of Laban's daughters. He desired only the younger daughter *Rachel,* for he loved her. But in this matter, he who had deceived in the past now became the victim of deception.

Jacob made a bargain with Laban to serve him for seven years as recompense for receiving Rachel in marriage. This was in lieu of the money usually paid by a man to his father-in-law. In making the contract, it was not mentioned to Jacob that the custom was to give daughters in marriage according to their seniority.

Laban took advantage of Jacob's passion for Rachel to trick him into taking as a wife his older daughter *Leah* as well. On Jacob's wedding night, Laban sent Leah veiled as a bride, into the darkness of the bridechamber. The groom did not discover the subterfuge until the next morning.

The outcome was that Jacob had to take the older daughter. But when the week of marriage festivities was completed, he was also given Rachel as his wife. However, he was required by Laban to serve another seven years for Leah, making a total of fourteen years of labor in all.

During the entire time Jacob was in Laban's house, eleven sons and one daughter were born to him. Leah gave birth to six boys and the one girl before Rachel, who was barren for many years, bore *Joseph,* her first child.

Each of the wives' maids had two sons by Jacob. The youngest and last son of the patriarch was Benjamin. He was to be born on their way back to Isaac's home in Canaan, and his mother Rachel was to die as a result of this birth.

But at the time of Jacob's second dream, his household is still in Haran. His management of Laban's flocks has been so successful that the uncle is unwilling to let him go, now that his fourteen years are fulfilled. A new agreement is made. Jacob will continue to work for Laban in return for all the animals of the flocks and herds which are of impure color. In this way Jacob can build up capital of his own from which to support his family.

Laban, at the very beginning of the agreement, again acts deceitfully. He removes all the stock to which Jacob might lay claim, thinking that no more of their kind will be produced.

But God sees to it that Jacob receives his just compensation. He gives him some advice in a dream. This enables Jacob to turn his father-in-law's trickery to his own advantage without infringing the agreement. We learn of the advice from the explanation Jacob later gives his wives Leah and Rachel.

"I had a DREAM at the time the flock conceived. I looked up and saw that the rams which mated with the she-goats were streaked, speckled, and spotted.

"The Angel of God said to me in the DREAM, Jacob. And I said, Here am I.

"He said, Look up and see, all the rams which mate with the flock are streaked, speckled, and mottled; for I have seen all that Laban does to you" (Gen. 31:10–12).

Assured of God's help, Jacob proceeded to carry out the strategy conveyed to him in the dream. Taking fresh tree branches, he peeled back the bark so that white streaks appeared in them. He placed these branches in front of the flocks at the watering troughs when the stronger ewes were breeding.

The result of Jacob's tampering with nature was remarkable. The animals produced many speckled, ring-streaked, and spotted lambs—all of which became Jacob's property. By this ingenious device, he gradually acquired large flocks of his own. His property increased exceedingly over a period of six years.

But Laban's sons grew more and more jealous of Jacob's prosperity. Laban himself began to treat Jacob less favorably than before. He had been in Haran twenty years when God told him it was time to leave.

"Then the Lord said to Jacob, Return to the land of your father and to your people, and I will be with you . . .

"I am the God of Bethel, where you anointed the pillar, and where you vowed a vow to me. Now arise, get out from this land, and return to your native land" (Gen. 31:3, 13).

In response to this divine command, Jacob took his wives, his sons, his livestock, and all that he had, and secretly departed from Haran.

Laban

Laban was away from home for sheepshearing at the time Jacob and his family fled from Haran. The older man knew nothing about the departure until three days later. When it was told him, he flew into a rage. Taking some kinsmen with him, Laban set off in hot pursuit, determined to compel Jacob to return everything he had accumulated.

For seven days Laban and his brethren swiftly traveled before catching up with Jacob. It was nightfall when they spotted his tents pitched on a hill of Gilead, over three hundred fifty miles south of Haran. Laban encamped nearby, planning how he would vent his fury on Jacob in the morning.

But God stepped into the picture—this time with another dream, a dream of divine warning. Genesis 31:24 tells about it in these concise words:

"God came to Laban the Syran in a DREAM by night, and said to him, Be careful that you do not speak from good to bad to Jacob—(peaceably, then violently)."

God was warning Laban to restrain his feelings of violence. Because of the impact of the dream, he did so. When he accosted his son-in-law the next day, Laban told him, "It is in my power to do you harm; but the God of your father spoke to me last night warning me not to do this."

Jacob replied, "And if the God of my father had not been with me, surely you would have sent me away now empty-handed. God has seen my humiliation and the wearying labor of my hands for the last twenty years, and He rebuked you."

The two men settled their differences. A peace agreement was made between them, and a pillar erected atop a heap of stones as a witness of their covenant. The pillar, or monument, Laban called MIZPAH. Its meaning is "watchpost"; for he said, "The Lord watch between you and me, when we are absent and hidden one from another."

This covenant signified that, as God was witness between them, neither one would pass that boundary line to make war on the other. It is considered to be the original settlement of the border between Israel and Syria, represented by Jacob and Laban. A sacrifice was offered on the mount, and the two parties shared the evening meal as a sign of their goodwill.

"Early in the morning Laban rose up, and kissed his grandchildren and his daughters, and pronounced a blessing (asking God's favor) on them. Then Laban departed and returned to his home" (Gen. 31:55).

But the story would never have ended so pleasantly had it not been for God's visit to Laban in a dream.

Jacob's Return to Canaan

After this the Bible records several manifestations of the divine presence to Jacob. The first occurred right after Laban's departure. Genesis 32:1 says:

"Then Jacob went on his way, and God's angels met him."

Jacob left Canaan a lonely wayfarer, with only his staff as a companion. Twenty years later he is returning to Canaan with a numerous family and large possessions. On the first trip the Lord gave Jacob the dream of angels on a ladder reaching from earth to heaven. This was to assure him of God's watchful love. Now, upon his return, the Lord renews that assurance—this time with a vision of angels coming to meet him.

"When Jacob saw them, he said, This is God's army! So he named that place Mahanaim (two camps) " (Gen. 32:2).

The angelic host of heaven met Jacob to verify the protection promised to him in his dream at Bethel. As he entered Canaan, the angels became visible on each side of Jacob's company, surrounding and protecting the divisions of his household.

But the vision did not entirely allay his fears. When he learned that his brother Esau was coming to meet him with four hundred men, he was greatly afraid and distressed. He remembered their hostile parting. Esau, in his hatred because of the stolen blessing, had planned to kill his brother.

Now, for the first time in his life, Jacob confessed his unworthiness of God's benevolence. He prayed for deliverance from the hand of Esau whom he had wronged in the past. Jacob sent very costly and generous presents before him to his brother. Then he retired for the night.

It was sometime in the midnight hours that God appeared to him in the form of an angel, and the two of them wrestled until the breaking of the day. Jacob prevailed in strength. He would not let the angel go until he had blessed him. The angel did bless him, and also changed his name from Jacob to Israel.

"And Jacob called the name of the place Peniel (meaning "face of God"). For I have seen God face to face, and my life is spared and not snatched away" (Gen. 32:30).

This was an actual physical experience, not a vision. As a result of the bodily encounter, Jacob's hip socket was dislocated, the thigh muscle shrank, and he was left with a decided limp.

The meeting with Esau turned out to be a reconciliation between the two brothers. Jacob's prayers were more than answered, for Esau greeted him with goodwill and affection.

Resuming his journey into Canaan, Jacob came to Bethel. Here in the place of his first dream twenty years before, God again appeared to him. The Lord confirmed his new name of Israel, and renewed the Abrahamic covenant with him.

Many years afterward Jacob is given a final vision. But preceding this, his son Joseph has two very significant dreams. In addition to these, three other interesting characters have dreams as well, which drastically alter the course of Joseph's life.

We're going to take a look at all six of these dreams right now, and then conclude the chapter with Jacob's last vision.

Joseph

The story of Joseph's life is one of the most graphic and attractive in the Old Testament. He is regarded as a type of Christ, for their lives have many resemblances.

At the time of his two dreams, Joseph was just seventeen years old. His family dwelt in Canaan, the land of Abraham and Isaac. All of Jacob's sons were shepherds of their father's flocks. Joseph was the eleventh son, but he was Jacob's favorite, for he was the firstborn of Rachel.

His father had given him a coat of many colors—a long robe with sleeves, which was a mark of honor and rank, meant to be worn only by the heir. This inflamed the jealousy of his brothers. They hated him, and could not speak peaceably to him.

The scripture tells us in the 37th chapter of Genesis, beginning at the 5th verse:

"Now Joseph had a DREAM, and he told it to his brothers, and they hated him still more. He said to them, Listen now and hear, I pray you, this DREAM that I have DREAMED:

"We brothers were binding sheaves in the field, and lo, my sheaf arose and stood upright; and behold, your sheaves stood round about my sheaf and bowed down!"

This was, of course, a prophetic dream, foreshadowing Joseph's pre-eminence among his brethren. But his brothers were furious when they heard it. They said to him, " 'Shall you indeed reign over us? Or are you going to have us as your subjects and dominate us?' And they hated him all the more for his DREAMS and for what he said" (Gen. 37:8).

The Bible goes on to relate his second dream.

"Joseph DREAMED yet another DREAM, and told it to his brothers also. He said, See here, I have DREAMED again, and behold, this time not only eleven stars but also the sun and the moon bowed down and did reverence to me."

The sun, moon, and twelve stars are a symbol of national Israel. This same symbol is seen by the apostle John in Revelation 12:1 when he writes of a great wonder in heaven—a woman clothed with the sun, and the moon under her feet, and upon her head a crown of twelve stars.

Joseph told this second dream to his father. Jacob gently rebuked him, asking, "Shall I and your mother (meaning Leah, for Rachel was dead) and your brothers actually come to bow down ourselves to the earth and do homage to you?"

Jacob rightly interpreted the dream as referring to himself and his family being humbled before Joseph. The dream obviously made a deep impression on all of them. Envy was now added to the brothers' jealousy. But Jacob gave the dream much thought. He took it as a divine indication of events that would affect his family.

There followed the plot of Joseph's brothers to kill him. When he was sent to where they were pasturing the flocks, they said one to another: "See, here comes this DREAMER and master of DREAMS.

"So, come on now, let us kill him and throw his body into some pit. Then we will say to our father, Some wild and ferocious animal has devoured him; and we shall see what will become of his DREAMS!" (Gen. 37:19, 20).

They stripped Joseph of his coat of many colors and threw him into a dry cistern, where it would be impossible for him to get out unaided. As they were eating, a caravan of Ishmaelite merchants approached. The brothers decided to sell Joseph to them as a slave. The traders took him to Egypt where he was sold to *Potiphar,* a high officer of Pharaoh.

Joseph found favor in his master's sight, and he was made an overseer in his household. It was here that the incident of Potiphar's seductive and untruthful wife caused Joseph to be thrown into prison.

And it is in this dungeon that we meet two individuals who are also to have some prophetic dreams . . .

The Butler and the Baker

The chief butler (or cup-bearer) to the king of Egypt, and his chief baker were important officials in Pharoah's court. But they offended their ruler, and he had them put in the same prison-house where Joseph was incarcerated.

"They both DREAMED a DREAM in the same night, each man according to (the personal significance of) the interpretation of his DREAM—the butler and the baker of the king of Egypt, who were confined in the prison" (Gen. 40:5).

When Joseph came in to them in the morning, he found them looking very downcast. "Why do you look so dejected and sad today?" he asked.

"We have DREAMED DREAMS," they answered, "and there is no one to interpret them."

Joseph replied, "Do not interpretations belong to God? It may be that God who sent the dreams will give me the interpretation of them." Then he urged them to tell him their dreams.

The chief butler, whose duty it had been to serve drinks to the king, said to Joseph: "In my DREAM I saw a vine before me;

"And on the vine were three branches. Then it was as though it budded, its blossoms burst forth, and the clusters of them brought forth ripe grapes (almost all at once).

"And Pharaoh's cup was in my hand. I took the grapes and pressed them into Pharaoh's cup. Then I gave the cup into Pharaoh's hand" (Gen. 40:9-11).

This was all there was to the dream, but the butler was perplexed and troubled as to what it could mean. Joseph immediately gave him the interpretation. He said that the three branches were three days. Within that time the butler would be restored to his place and would be delivering Pharaoh's cup into his hand, just as he had formerly done.

"But think of me when it shall be well with you," requested Joseph. "I beg of you, be kind enough to mention me to Pharaoh and get me out of this prison."

When the baker heard that the butler's dream meant good news, he lost no time in telling Joseph his dream: "I also

DREAMED, and behold, I had three cake baskets on my head.

"And in the uppermost basket were some of all kinds of baked food for Pharaoh; but the birds of prey were eating out of the basket on my head" (Gen. 40:16, 17).

Joseph told him that the three baskets represented three days. Carrying loads on the head was a custom in Egypt, but the part of the baker's dream where the birds came and ate out of the basket was not a customary happening. Joseph said it meant that within three days Pharaoh would take his office from him, have him beheaded and hung on a tree! He would not so much as be given burial. The birds would eat his flesh from off the bones.

The offense of the baker must have been very great to be punishable by such a death, for the Egyptians took considerable pains to preserve the bodies of the dead. To have one's body devoured by the birds, as Joseph foretold, would be regarded as a terrible doom.

Everything came to pass exactly as Joseph had predicted. The butler was restored to his former position, and the baker was hanged. But when all was well with the butler, he forgot about Joseph's request to help him get out of prison. And so for two additional years Joseph remained in that dungeon.

Pharaoh

Do you know what caused Joseph to be delivered at last? It was two more dreams—these by Pharaoh himself! Genesis chapter 41 gives this account:

"After two full years, Pharaoh DREAMED that he stood by the river (Nile).

"And behold, there came up out of the river seven well-favored cows; sleek and handsome and fat. They grazed in the reed grass (in a marshy pasture)."

Egypt is dependent upon the Nile River for good crops. In the middle of summer this great body of water rises and overflows its banks, then recedes, leaving the land very fertile. Without that rise, famine could result. Cows were Egyptian emblems of agriculture and prosperity. The fact that the cows in the dream were fat and were feeding on marsh grass, which was

growing profusely along the Nile, signified an abundant overflow. All of this made a very pleasant picture . . .

If the dream had ended there, Pharaoh wouldn't have been
so troubled when he awoke. But this was the rest of the dream:

"And behold, seven other cows came up after them out of the
river, ill-favored and gaunt and ugly. They stood by the fat cows
on the bank of the river Nile.

"The ill-favored, gaunt and ugly cows ate up the seven well-
favored and fat cows . . . Then Pharaoh awoke."

As if this weren't nightmare enough, he fell back to sleep and
dreamed the second time. "And behold, seven ears of grain
came out on one stalk, plump and good. After them seven ears
(of grain) sprouted, thin and blighted by the east wind.

"The seven thin ears (of grain) devoured the seven plump and
full ears . . . And Pharaoh awoke, and behold, it was a
DREAM."

The east wind in Egypt is dry and parching. It prevents the
dew, hardens the earth, and shrivels the grain. No wonder
Pharaoh was so disturbed the next morning that he sent for
all the magicians and wise men of the country. They were supposed to be able to reveal secrets, interpret hidden things, and
foretell the future. But when Pharaoh told them his dreams,
none of them could give an interpretation.

About this time the chief butler finally remembered the young
Hebrew who had correctly interpreted his and the baker's
dreams while they were imprisoned together. When Pharaoh was
told about Joseph, he hastily sent for him.

"Pharaoh said to Joseph, I have DREAMED a DREAM, and
there is no one who can interpret it. I have heard it said of you
that you can understand a DREAM and interpret it.

"Joseph answered Pharaoh, It is not in me; God (not I) will
give Pharaoh a (favorable) answer of peace."

Joseph spoke of the God of Israel, giving glory to Him, and
expressing absolute faith in His power. He listened to Pharaoh's
narration of the two dreams. Then he said that both of them
signified the same thing. They were repeated for emphasis to
establish the truth of what God was about to do.

"The good cows are seven years; and the good ears of grain

are seven years. The ill-favored cows that came up after them are seven years; as are the empty ears of grain blighted and shriveled by the east wind. But they are seven years of hunger and famine.

"Take note! Seven years of great plenty throughout all the land of Egypt are coming. Then there will come seven years of hunger and famine. There will be so much want that all the great abundance of the previous years will be forgotten. Hunger, destitution, starvation will exhaust and consume the land.

"And the plenty will become quite unknown in the land because of that following famine, for it will be woefully severe."

Then, still speaking with the authority born of inspiration and faith in God, Joseph recommended a line of action that would save the nation from famine. Pharaoh was so impressed by Joseph's wisdom, for he felt that it had a divine source, that he made him prime minister of Egypt. He gave him a ring with the king's seal, by which he could transact all business for Pharaoh. He dressed Joseph in fine garments, with a gold chain around his neck. He was to ride in a royal chariot, and the people would have to bow the knee to him throughout all the land.

The daughter of one of the most influential and noble families in Egypt, that of the chief priest, was given to Joseph in marriage. Thus, at only thirty years of age, Joseph was highly exalted in the eyes of all the surrounding countries.

When the seven years of plenty were ended, and the seven years of dearth began, there was famine everywhere. But because of Joseph's bulging storehouses, there was bread and to spare in Egypt.

Joseph's brethren in Canaan were forced to come to Egypt to buy corn. There ensues the intensely dramatic story of his two encounters with them. *On their first visit they bowed themselves before him with their faces to the earth, thereby literally fulfilling Joseph's dream of long ago.*

"Joseph knew his brethren, but they did not know him. And Joseph remembered the DREAMS he had DREAMED about them . . ." (Gen. 42:8, 9).

So many years had passed since their last meeting, and so greatly was Joseph's appearance changed, that they did not recognize him.

He was now thirty-nine years of age, dressed as an Egyptian, speaking Egyptian and addressing himself to them through an interpreter.

He did not make himself known to them, but he deftly questioned them regarding the family. When he learned that his father was still alive and was with his younger brother Benjamin at home, he devised a plan where they would have to bring Benjamin with them the next trip.

On their second visit they were taken into Joseph's house. *Here they again bowed down their heads and made obeisance to him.* They were served a banquet, and then tested in various ways. Finally when Joseph could restrain himself no longer, he wept aloud and told them who he was. What they must have experienced in that moment of revelation!

Joseph generously invited them to bring their father Jacob and come and live in Egypt. He promised that all their needs would be abundantly supplied.

The brothers returned and told their elderly father that Joseph, the son whom he had believed dead all these years, was alive and governor over all the land of Egypt!

"Jacob's heart began to stop beating and fainted, for he did not believe them. But when they told him all the words of Joseph which he had said to them, and when he saw the wagons which Joseph had sent to carry him, the spirit of Jacob their father revived. Warmth and life returned.

"And Israel said, It is enough; Joseph my son is still alive. I will go and see him before I die.

"So Israel made his journey with all that he had, and came to Beer-sheba (a place hallowed by sacred memories), and offered sacrifices to the God of his father Isaac" (Gen. 45:26–28; Gen. 46:1).

Jacob's Final Vision

It was here, about twenty-five miles from home, on the night of his first stop enroute to Egypt, that Jacob is granted a final vision from God.

What was the reason for this vision?

Well, if you can imagine what your state of mind would be if you were a very elderly person just starting out with all you possessed (which in Jacob's case as head of a large tribe was considerable), and you were moving to a strange land—then you can begin to understand the old man's mental and emotional condition at this moment . . .

In back of his thoughts must have been the remembrance that when his father Isaac undertook a similar journey to that same country because of a faminine in his time, God stopped him and forbade him to go down to Egypt. Jacob also recalled what happened to his grandfather Abraham and his grandmother Sarah when they failed to remain in the promised land during a famine in their day and went to Egypt for help.

Naturally he was haunted by fears and uncertainties about the whole thing. Yet his heart cried out to see once more the son he loved above all the others.

We read in Genesis 46:2: "God spoke to Israel in VISIONS of the night, and said, Jacob! Jacob! And he said, Here am I.

"And He said, I am God, the God of your father. Do not be afraid to go down to Egypt; for I will there make of you a great nation.

"I will go down with you to Egypt, and I will also surely bring you (your people Israel) up again. And Joseph shall put his hand upon your eyes (when they are to be closed in death)."

Here the Lord came personally in a vision and spoke to Jacob, assuring him that it was in the divine will and plan for him to go to this strange land. The God of his father Isaac would go with him. Since Canaan was the place for fulfillment of the covenant, God declared that Jacob would be brought back there, and his descendants as well.

Then the Lord added a tender promise. He said that Jacob's long-lost son Joseph would be the one to close his father's eyes in death. How kind and lovingly compassionate is our God!

Jacob's reunion with his son, the firstborn of his wife Rachel, is touchingly told in these simple verses:

"Then Joseph made ready his chariot and went up to meet Israel his father in Goshen. He presented himself and gave distinct evidence to him (that he was Joseph). And each fell on the other's neck and wept on his neck a good while.

"Israel said to Joseph, Now let me die, since I have seen your face, (and know) that you are still alive" (Gen. 46:29, 30).

Jacob continued to live for seventeen years after this, bountifully cared for by Joseph. When the time drew near that Jacob must die, he called Joseph to his bedside and made him promise to bury him in the land of Canaan with his ancestors. In his dying hour he mentioned his beloved Rachel, showing his never-failing love for her.

Then he laid his hands in blessing on her grandchildren—*Ephraim* and *Manasseh,* the two sons of Joseph. Jacob adopted them as his own sons with privileges equal to the others, thus making them heads of distinct tribes. By so doing, he gave to Joseph—the elder son of Rachel, whom Jacob regarded as his true wife—the position of firstborn with a double portion of his inheritance. (Reuben was actually the eldest of Jacob's twelve sons, but he was disinherited because of his sin with his father's concubine.)

After this, all the sons were called in. Jacob said to them: "Gather yourselves together (around me), that I may tell you what shall befall you in the latter or last days" (Gen. 49:1).

His prophecy outlined the future history of each one and the tribe he would head. When he came to *Judah,* he predicted the advent and coming reign of the Messiah, who was to descend through that branch of the family.

At the conclusion of the prophecy, the Bible says: "When Jacob had finished commanding his sons, he drew his feet up into the bed, and breathed his last, and was gathered to his (departed) people.

"Then Joseph fell upon his father's face, and wept over him and kissed him" (Gen. 49:33; Gen. 50:1).

Jacob's request to be buried in Canaan was carried out. When the family returned to Egypt, the brothers sent a message to Joseph telling him of another request their father had made—that he, Joseph, forgive them for the sin they had done to him in the past.

Joseph had forgiven them long ago. But now he summed up the great lesson of this experience. He said to them, without any trace of bitterness: "You thought evil against me; but God meant it for good" (Gen. 50:20).

More than a half century later it came Joseph's turn to die. He spoke these last words to his brethren: "God will surely visit you and bring you out of this land to the land He swore to Abraham, to Isaac, and to Jacob (to give you)" (Gen. 50:24).

Then he elicited from them the same solemn promise he had given his father that his body also be taken back to Canaan for burial. The closing verse of the book of Genesis reads:

"So Joseph died, being 110 years old. And they embalmed him, and he was put in a coffin in Egypt" (Gen. 50:26).

We learn from the book of Exodus that his body stayed in Egypt for several hundred years. It was taken out by Moses when the children of Israel left that land of bondage. In the last chapter of the book of Joshua, we have the final reference to the bones of Joseph being deposited at Shechem in the portion of ground that Jacob had bought long before.

*   *   *

Thus far we have studied *thirteen dreams and visions*. Through them we have seen how God has made Himself known in a variety of ways . . .

In them He has spoken gracious words of everlasting covenant, of protection and blessing—as well as stern words of divine warning. His messages have touched upon birth and upon death. In one He gave clever instructions about sheep-breeding. Many dreams contained prophecies foretelling the destiny of individuals and of the land of Egypt.

As men have slumbered upon their beds, God has indeed opened their ears—and imparted quite an assortment of material, has He not?

CHAPTER TWO

Strange Happenings In The Night

There are three people in the Bible who have visions while in a state specifically designated as a "trance." One is *Balaam,* the backsliding prophet of God in the Old Testament. The other two are the apostles *Peter* and *Paul* in the New Testament. The prophet Ezekiel had visions while in a trance, but the scriptures do not use the word in connection with him.

A trance differs from a dream or vision, in that it is an abnormal state which is neither sleep nor wakefulness. The entranced person is insensible to ordinary surroundings, the mind or spirit being withdrawn from bodily consciousness. The individual may appear to be in a daze or an ecstasy. Sometimes the eyes are open; sometimes they are closed.

In Numbers 24:4 and 16 Balaam is called "the man which heard the words of God, and knew the knowledge of the most High, which saw the VISION of the Almighty, falling into a trance, but having his eyes open" (KJV).

Balaam

Balaam lived in Mesopotamia, on the west bank of the Euphrates river, about 1400 B.C. He was not an Israelite. Known as a diviner, one who practiced divination, he partially obeyed God but eventually betrayed Israel for a reward. God left him as a result of this sin and ceased to inspire him by the Holy Spirit. Then he reverted to being a mere fortuneteller, a soothsayer, an instrument of Satan.

Before he went into error, God visited him a total of seven times. It is evident that at least two of those occasions were by means of a vision or a dream, for we read: "And God came to

Balaam *at night,* and said to him . . ." (Num. 22:9 and 20). Although they are not explicitly called dreams or visions, we include them in our study, for Balaam definitely was one of the visionaries of the Bible.

His story is famous because of a miracle that occurred following the second visit of God to Balaam at night.

The first night He came to the prophet, the Lord conversed with him regarding messengers dispatched by the king of Moab. *Balak,* the Moabite ruler, was afraid of the Israelites who were camping in his land on their way to Palestine. He sent princes to Balaam to offer him rewards if he would come back with them and bring a curse upon Israel.

"God said to Balaam, You shall not go with them. You shall not curse the people, for they are blessed" (Num. 22:12).

Balaam told the princes to return to Moab without him. But the king sent more of them the next time, with greater offers of reward. The prophet did not send these messengers back. Instead he asked them to stay overnight. He said he wanted to inquire of the Lord once more regarding the matter. The promise of riches and honor was beginning to be very tempting.

God, knowing that Balaam would eventually yield and go anyway, granted him permission to go to Moab. But the Lord specified that Balaam speak only what would be given him to say.

"God came to Balaam at night, and said to him, If the men come to call you, rise up and go with them. But still only what I tell you may you do" (Num. 22:20).

Balaam was so anxious to go with the enemies of Israel that he rose early the next morning and departed with them for Moab. God's anger was kindled when He saw the covetousness in the heart of the prophet and his intention of satisfying Balak despite the word of the Lord.

Then we read that: "The Angel of the Lord stood in the way as an adversary against him" (Num. 22:22).

Balaam did not see the Angel standing in the road with drawn sword in hand; but the ass upon which he was riding did. The animal turned aside and went into a field. Balaam struck her to turn her back. But the Angel stood in the field as well. When the ass saw him there, she thrust herself into a wall, crushing Balaam's foot. He smote her again.

The Angel of the Lord went farther and stood in a narrow place. With no way to turn, the ass fell to the ground. Balaam struck her a third time. At this point God performed a miracle . . .

He opened the mouth of the ass and enabled her to speak. She reproved Balaam for his injustice to her. As the apostle Peter put it when referring to the incident in 2 Peter 2:16: "He was rebuked for his own transgression when a dumb beast of burden spoke with human voice and checked the prophet's madness."

Balaam was brought low before the Lord. His eyes were opened, and he beheld the Angel for himself. He confessed his sin and said he would go back if it was required of him. But God allowed him to proceed on his journey—because the Lord wanted him, as His messenger, to bless His people.

When he arrived in Moab, rather than cursing Israel, Balaam delivered three phophecies of blessings for them, according to the words the Lord put in his mouth.

The Spirit of God came upon him and he fell into a trance, his eyes being open. He brought forth two powerful oracles of prophetic utterance regarding Israel. The opening words of the last prophecy were these:

"I see Him, but He is not now. I behold Him, but He is not near. *A star* shall come forth out of Jacob, and *a scepter* shall rise out of Israel and shall crush all the corners of Moab, and break down all the sons of Sheth (Moab's sons of tumult)" (Num. 24:17).

This was a far-reaching prediction of the coming of the Messiah out of Israel, and the extent of His kingdom. The prophecy went on to foretell the captivity of Edom and the destruction of the people who were Israel's enemies.

As might be expected, the Moabite king reacted to these prophecies with wrath. He had offered a reward to Balaam to curse the Israelites, and instead he had pronounced blessings upon them. Nevertheless, before Balaam left for home, he succeeded in receiving the reward from Balak after all! But in obtaining the wages of unrighteousness, he forsook the Lord. And because of what he did, his name is one of the blackest in all the Bible.

More than fourteen hundred years after his death, Balaam was still mentioned as a symbol of infamy. Both Peter and Jude, in speaking of various evil acts, referred to him as an outstanding example of greed and corruption (2 Pet. 2:15; Jude 11). But it is the condemnation of Christ Himself that is the most significant.

In His last seven messages to His church, there are three individuals whom Christ denounces by name. One of them is *Satan*. The second is "that woman *Jezebel*, who calls herself a prophetess, but who teaches my people sexual immorality, and to eat things sacrificed to idols" (Rev. 2:20). The third person is *Balaam* (Rev. 2:14).

Why is his name again recalled and branded with disrepute?

It is not because of his avarice or apostasy, though he was guilty of both. The reason is that he caused God's people Israel to go into idolatry. The Lord hates idolatry above every sin. It is the chief of abominations in His sight.

The Israelites whom Balaam led astray were not the Israelites who had worshiped the golden calf at Mount Sinai. All who participated in that shameful episode were dead, including Aaron. Out of the generation who left Egypt, only Moses, Joshua, Caleb, and those who were under twenty years of age at the time of the exodus were left. This was a new generation, and they had no blot of idolatry on their record. Up to this point they had resisted all forms of heathen worship.

But Balaam caused many of these children of Israel to sin grievously against God. For this they were severely punished. And for this, Balaam was generously rewarded by the Moabite king.

How did he go about turning Israel from the Lord and leading them into idolatry? Was it through some captivating false teaching, or the working of miracles by demon power?

No . . . He simply gave some advice to Balak, the Moabite king—and it proved to be very effective.

Balaam understood human nature. He knew that the lust of

the flesh is stronger in most men than is their consecration to God. And so he suggested to the king that prostitutes from their pagan cult be introduced to the men of Israel. These prostitutes of Moab and Midian were the most beautiful women of the land. They were set apart to commit sexual sin in order to attract more devotees to their religion.

Lured by the prostitutes and by their own lust, Balaam knew that the men of Israel would soon be committing adultery with them. The next step would be to join in with their heathen practices of worship, in which sex orgies played a prominent part. This would lead to outright idolatry. Then God Himself would destroy them.

Unfortunately, that is exactly what happened, and it took place at Baal-peor.

Baal is the name of a Canaanite god supposedly responsible for fertility of family, flock, and field. He was worshiped in hill-tops or in groves of trees, with licentious rites and ritualistic feasting. *Peor* was the name of one of these places. It was located across the Jordon from Jericho. The Israelites were encamped nearby preparatory to their entrance into Canaan.

Here, the scriptures tell us, "The people of Israel began to commit whoredom with the daughters of Moab" (Num. 25:1, KJV).

In accordance with the counsel of Balaam, the beautiful pros-titutes invited the Israelites to their feasts. Those who accepted the invitation ate food that was sacrificed to idols. As part of the ritual, the guests bowed down to heathen gods. The next step in the seduction followed. The men of Israel began to commit fornication with these prostitutes. It wasn't long after that until great numbers of Israelites united with Baal worshipers.

"So Israel joined himself to (the god) Baal of Peor. And the anger of the Lord was kindled against Israel" (Num. 25:3).

Balaam's strategy worked perfectly. The children of Israel cor-rupted themselves and went into the depths of idolatrous prac-tices and moral depravity. God's judgment upon them was in-evitable, and it was quick.

"The Lord said to Moses, Take all the leaders or chiefs of

the people, and hang them before the Lord in the sun (after killing them), that the fierce anger of the Lord may turn away from Israel" (Num. 25:4).

The Moabites and the Midianites had concentrated their efforts on getting the leaders of Israel to sin, knowing that the rest of the Israelites would soon follow. Moses ordered the judges of Israel to slay every man who had joined himself to Baal of Peor. One thousand of these leaders were hung. In addition twenty-three thousand others were killed, making a total of twenty-four thousand Israelites who died in one day (Num. 25:9).

And it all began with Balaam's advice.

The glorified Christ says of Balaam: "He taught Balak to set a trap and a stumblingblock before the sons of Israel, (to entice them) to eat food that had been sacrificed to idols, and to practice lewdness—giving themselves up to sexual vice" (Rev. 2:14). Jesus condemns those who "hold to the doctrine of Balaam."

Does all this have anything to do with us today? Most assuredly it does. Remember that Christ, as Lord of the churches, is talking to *Christians*. And the apostle Paul is writing to *born-again Christians* when he refers to the same incident:

"From this we learn a terrible lesson: that we must not desire evil things as they did" (the Israelites who corrupted themselves and fell into idolatry).

"All these things happened to them as examples, as object lessons to us, to warn us against doing the same things. They were written down so that we could read about them and learn from them in these last days as the world nears its end" (I Cor. 10:6, 11, Living Letters).

Paul cautions anyone who thinks he is immune to such temptation to take heed lest he fall. He tells us to shun any sort of idolatry, which means loving or venerating anything more than God.

As for what happened to Balaam—of course from then on the Spirit of God did not speak through him, and he had to turn to demon powers for inspiration. He went to sojourn with the Midianites. Not long afterward God commanded Israel to wage war on Midian to destroy the people who had caused them to sin. In battle they killed all the males, the five kings of Midian, all the women except the young girls who were virgins—and also Balaam the ex-prophet.

Thus the man who was once used of God in many ways, was put to death while fighting against God's people as an ally of Midian. His life serves graphically to illustrate the truth of the warning in the 13th chapter of Deuteronomy:

"If a prophet arises among you, or a DREAMER of DREAMS, and gives you a sign or a wonder, and the sign or the wonder he foretells to you comes to pass; and if he says Let us go after other gods, which you have not known, and let us serve them;

"You shall not listen to the words of that prophet, or to that DREAMER of DREAMS. For the Lord your God is testing you, to know whether you love the Lord your God with all your mind and heart and with your entire being . . .

"But that prophet, or that DREAMER of DREAMS, shall be put to death; because he has talked rebellion and turning away from the Lord your God" (Deut. 13:1–3, 5).

These verses clearly explain why Balaam was put to death. They also show us that among the Hebrews there was a close association between dreams and the functions of a prophet. The dreamer and the prophet are classed together.

Moreover, these passages point out that false religions and satanic powers *do* perform signs and wonders. God permits this in order to prove men, to know whether they really love Him. If there was no darkness, we could not know what light was. But if we deliberately choose darkness rather than light, we fail to pass the test, and real love for God is not in us.

Such proved to be the case with Balaam the prophet. For the sake of material gain, he chose to be on the side of darkness rather than remain true to God.

Joshua

In sharp contrast with Balaam is a man who chose to serve God all the days of his life. He it was who voiced the familiar words: "Choose you this day whom you will serve . . . but as, for me and my house, we will serve the Lord." His name is

Joshua, and he lived during the same period of time as Balaam —around 1400 B.C.

Joshua was born a slave in Egypt. A Hebrew of the tribe of Ephraim, he was a young man when the exodus from Egypt took place. From the very beginning he exhibited valiant leadership.

When the Amalekites, first of the enemies to battle Israel in the wilderness, attacked at Rephidim, it was Joshua whom Moses appointed captain of the army. "Choose your men and go out and fight Amalek," Moses said to Joshua. "Tomorrow I will stand on the top of the hill with the rod of God in my hand."

The Amalekites were a fierce and warlike nomadic tribe of Bedouins, descendants of Esau. Joshua led the bitter fighting against them in the valley, while Moses prayed from the hilltop above. When his uplifted arms grew weary, Aaron and Hur held them up as they stood on either side of him.

The rod in Moses' hand not only signified an appeal for God's intercession on Israel's behalf, but the sight of it was a steady encouragement to the warriors. They remembered how that rod was used in the parting of the Red Sea when they were delivered from Pharaoh and his hosts. And it had recently been used to strike the rock out of which flowed water in the desert.

All day the battle raged. But at the going down of the sun, Joshua won a decisive victory for Israel.

A little later Joshua was one of twelve men sent into Canaan to spy out the land. He and Caleb brought back a report that the promised land was truly all that God said it was. The report of the other ten spies was pessimistic and fearful. They said Israel was not able to come against such huge inhabitants in their walled cities. They completely disregarded the promise of God that He would destroy the power of the Canaanites and give their land to the children of Israel.

The Canaanites were a wicked and idolatrous people. God had warned them in the destruction of Sodom and Gomorrah, but they had not changed a bit. Joshua and Caleb urged Israel to believe God for victory and advance into Canaan.

The people sided with the unbelieving spies. In a spirit of

despair and rebellion they demanded that Joshua and Caleb be stoned to death. But God intervened to protect them. The ten fearful and cowardly spies were killed by a plague sent from the Lord. As further judgment, Israel's entrance into Canaan was delayed thirty-eight years. They would not possess the land until after the death of all the disbelieving men over twenty years of age.

Joshua was Moses' right-hand man, and his attendant in the tabernacle in the wilderness. His intimate relation to the great law-giver—like that of Elisha to Elijah—afforded a unique education for him. When the time came for Moses to turn over the reins of leadership, he knew that the man divinely designated as his successor was Joshua. God had chosen him to complete what Moses began.

In a solemn ceremony of consecration, and by the laying-on of hands, Moses charged Joshua with the responsibility of leading God's people into their inheritance in the promised land. He assured him of the Lord's presence. "Be strong and of a good courage, for God will be with you."

With these words of Moses still echoing in his ears, Joshua took up his work. A spirit of wisdom and a noble bearing rested upon him from first to last, and he won the unquestioning obedience of the wayward Israelites.

After the death of Moses and the end of the period of mourning for him, Joshua told the priests to take up the ark of the covenant and step into the Jordan. The river was overflowing all its banks. *But when the soles of the priests' feet touched the waters of the Jordan, they parted!* All Israel passed over on dry ground. From the river bed, the place where the priests' feet stood firm, twelve stones were taken. These stones were piled up on the other shore, as a lasting memorial of this miracle that God had done for them.

News of the notable wonder of the drying up of the Jordan in the time of its flooded state reached the ears of the Canaanite kings in the surrounding plains. They realized that a powerful God was on the side of Israel. This discouraged them from attacking the Israelites as they camped at Gilgal near the eastern border of Jericho.

It was here at Gilgal that the Lord instructed Joshua to renew the rite of circumcision. All bondage to Egypt was rolled away as the males born in the wilderness during the forty years of wandering were circumcised. Henceforth the new generation would bear the visible token of belonging to the Lord in covenant relationship with Him.

Four days after crossing the Jordan, the men having been circumcised, Israel was ready to keep the passover. This was the annual feast commemorating their deliverance from Egypt.

On the day following the passover celebration, the people ate of the crops of the land—unleavened cakes and parched grain —for the first time. The very next day the manna, which had fallen six times a week for forty years to sustain them, ceased. The children of Israel never ate manna again; they ate of the fruit of the land of Canaan.

At Gilgal Joshua knew that he must face the first serious obstacle after crossing the Jordan River. The initial strong point to be overcome on the way to the promised land was the city of Jericho. Located about four miles from the Jordan, and approximately twenty miles northeast of Jerusalem, Jericho was a formidable, high-walled city.

Incidentally, archeologists tell us that this "city of palm trees," as it is called in the Bible, can lay claim to being one of the oldest occupied sites in the world. Its lowest levels of occupation date back to 7000 B.C.

While he pondered his strategy regarding the taking of Jericho, a remarkable vision was granted to Joshua. The scripture reads:

"When Joshua was by Jericho, he looked up, and behold a Man stood near him with His drawn sword in His hand. Joshua went to Him, and said to Him, Are you for us, or for our adversaries?" (Josh. 5:13).

This Man with the drawn sword in hand was none other than the Lord Himself, the pre-incarnate Christ in visible form. But from all outward appearances He looked like any other man of war. Joshua approached Him, inquiring whether He was friend or foe.

"And He said, No (neither); but as Prince of the Lord's host am I now come" (Josh. 5:14a).

This statement of being the Prince or Captain of the army of the Lord immediately identified Him to Joshua as God, for God was the heavenly Captain of Israel. He had promised to go before them and lead them into Canaan. This was a marvelous confirmation of that promise given to Israel through Moses:

"Behold, I send an Angel before you to keep and guard you on the way and to bring you into the place I have prepared . . . Obey His voice, for My name is in Him . . . I will deliver the inhabitants of the land into your hand, and you shall drive them out before you" (Ex. 23:20, 21, 31).

Joshua fell on his face to the earth and worshiped the Lord. Such reverence belongs only to deity. If this had been an angel acting as God's messenger, he would not have permitted worship.

"What says my Lord to His servant?" inquired Joshua.

"The Prince of the Lord's host said to Joshua, Loose your shoes from off your feet; for the place where you stand is holy. And Joshua did so" (Josh. 5:15).

This same command was spoken to Moses at the burning bush when the pre-incarnate Christ appeared to him. Only God could make such a demand. The appearance of the divine Captain in this vision was to show Joshua that He who marshals the armies of heaven was fighting for Israel.

Thus was confidence firmly imparted to Joshua to begin the conquest and occupation of Canaan.

In obedience to God's direction, Joshua and the men of Israel circled the city of Jericho once each day for six days. On the seventh day they encompassed it seven times. When the priests blew their trumpets, and the people shouted a great shout, *the walls of the city fell down flat!*

Many other victories followed. The Lord was indeed with Joshua. On one occasion the sun and the moon stood still for a day in order that Israel might finish killing and scattering her enemies. The promised land was conquered and divided among the tribes. At long last Israel entered into rest.

When Joshua's task was fulfilled, after thirty years of leadership in Canaan, he dissolved his command. The great spiritual leader, advanced in age, assembled all Israel for his farewell address. In his exhortation he reviewed the goodness and faithfulness of the Lord, admonished Israel to obey God's laws, and warned them against disobedience, idolatrous practices, and apostasy.

Joshua then retired to his own land in Ephraim. Here, at the age of one hundred ten, he died. Israel's beloved military leader, who chose to serve God all the days of his life, was buried on the side of a hill at the edge of his inheritance.

A Midianite Soldier

Strangely enough, it is another military man who has the next dream recorded in the scriptures. We do not know his name; we simply know him as a "Midianite."

Descended from Abraham by Keturah, the concubine he wed after the death of Sarah, Midian became a bitter enemy of Israel in the days of Moses. Previous to this, Moses had married a Midianite woman. It appears from Numbers 31 that Midian was destroyed as a nation in the war in which Balaam was killed, but a remnant of this nomadic tribe escaped the sword. They multipled again and became the leaders of the vast multitude that came against Israel in the time of Gideon.

This was somewhere around the year 1200 B.C.

Gideon—a humble farmer of the tribe of Manasseh, the elder son of Joseph—lived during a very dark period of Israel's history. Their great leaders, Moses and Joshua, were dead. The nation was ruled by judges, whom God raised up from time to time to deliver His people from their enemies.

The Lord allowed these heathen nations to oppress Israel for the same reason noted in connection with satanic powers and false religions. God used these enemies to prove Israel, to see if they would be obedient and faithful to Him. They failed the test repeatedly. They forgot the one true God and worshiped the gods of the nations round about them.

By the time Gideon appeared on the scene, Israel had a lengthy record of disobedience, apostasy, servitude, then deliverance— only to be succeeded by a lapse into apostasy again.

They were presently under terrible oppression by the Midianites, who had held them in bondage for seven years. Many of

the people were hiding in caves and dens in the mountains. All
of them were impoverished, for the enemy had stolen their stock
and destroyed their crops. As usual in distress, Israel cried unto
the Lord for help; and once again God was compassionate and
merciful to them.

There follows the fascinating story of how rescue came
about . . .

One day Gideon was furtively threshing what little wheat he
had in the wine press—a place the Midianites would not suspect,
because there were no grapes left from which to make wine.
Suddenly there came the Angel of the Lord and sat under a
nearby oak tree.

We read in Judges 6:12: "The Angel of the Lord appeared
to Gideon and said to him, The Lord is with you, you mighty
man of (fearless) courage."

Gideon's response was a perfectly natural one in view of
Israel's state at the time. "If God is with us, why has all this
befallen us?" he questioned the Angel. "Where are all the
miracles our fathers told us about? Why has the Lord forsaken
us and given us over to the hand of Midian?"

"The Lord turned to him and said, Go in this your might,
and you shall save Israel from the hand of Midian. Have I not
sent you?" (Judg. 6:14).

"How can I deliver Israel?" exclaims Gideon. "My clan is the
poorest in Manasseh, and I am the least in my father's house!"

"The Lord said to him, Surely I will be with you, and you
shall smite the Midianites as one man" (Judg. 6:16).

Gideon felt that he needed further proof that this was really
the Lord speaking to him. He said to the Angel of God, "If I
have found favor in Your sight, then show me a sign that it is
You who talks with me. Stay here until I come back with an
offering and set it before You."

"I will wait until you return," came the reply.

Gideon prepared a kid, placing it in a pot with some broth.
Then he put some unleavened cakes in a basket. He brought
these to the Personage under the oak and presented them.

The Angel instructed him to put the food on a rock close at
hand. The broth was poured out upon the meat and bread. As

the Angel touched the soaked food with the staff He carried, fire blazed up from the rock and consumed the offering!

This miraculous demonstration convinced Gideon that the Person talking with him was God in angelic form. When he realized that his eyes had looked upon a manifestation of deity, he was afraid he would die because of seeing God.

"The Lord said to him, Peace be to you; do not fear, you shall not die" (Judg. 6:23). Then the heavenly Being vanished from sight. Gideon built an altar there to the Lord and called it "The Lord is peace."

That same night Gideon carried out the first instructions God gave him. He took ten servants with him, and they tore down the altar of Baal (the chief Canaanite god) located on his father's land. They also destroyed the wooden image of Asherah (the chief goddess) that was beside it. Gideon replaced these with an altar to the Lord.

A little later an army of one hundred thirty-five thousand Midianites came down to attack Israel. Gideon hastily mobilized thirty-two thousand men to meet them. He asked God for a sign that Israel would be saved despite the terrific odds. God answered by two miracles of confirmation. Dew fell on a fleece of wool and not on the floor. The next night dew fell on the floor but not on the fleece. Gideon was convinced, and he made ready to go into battle.

Realizing that prideful Israel would boast that they had achieved the victory by themselves, the Lord gave some instructions designed to make such a claim preposterous.

Gideon was told to thin out his army. All who were fearful or afraid should return home; and twenty-two thousand of them did. The remaining ten thousand men were brought down to a spring of water. Here their number was further reduced by a second requirement.

Only those who would lap up water from their hands, like a dog, instead of kneeling down to drink, were to be retained. This cut Gideon's army down to three hundred men. How could that mere handful possibly defeat a multitude?

But God promised Israel that victory would be theirs. He gave additional personal assurance to Gideon in the most surprising manner. He directed him to take his servant, and under cover of darkness, go down to the enemy's camp in the valley below. There he would hear what they were saying.

When the two of them reached the outskirts of the camp, a man was telling a dream to his comrade:

"And he said, Behold, I DREAMED a DREAM; and lo, a cake of barley bread tumbled into the camp of Midian, and came to the tent, and struck it so that it fell, and turned it upside down, so that the tent lay flat.

"His comrade replied, This is nothing else but the sword of Gideon son of Joash, a man of Israel! Into his hand God has given Midian and all the host" (Judg. 7:13, 14).

It was obvious that God had inspired both the dream and the interpretation. All Gideon needed to do was to apply it to himself, and he would see God's plan for the defeat of the Midianites. The cake of barley bread symbolized the Israelite peasants, as the tent represented the Midianite nomads. When the bread fell into their midst and flattened them, it signified their downfall.

"When Gideon heard the telling of the DREAM and its interpretation, he worshiped. He returned to the camp of Israel, and said, Arise; for the Lord has given into your hand the host of Midian" (Judg. 7:15).

That very night Israel made their attack. They surrounded the camp of the sleeping enemy. Each man was armed only with a sword, a trumpet, and an earthen lamp. At a given signal they all blew their trumpets at once, broke open their pitchers, and held aloft the lamps that were burning within. Then in unison they shouted with a loud voice, *"The sword of the Lord, and of Gideon!"*

Such piercing noise and sudden flame of torches was startling enough, but the Lord added mass confusion to the Midianites. They began to kill each other, while fleeing in every direction.

This spectacular victory was followed by others of lesser degree. Finally Gideon's fame as a hero reached such proportions that Israel sought to make him king over them. He refused to be king, but consented to become a judge. As such he ruled for forty years.

Since the Bible often tells the bad as well as the good about an individual, we learn that Gideon's subsequent career was not so admirable. He made an image from the golden earrings taken as spoil in battle, and set it up in his own city. This turned out to be a source of apostasy to himself, his house, and to the nation.

Thus the old cycle of disobeying God, being delivered by Him, and then disobeying Him again, was repeated. Nevertheless, Gideon's name has been placed in the eleventh chapter of Hebrews among the heroes of faith.

And we have been introduced to him in this study because one night a Bedouin soldier had a dream.

Samuel

The last and greatest of the judges was Samuel. He was also a prophet, and considered the most outstanding figure in the Old Testament since Moses. He is the next personality we are to meet.

Samuel was one of three *Nazirites* in the Bible. The other two were *Samson* and *John the Baptist*. It would appear that the apostle Paul took a Nazirite vow for a period of time, but he was not a life-long Nazirite as were the others.

Nazirites had much in common with the prophets, with whom they are classed as being raised up by God Himself (Amos 2:11). A Nazirite meant a separated or consecrated person, one who abstained from all fruit of the vine, no razor came upon his head, and he was not to be defiled by touching a dead body.

Born somewhere around 1100 B.C., Samuel belonged to the Lord from birth. His mother *Hannah,* who long had been childless, made a vow that if God granted her a son, he would be dedicated to the service of the sanctuary. So when Samuel was about two or three years old, Hannah brought him to the tabernacle at Shiloh and left him with *Eli* the priest.

From early childhood Samuel ministered in the house of the Lord. He received his training from Eli, and they resided in the living quarters adjoining the tabernacle. Every year Samuel's mother made him a little robe, and brought it to him when she came with her husband to offer the annual sacrifice. God blessed Hannah, and she bore three other sons and two daughters.

I Samuel 3:1 tells us: "The word of the Lord was rare and precious in those days; there was no frequent or widely spread VISION."

Because of sin among God's people, the word of the Lord was seldom heard. Revelations, prophecies, visions, and contacts with God were scarce. Consequently they were very valuable. There was no accredited prophet, one who sees beyond ordinary things, and therefore no vision was breaking through.

One night as Samuel lay sleeping, the Lord spoke to him in an audible voice, loud enough to awaken him. He thought it was Eli who had called. He ran to the priest and said, "Here I am, for you called me."

"I did not call you," responded Eli. "Lie down again."

It took three of these summons before the old priest realized that it was God who was speaking to Samuel. He advised the lad what to reply if the Lord called again.

"So Samuel went and lay down in his place. The Lord came, and stood, and called as at other times, Samuel! Samuel! Then Samuel answered, Speak, Lord, for Your servant is listening.

"The Lord told Samuel, Behold, I am about to do a thing in Israel, at which both ears of all who hear it shall tingle . . ." (I Sam. 3:9-11).

The prophecy that followed concerned the judgment that was to befall Eli's house. His sons had vilely corrupted the priesthood, and Eli had not restrained them. The Lord had previously warned Eli that his family would fall into poverty and obscurity, even telling him that in one day both of his sons would die.

Still Eli did not remove his sons from the position they disgraced. He could not bring himself to humiliate them and lower his own standing in the sight of the people. Now God declared through Samuel that He was going to put an end forever to the house of Eli. Their iniquity could not be atoned for or purged with sacrifice.

"Samuel lay until morning; then he opened the doors of the Lord's house. And (he) was afraid to tell the VISION to Eli" (I Sam. 3:15).

Samuel loved Eli, and was reluctant to give him the message.

He did not want to distress the man whom he reverenced as a father and spiritual guide. But when Eli commanded that Samuel tell him, he did so. The old priest submitted to God's pronouncement of judgment, for he knew it was justified.

The disclosure of this vision caused all Israel—from Dan to Beersheba—to know that Samuel had been entrusted with a prophet's office by the Lord. The people recognized that he was God's chosen human instrument of prophetic revelation.

Fulfillment of the prophecy began when both of Eli's sons were slain on the same day in battle against the Philistines. Eli learned of their death as he sat by the road at the city gate. When he received the additional news that the ark of God had been captured, he fell backward off his seat and died with a broken neck.

The wife of one of Eli's sons was about to give birth to a child. The report came to her that her husband, her brother-in-law, and her father-in-law were all dead, and that the ark of God had been taken away. Immediately her labor pains commenced, and she died in childbirth.

Although the posterity of Eli continued to be priests until the time of Solomon, they all died young. When Solomon expelled the last descendant of Eli from the priesthood, the prophecy was completely fulfilled.

Samuel took over the reins from the deceased Eli. For many years thereafter he was judge, prophet, and priest. But when Samuel was advanced in years, he made the mistake of appointing his sons as judges over Israel. They were unfit for the office, being little better than Eli's sons. Their wickedness helped to bring about Israel's demands for a monarchy—the common form of rule in neighboring nations.

Samuel warned the people of the price they would have to pay for a king—conscription into the army, heavy taxation, enforced labor, and oppression. But his words went unheeded. The people would have their king.

And so Samuel anointed *Saul* the first king of Israel. For thirty-eight years of Saul's reign. Samuel continued to be a respected judge of Israel, in addition to being highly esteemed as a prophet of God.

Saul

Saul was just a farm boy from the tribe of Benjamin when he was chosen to become Israel's king. He was a handsome young man, gifted with an imposing appearance and a magnificent physique. Standing head and shoulders above his brethren, he was easily the finest physical specimen in the land.

In the beginning he was humble in spirit. When Samuel indicated to Saul that he was the one whom God had appointed to be the ruler over Israel, he answered, "Am I not a Benjamite, the smallest of the tribes; and is not my family the least of all the clans of Benjamin? Why then do you speak this way to me?"

Samuel had a long talk with Saul, revealing to him the word of the Lord. Before the assembly of Israel met officially to choose a king and establish the monarchy, the old prophet privately anointed Saul.

"Then Samuel took the vial of oil, poured it on Saul's head, and kissed him, and said, Has not the Lord anointed you to be prince over His heritage Israel?" (I Sam. 10:1). Samuel went on to tell Saul, "The Spirit of the Lord will come upon you mightily, and you will prophesy, and you shall be turned into another man."

All this came to pass. The people were called together to present themselves before the Lord at Mizpah. Lots were drawn, and they fell upon the tribe of Benjamin. Then Saul's name was singled out as further confirmation that he was the one divinely chosen. But when they looked for him, he could not be found. He was so timid he had hidden himself among the baggage.

Samuel brought him before the assembly and publicly proclaimed him king of Israel. Peace offerings were made, and a great feast was held in Saul's honor. The people hailed him as their ruler, shouting "God save the king!"

Saul began his reign about 1040 B.C. His outstanding courage and military prowess made him a national hero. He successfully fought against many of Israel's enemies, but his most important victories were over the Philistines. He was a strong and gallant leader.

But in time his pride and disobedience to the Lord's commands caused God to reject his rulership. Twice Samuel had to rebuke him for his flagrant violations of divine instructions. The first occasion was when Saul, through impatience, presumptuously took over the duties of priest, offering sacrifice at Gilgal. For this sacrilege his rejection from the kingdom was prophesied by Samuel.

The second occasion was Saul's deliberate disobedience of the Lord's command to exterminate the Amalekites. Samuel sternly censured him for this, and told him again that God had rejected him. After that Samuel made no more official visits to him.

God selected Saul's replacement—*David,* "a man after God's own heart." The Lord told Samuel to fill his horn with oil, and go to the house of Jesse in Bethlehem, "for I have provided me a king among his sons."

These instructions regarding the anointing of David must have been given to the prophet in a vision. In one of the Psalms, we read these words addressed to God:

"Once You spoke in a VISION to Your devoted one (obviously a reference to the prophet Samuel) and said, I have endowed one who is mighty (a hero), giving him the power to help—to be a champion for Israel.

"I have exalted one chosen from among the people. I have found David, My servant; with My holy oil have I anointed him" (Ps. 89:19, 20).

In the midst of his brethren, Samuel privately anointed the boy David. Afterward the young shepherd lad was brought into King Saul's court. There he played upon the harp to soothe the troubled and melancholy king. Later David was given Saul's daughter Michal in marriage.

Saul's character became less and less favorable as time went on. His health broke, and he grew increasingly morose. Often he was violent in his fits of anger. He was one of the most insanely jealous persons on record, and he came to hate the popular young warrior David. Again and again he tried to kill him, but failed every time.

Before David could publicly be made king of Israel, Samuel the prophet died. Notwithstanding, there was one more encounter between him and Saul . . .

After Samuel's death, no word came from the Lord for the king. "When Saul inquired of the Lord, He refused to answer him, either by DREAMS, or by Urim (a symbol worn by the priest when seeking the will of God for Israel), or by the prophets" (1 Sam. 28:6).

The Urim and Thummim were stones worn in the breastplate of the high priest. They were encased in a pouch fastened to the ephod. Apparently a direct question was asked, to which a simple affirmative or negative reply could be given. The particular stone drawn from the pouch was supposed to give the divine answer.

With Samuel dead, and inquiry of the Lord closed to him by any other means, Saul was beside himself with fear and indecision. He had to know what to do about the Philistines who were about to attack Israel. In desperation, even though he himself had outlawed pagan occultism, he sought out a spiritualist medium—the witch of Endor.

Disguised so as not to be recognized, he asked the woman to call up the spirit of Samuel. The medium went into a trance. Suddenly, to her extreme fright, the spirit of Samuel actually appeared!

When she saw him, the witch screamed. She had expected a demon impersonator, not the great prophet himself. It was clear to her that this had been accomplished by God, not by traffic with demons. She knew then that the man inquiring for him could be no less person than the king of Israel.

"Why have you deceived me?" she demanded. "You are Saul!"

The king said to her, "Don't be afraid. What do you see?"

"I see a god coming up out of the earth!" the woman exclaimed. (In those days judges were called "gods.")

Saul asked, "In what form is he?"

"An old man comes up, covered with a mantle."

From this description, Saul perceived that it was Samuel. He bowed in obeisance with his face to the ground.

Samuel said to Saul, "Why have you disturbed me, to bring me up?"

Saul answered: "I am bitterly distressed; for the Philistines make war against me, and God has departed from me, and answers me no more, either by prophets, or by DREAMS. Therefore I have called you, that you may make known to me what I shall do" (I Sam. 28:15).

Samuel said, "What then do you ask of me, seeing the Lord has turned from you and become your enemy? He has done to you what He said through me He would do. He has torn the kingdom out of your hand and given it to David. You did not obey His voice, or execute His furious wrath upon Amalek; therefore the Lord has done this thing to you.

"Moreover," Samuel added, "the Lord will also give the army of Israel into the hand of the Philistines. And tomorrow you and your sons shall be with me among the dead."

Samuel, in spirit form, pronounced impending doom upon Saul. The king fell to the floor in fear and weakness. Seeing him in such a state, the medium insisted on providing food for Saul and his servants. When they had eaten, they rose up and departed into the night.

The next day in a fierce battle on Mount Gilboa, the king's three sons were slain. Saul himself was severely wounded. He commanded his armor-bearer, "Draw your sword and finish killing me. If you don't, the enemy will come and make sport of me by slowly torturing me to death."

The armor-bearer was too terrified to carry out the order. He could not bring himself to kill his king. Whereupon Saul grasped his sword and fell on top of it, committing suicide. When the armor-bearer saw that Saul was dead, he likewise fell upon his sword and died with him.

Saul, his three sons, his armor-bearer, and all his men died that day together. Samuel's prophecy was fulfilled to the letter.

So ends the story of Saul, the first king of Israel—a mighty man of power, head and shoulders above his brethren—yet one of the most pathetic figures in all the Bible. He died as he had lived—self-willed, disobedient to God, never having truly repented before the Lord.

Nathan

Samuel's successor, to whom and through whom the Lord spoke, was the prophet Nathan. He first appeared on the scene in the early years of David's reign.

Only recently David had been crowned king over all Israel. With the capture of the stronghold of Zion in Jerusalem, the last vestige of Canaanite power was routed out. The new monarch set up residence in this stronghold, calling it The City of David. There Hiram, king of Tyre, built a beautiful house of cedar for him.

After two major victories over the Philistines, David turned his attention to the restoration of the religious life of his people. He had the ark of the covenant brought from the house of Abinadab, where it had remained for twenty years following its return by the Philistines. With much rejoicing, the ark was carried into Jerusalem and set in place inside the tent which David had pitched for it.

Now David was dwelling in his beautiful home in Jerusalem in comfort and in peace, the Lord having given him rest from all his surrounding enemies. He began to think about the contrast between his brand new house of cedar and the tent which housed the ark of God.

Centuries ago the Lord had promised to dwell between the cherubim above the mercy seat. Yet in all this time He had never had a house. Ever since his people came out from Egypt, God's dwelling place had been in a tabernacle which was moved from place to place.

David called Nathan the prophet and told him of his desire to build a permanent and worthy house for God. The prophet encouraged David to do all that was in his heart. He told the king, "The Lord is with you."

That same night an important message came to Nathan regarding his conversation with David about building a house for God. The prophet received the communication by hearing the actual words spoken in a vision.

II Samuel 7:5 reads: "That night the word of the Lord came

to Nathan, saying, Go and tell My servant David, thus says the Lord . . ."

In the message that followed, God reminded David that He took him from the pasture, from keeping the sheep, to be a prince over His people Israel. He said that He had been with him wherever he went, and had cut off all his enemies from before him. Then the Lord stated: "I will make you a great name, like that of the great of the earth."

As for Israel, God promised that He would someday plant them in a land of their own, from which they will never have to move again. Neither shall the wicked afflict them any more. This is, of course, a reference to Israel's future during the millennium.

Then, as a further prophecy for David, the Lord declared: "I will make you a house. When your days are fulfilled, and you sleep with your fathers, I will set up after you your offspring who shall be born to you. He will be the one who shall build a house for My name and My presence, and I will establish the throne of his kingdom for ever. My mercy and loving-kindness shall not depart from him, as I took them from Saul."

God loved David, and approved his desire to build a temple. He was to permit him to collect materials for it, but the Lord said he was not the one to build it. Because David was a man of war, whose hands had shed much blood, the privilege of building God's house could not be his. This must go to David's offspring. The Lord pledged that He would not completely remove His mercy from David's son, as He had done with Saul.

As His concluding remark, God made a striking announcement. He declared: "And your house and your kingdom shall be made sure for ever before you. Your throne shall be established for ever" (2 Sam. 7:16).

Here God promised three things that are to be eternal for David—his house, his kingdom, and his throne. It is interesting to note that it was on the occasion of David's desire to build God a house, that *the Lord revealed He would build David a house*. It would not be made of material, dead substance. It would be made of spiritual, living substance—a human house to live eternally.

What a decree of sovereign grace and everlasting blessing!

Thus in a vision God delivered what is known as the Davidic covenant. We remember that the Abrahamic covenant was also established in a vision. Both of them promised an *eternal seed.* The Abrahamic covenant included an *eternal land,* while David's covenant included an *eternal throne.* This great covenant of kingship centers in Christ, for it will not be fulfilled until His second advent. At that time Christ will rebuild the house of David and set it up forever.

"In accordance with all these words and all this VISION, Nathan spoke to David" (2 Sam. 7:17).

All that God had spoken to Nathan in the vision was passed on by the prophet to the king, and David knew that the Lord was speaking directly to him in this manner. When Nathan had told him everything that God said, David went in to worship the Lord in holy humility and awe.

His prayer was one of praise and thanksgiving to God for the covenant:

"Who am I, O Lord God, and what is my house that You have brought me this far? Then as if that weren't enough, You have spoken also of Your servant's house in the far distant future. And because You have spoken it, I know it will come to pass.

"You are great, O Lord God. There is none like You. You have established Israel to be Your people for ever; and You became their God. Your name and Your presence shall be magnified for ever.

"Now You have revealed this to Your servant: *I will build you a house!*

"O Lord, You are God and Your words are truth, and You have promised this good thing to Your servant. Therefore, let it please You to bless the house of Your servant, and with Your blessing let his house be blessed for ever" (2 Sam. 7:18–29 abbr.).

Nathan the prophet played an important part all during David's reign. His messages from God to the king were bold and to the point. He is best known for his fearless denunciation of David's double sin against Uriah the Hittite, and the parable in which it was couched—that of the rich man who killed the poor man's one little lamb.

At the close of David's life, his son Adonijah plotted to seize his father's throne. It was Nathan who took prompt action to stop the intrigue. The prophet advised Bathsheba to remind David of his promise to name Solomon his successor. The king kept his promise. He instructed Nathan to make the proclamation that he had appointed Solomon as ruler over Israel.

Nathan, along with Zadok the priest, anointed Solomon with holy oil from the tabernacle. Afterward the trumpets were blown, the people came out in great numbers and began to make merry. They played their musical instruments and rejoiced and shouted, "Long live king Solomon!"

And the earth resounded with the joyful noise.

Solomon

Our next Bible personality received his religious training from Nathan the prophet. It was Nathan who gave him a pet name.

At the birth of this child, about 991 B.C., his father—*King David*—called him Solomon. But Nathan named him *Jedidiah,* which means "beloved of the Lord." The child's mother was *Bathsheba,* former wife of Uriah the Hittite.

Truly Solomon was favored of God from his early years to the end of his life. When Saul and David, like the judges, were first chosen to rule Israel, God gave them a special measure of power. Solomon ascended the throne without this anointing. But soon after he began his reign, God Himself personally appeared to the young king in a dream.

This happened in the city of Gibeon, about four miles from Jerusalem. Here was located the original tabernacle Moses had made in the wilderness, with its altar of burnt offering. The ark of the covenant was at that time in a tent of meeting at Jerusalem. Solomon came to Gibeon to worship and to offer sacrifices. He presented a thousand burnt offerings upon that altar.

I Kings 3:5 states: "In Gibeon the Lord appeared to Solomon in a DREAM by night. God said, Ask what I shall give you."

God told him to ask whatever he wanted, and it is plainly implied that it would be granted him. Solomon's request was for an understanding heart, that he might judge Israel with true justice. One of the chief functions of an Oriental monarch was to hear and decide cases. Solomon knew he would need divine inspiration to wisely and fairly govern so great a people as Israel.

Such an unselfish request pleased the Lord. God promised to grant him not only what he asked for, but to give him all these other things as well—long life, riches, honor, and victory over his enemies.

"Solomon awoke, and behold, it was a DREAM" (I Kgs. 3:15). He returned to Jerusalem and stood before the ark of the covenant and offered up more sacrifices. Then he made a feast for all his servants.

God had declared that Solomon would be greater than any earthly king, and certainly he has never had an equal. His ivory throne was the grandest this world has ever seen. His palace, which took thirteen years to build, was dazzling. All of the household vessels were of pure gold. His annual income exceeded twenty million dollars.

The splendor of the temple, which he was seven years in building, was unparalleled in magnificence. His wisdom and fame were so great that kings from all over the world came to hear him.

Even Jesus referred to "Solomon in all his glory" in the sermon on the mount. On another occasion He spoke of the visit of the Queen of Sheba, who "came from the uttermost parts of the earth to hear the wisdom of Solomon." Then, because He was speaking to unbelieving scribes and Pharisees, Jesus added these words: "And, behold, a greater than Solomon is here."

God appeared a second and final time to Solomon when the temple was completed, following the feast of dedication and the feast of tabernacles. The scripture does not use the word "dream" or "vision" in connection with this appearance. But it does say that it was *by night*—indicating that it was very likely in a dream, as was the first appearance.

God assured Solomon that He had heard his prayer. He told him that He had hallowed the temple, and that His eyes and heart would be there continually. He renewed the Davidic covenant with Solomon, as He had renewed the Abrahamic covenant with Isaac and Jacob.

But the Lord also warned Solomon that if Israel turned away from Him to serve other gods, they would be cut off from the land, and the temple would be cast out of His sight.

Regrettable as it is to relate, Solomon later compromised the convictions he had expressed in his dedicatory prayer for the temple. To placate the many foreign wives he had married, he began to engage in their heathen practices of worship.

The Bible tells us in I Kings 11:4 and 6: "When he was old, his wives turned away his heart after other gods . . . and Solomon did evil in the sight of the Lord."

God was angry with Solomon because of this. But for the sake of his father David, He did not wrest the kingdom from him. However, He announced that He would rend it out of the hand of his son.

Solomon's idolatry was the beginning of Israel's decline. From glory and greatness, peace and plenty, and worship of the Living God, the kingdom fell into division and the people into apostasy. There ensued civil strife, war, and invasion from various enemies. Finally both Israel and Judah were utterly defeated, led into captivity, their cities taken, and the magnificent temple demolished.

What an ignominious end to that which had begun so auspiciously, and had attained such splendor!

Micaiah

About a hundred years after Solomon's temple was finished, and of course long before it was destroyed, there was a prophet who had a vision guaranteed to engage our attention. This man's name was *Micaiah.* The time of his vision was around 850 B.C.

Micaiah lived during the reign of the wicked king *Ahab,* whose queen was the infamous *Jezebel.* Ahab, king of Israel, had successfully fought two wars with Syria, but the city of Ramoth in Gilead had remained in Syrian hands. After a three-year interval of peace between the two countries, Ahab decided to undertake a third war for the purpose of re-capturing the city.

He made an alliance with the wealthy and powerful king of Judah, *Jehoshaphat.* Ahab asked the Judean ruler if he would join forces with him to fight against Syria. Jehoshaphat said that he was willing, but he thought they ought to inquire of the Lord first. So Ahab gathered all his prophets together, about four hundred men, and questioned them whether or not he should go to war.

These were false prophets, but they were very popular with the king because their advice was always what he wanted to hear. True to form, all four hundred were in agreement that Ahab should go to war. They confidently predicted that the Lord would give him victory.

Jehoshaphat evidently sensed something wrong with so many prophets being united regarding the matter. Or perhaps he detected a hollowness and unreality in their predictions. He asked Ahab if there wasn't a prophet of the Lord in the kingdom, besides these prophets of Baal.

Ahab answered that there was one man, Micaiah by name. But he said he hated him, because he did not say good things like the others. Although Elijah was alive at this time, and had already given several messages to Ahab, he was not mentioned. However, in order to satisfy Jehoshaphat, Micaiah was sent for.

Since he was known to be a man who stood for the truth in the midst of widespread apostasy, the messenger who came to call him warned him that he had better predict victory like the others. Micaiah replied that he would speak only what the Lord told him.

When he was brought before the two kings, they were attired in their royal robes and seated on their thrones in the entrance to the gate of Samaria, the capital city of Israel. All around them were the false prophets continuing their forecasts of victory.

At first, in a spirit of irony, Micaiah prophesied the same as the rest. But Ahab knew this was not like him. He commanded him to tell the truth in the name of the Lord. Then Micaiah revealed his vision. We read his words in I Kings 22:17:

"And he said, I saw all Israel scattered upon the hills, as sheep that have no shepherd. And the Lord said, These have no master. Let them return every man to his house in peace."

This was a shocking prophecy. It pictured Israel defeated and scattered. Furthermore, it predicted the death of Ahab, for the sheep had no king and therefore could go home.

Then the king of Israel said to Jehoshaphat, "Did I not tell you that he would prophesy no good concerning me, but evil?" Ahab was as displeased with the true prophecy as he was with the false one. But there was more to come.

"Micaiah said, Hear the word of the Lord: I saw the Lord sitting on His throne, and all the host of heaven standing by Him on His right hand and on His left.

"And the Lord said, Who will entice Ahab to go up and fall at Ramoth-Gilead? One said this way, another said that way. Then there came forth a spirit who stood before the Lord, and said, I will entice him.

"The Lord said to him, By what means? And he said, I will go forth and be a lying spirit in the mouth of all his prophets. The Lord said, You shall entice him, and succeed also. Go forth and do it" (I Kgs. 22:19–22).

From these verses we learn that, on occasion, God and the many spirits in the heavenlies have conferences concerning the affairs of men on earth. Sometimes demons have access to these gatherings.

When the Lord asked for someone to persuade Ahab to go to Ramoth, various spirits gave their suggestions. Finally there came a demon who volunteered to be a lying spirit in the mouth of Ahab's prophets to urge him to go to battle. The Lord gave him permission to carry out his plan.

All during Ahab's reign he refused to obey God. He was in league with idol-worshipers, and listened to their prophets instead of the true prophets of the Lord. So God permitted him to be deceived, according to his own choice.

After hearing the vision, the king ordered Micaiah put in prison on a diet of bread and water until he (Ahab) would return victorious from Ramoth-Gilead. Then, spurning the prophet's warning, he and Jehoshaphat went into battle.

This ill-advised act nearly cost Jehoshaphat his life. Indeed, he would have been killed if he had not cried out to God. The Lord caused his pursuers to turn back. Ahab, even though in disguise, was mortally wounded by a random arrow, and he died in his chariot at sundown.

Thus were the prophecies of both Elijah and Micaiah fulfilled regarding this wicked king of Israel. And through the vision of

Micaiah, we are given a startling glimpse behind the scenes in the realm of the spirit world . . .

In thinking over the implications of this vision, do you suppose it is possible that sometime, in some heavenly conference, you and I have been the subjects under discussion?

We know from the Book of Job, as well as from this section of scripture, that there are assemblies in the heavenlies. There the sons of God, and Satan among them, are described as coming to present themselves before the Lord. In each of these cases the council, so far as its purposes are revealed to us, had reference to an inhabitant of earth. And its decisions were of gravest consequence to him.

We learn from the Books of Daniel and Zechariah that angelic "watchers," as they are called, walk to and fro upon the earth and oversee the affairs of men. They are sent by the Lord to observe conditions and to gather information. They pass on their reports to superior angels, who deliver them to the Most High.

We know also that angels are aware of us personally and individually, for Jesus said there is joy in the presence of the angels of God over one sinner that repents. We are told that angels have charge over us. They assist, guide, strengthen, and protect the saints. They bring answers to prayers.

But the Bible also tells us that Satan, our adversary the devil, as a roaring lion walks to and fro upon the earth seeking whom he may devour. In the heavenlies he is the accuser of the brethren, bringing charges against them before God day and night.

Now, in light of all this, how thankful we should be for the ministry of angels. If our name *is* actually brought up in some heavenly council, and Satan accuses us, how much more grateful we should be that we have an advocate with the Father—One who will intercede for us, One who is able to present us faultless before the presence of His glory—Jesus Christ, the righteous.

What a friend we have in Him! What a wonderful mediator!

Elisha's Servant

Micaiah was not the only one of his day to look into the ordinarily invisible world of spirit beings. In that same ninth century, a momentary glimpse into this realm was granted a servant of Elisha the prophet.

Elisha was successor to the great prophet *Elijah*. He asked for, and received from the Lord, a double portion of the Spirit that rested upon the older man of God. Because of this, Elisha's ministry was characterized by many miracles. One of these miracles concerned the vision received by his servant.

This happened during a period of hostilities between Syria and Israel (the northern kingdom to which Elisha ministered). Ahab, king of Israel in Micaiah's time, had been dead for several years. The second of his sons was now on the throne. *Jehoram* was his name. He succeeded his elder brother, who died childless after reigning only two years.

Israel was being warred against by the king of Syria. But the Syrian camps and places of planned attack were made known in advance to Elisha by divine revelation. The prophet passed this information on to Jehoram. Three times Israel was saved as a result of Elisha's supernatural knowledge and warnings.

Although the prophet was against many things the Israelite kings did, particularly the pagan religions they favored, he often came to their rescue. Kings and peasants alike turned to him for help.

When the Syrian ruler learned who was telling his military secrets, he sent spies to find out where Elisha was. They reported that he was in Dothan, a town about ten miles north of Samaria. Immediately the king dispatched horses, chariots, and an army of soldiers to capture the prophet.

They came by night to Dothan and surrounded the city. In the morning when Elisha's servant rose early and went outside, he saw the Syrians. Trembling with fright, he ran to awaken the prophet, telling him that a host of men, horses, and chariots encircled them.

"Alas, my master!" the servant cried out, "What shall we do?"

Elisha calmly answered, "Fear not; for those with us are more than those with them."

"But there isn't anyone with us!" protested the panic-stricken servant.

Then Elisha prayed: "Lord, I pray You, open his eyes that he may see. And the Lord opened the young man's eyes, and he saw. And behold, the mountain was full of horses and chariots of fire round about Elisha" (2 Kgs. 6:17).

The prophet knew that he was safe. He could see into the world of the spirit, and the angelic army that was with him far outnumbered the earthly army gathered against him. God was infinitely more powerful than the prophet's enemies. But the servant knew nothing about this.

Elisha asked the Lord to permit his servant to witness what he, as a seer, was privileged to perceive. By divine intervention the servant's eyes were opened, and he was enabled to view that which could not be seen with the natural eyes. A guard of angels stood by to protect Elisha. Countless horses, and chariots so bright they appeared like fire, encompassed him.

This vision of heavenly forces arrayed on the hill east of town was the best possible encouragement and assurance that could be given the frightened servant.

The Syrians came down to the wall of Dothan demanding that the city surrender Elisha to them. Again the prophet prayed to the Lord. He asked that the attackers be smitten with blindness. God answered by doing that very thing.

Then the prophet took the entire Syrian army which had been sent to apprehend him, and personally led them as prisoners to Samaria. After he delivered them into the hands of Jehoram, Elisha prayed that God would open their eyes. The Lord did so, and the Syrians looked upon the two men they wanted—the king of Israel, and the prophet who had revealed their secrets to him.

"Shall I kill them all?" the Israelite king inquired of Elisha.

"Do not smite them," advised the prophet. "Set bread and water before them, that they may eat and drink, and let them return to their master."

This goodness on the part of Israel made the Syrians ashamed of their plans of war, and they came no more into the land of Israel for some time . . .

The actual account of this vision is told in one verse of scripture, and the Bible does not even mention the name of the servant to whom it came. But what an unusual privilege was his, and what a wondrous sight he beheld!

Imagine seeing with your human eyes the armies of heaven marshaled nearby to deliver you from those who would destroy you! It would indeed be marvelous comfort, and visual proof that "The Angel of the Lord encamps around those who fear Him— who revere and worship Him with awe; and each of them He delivers" (Ps. 34:7).

Eliphaz

There was another man who had a glimpse into the spirit world, this one of quite a different nature, and it happened in the dead of night.

The man's name was Eliphaz. He was *a friend of Job,* one of his so-called "comforters." The events in the Book of Job took place in the time of the patriarchs. But since our study follows Biblical sequence, we just now come to them.

As background for the appearance of Eliphaz, we must relate what has happened to Job, for this is the reason Eliphaz came on the scene . . .

Job was a man of great wealth and high social position. He was also a very pious man, upright, one who feared God and shunned evil. He had a large family and possessed much property. But in one day all this changed!

Unknown to Job, there was an episode in the heavenlies when Satan presented himself before God and asserted that Job's piety was dependent upon his prosperity. Satan maintained that if God were to withhold His blessings, Job would curse God to His face. The devil was given permission to put Job to the test.

From the height of prosperity and happiness, Job was suddenly plunged into the depths of sorrow and misery. Within an hour he lost all of his property, and all of his children. Nothing was left. Although he was profoundly grieved, Job submitted reverently to the will of God. He stood the test.

In a second heavenly council Satan insisted that the trial had not been severe enough. He received permission to afflict Job's person, but was forbidden to take his life. Satan then smote Job with loathsome and painful boils from the soles of his feet to the crown of his head.

This added misfortune was interpreted by his relatives and fellow citizens as divine punishment for gross sin, and they threw him out of town. Job sat on the dung-hill outside the city gate, scraping his sores with a piece of broken pottery. His wife urged him to curse God and thus hasten the inevitable end.

Still Job was resigned. His faith remained unshaken. He made no complaint against the Almighty.

At this point three of his friends entered the picture—*Eliphaz, Bildad,* and *Zophar.* They were members of the rich, wise, and affluent class, as Job had been. Having heard of the great calamities that had befallen him, they came to console the ruined and bereaved man.

When they arrived upon the scene, Job was hardly recognizable, so emaciated and disfigured was he by sickness and suffering. They sat down beside him and wept. The appalling sight shocked and grieved them into speechlessness for a week.

Finally the silence was broken by Job. Until now he had been able to restrain himself; but in the presence of his friends, anguish overwhelmed him. Their silent horror was like a mirror in which he saw the extent of his misery. In an outburst of agony, he poured forth his heartache and despair, cursing the day he was born. He called for death to put an end to his plight.

Eliphaz, being the oldest of the group, was the first to give an answer to this pitiful lament. While admitting that Job was fundamentally a good man, Eliphaz inferred that his sufferings must be punishment for some sin. He maintained that the godly do not perish under affliction. It is the wicked who reap the evil they have sown.

Then to back up his argument that Job needed to recognize his sinfulness, Eliphaz cited a dream, or a vision, that he had had. In his opinion, this awe-inspiring experience qualified him for exhortation.

Reading from Job 4:12-21, we encounter one of the most weirdly descriptive passages in all the Bible. Eliphaz is speaking:

"Now a thing was secretly brought to me, and my ear received a whisper of it. In thoughts from the VISIONS of the night, when deep sleep falls on men, fear came upon me and trembling, which made all my bones shake.

"Then a spirit passed before my face; the hair of my flesh stood up!

"The spirit stood still, but I could not discern the appearance of it. A form was before my eyes. There was silence . . ."

Can't you just feel the mysterious atmosphere of the night—the hush of deep sleep—and then the sudden terror when Eliphaz beheld the shadowy figure of a spirit, and felt its breath on his face . . . ? No wonder his bones shook, and his hair stood on end!

". . . Then I heard a voice saying, Can mortal man be just before God, or be more right than He is? Can a man be pure before his Maker, or be more cleansed than He is?"

The voice that broke the midnight silence posed the questions: Can a man be justified or righteous before the Lord? In the eyes of a holy God, how can mortal man be pure or clean?

The spirit in the vision continued speaking: "Even in His (heavenly) servants He (God) puts no trust or confidence, and His angels He charges with folly and error; how much more those who dwell in houses (bodies) of clay, whose foundation is the dust, who are crushed like the moth, and by it!"

It is quite evident to us that this spirit was *not* from the Lord. Many dreams and visions have a satanic source—and this is a good example of one. The vision struck Eliphaz with fear from the very beginning. Then, clothed in darkness, the evil spirit insinuated that man can never be right with God. He pictured the Lord as distrustful of His celestial servants, and harshly condemnatory of angels.

Of course, there was *some* truth in what he said. The fall of angels was one of the earliest facts of history. God did charge with folly and error the angels who rebelled with Lucifer. But the spirit used this to imply that if God placed no confidence in spiritual beings like angels, accusing them of sin—how much greater is His accusation against man! As further belittlement, the spirit emphasized that man dwells in a body of clay, which was made of the dust. He said man can be crushed like a moth, or even by one!

The spirit then pronounced his concluding observation:

"Between morning and evening they (men) are destroyed. Without anyone noticing it, they perish for ever. Is not their tent cord plucked up within them, so that the tent falls? Do they not die, and that without acquiring wisdom?"

In a day men are destroyed, the voice informed Eliphaz. No one pays any attention, and they are gone forever. The falling tent is a figure of their collapse and death. And, according to the night visitor, men die without even learning the lessons of life.

Having filled the mind of Eliphaz with this assortment of negative, gloomy, and hopeless thoughts, the shadowy figure vanished into the blackness from whence it came.

Eliphaz lived in Teman, a city whose inhabitants were famous for their wisdom, their skill in proverbs and dark sayings. From a purely mental standpoint, Eliphaz was worthy of being called "a Temanite." But from a spiritual standpoint, the fact that he would pass on the philosophy expressed in this vision shows that he certainly did not possess the wisdom of God. Eliphaz reveals how utterly bankrupt is man's wisdom when it attempts to comfort a human being faced with extreme misfortune and prolonged physical suffering, as Job was.

At one point Job himself makes a comment about dreams and visions. In the 7th chapter, beginning at verse 13 where he is addressing God, we read:

"When I say, My bed shall comfort me, my couch shall ease my complaint, then You scare me with DREAMS, and terrify me through VISIONS."

Poor Job . . . Just when he thinks he will get some relief from his sufferings in sleep, and escape the torment for a while, then he is scared stiff by nightmares and frightened by dreadful visions! Of course, these bad dreams came from Satan, who delights in adding terror to affliction. But Job made the mistake of attributing them to the Lord.

So distressed was he by these dreams and visions that he said, "I would choose strangling and death rather than these my bones. I loathe my life. I would not live for ever. Let me alone, for my days are a breath."

The third friend to speak to Job was Zophar the Naamathite. He mentioned dreams to illustrate his firm opinion that the triumph of the wicked is short, and the joy of the hypocrite is but for a moment. Zophar's inference was that Job must be both a wicked person and a hypocrite, or he would not be suffering their punishment.

This is what he said in Job 20:6–8:

"Though his (the wicked man's) proud height mount up to the heavens, and his head reach to the clouds, yet he will perish for ever like his own dung. Those who have seen him will say, Where is he?

"He will fly away like a DREAM and will not be found. Yes, he will be chased away as a VISION of the night."

Zophar minced no words. He classified Job with the wicked and consigned him to their fate—that of passing out of existence, just as dreams and visions do. Pronouncements like that could have been of little comfort to Job in his misery. Zophar's explanations and arguments were as inadequate as were those of Eliphaz and Bildad. Being ignorant of the true cause of Job's suffering, they all drew totally false conclusions.

Job was not the unrighteous man Zophar presumed him to be. But in regard to the wicked and the conviction that their prosperity will come to an end as suddenly as a dream, the writer of the 73rd Psalm is in complete agreement with Job's friend. The 19th and 20th verses exclaim:

"How are they (the wicked) become a desolation in a moment! They are utterly consumed with terrors.

"As a DREAM which seems real until one awakens, so, O Lord, when You arouse Yourself to take note of the wicked, You will despise their outward show."

We conclude this chapter with one other reference to dreams. It is found in the opening lines of the 126th Psalm:

"When the Lord brought back the captives who returned to Zion, we were like those who DREAM, it seemed so unreal."

Israel's deliverance from captivity seemed too good to be true. Being freed was so unexpected and sudden that they doubted the reality of it for a time. They thought they were dreaming.

*   *   *

In this variety of nocturnal communications, we have seen where God continued to use dreams to give specific commands and directions to certain individuals. By means of dreams He imparted assurance of blessings, protection, and victory. In one dream the Lord offered to grant anything the person might ask of Him. Another dream warned of the consequences of disobedience.

God used visions to counsel rulers and prophets, and to make pronouncements of judgment. In a vision He promised to David an eternal house, kingdom, and throne. Two of the visions provided an amazing glimpse into the heavenlies and what was taking place there.

We even had samples of Satan's use of dreams and visions in this abundance of "Strange Happenings in the Night"!

CHAPTER THREE

Visitations From The Most High

Do you know who said: "Where there is no VISION, the people perish"?

It was King Solomon, the wisest mortal who ever lived. These words are found in the 29th chapter of Proverbs, verse 18. How often we have heard them quoted. Not so often do we hear the remainder of the sentence. It is this: "But he that keepeth the law, happy is he" (KJV).

The word that is translated *"vision"* in this proverb has no connection whatsoever with the meanings some have attached to it. It does *not* denote "power or activity of the imagination," or "unusual discernment or foresight," or anything of that nature. It is a Hebrew word meaning *"a dream, oracle, or revelation."* It refers to the redemptive revelations that came through the visions of the prophets.

It was the vision of the prophet and the instruction of the law that deterred the people from immorality. The literal interpretation of this part of the scripture is: "Where there is no prophetic revelation, the people cast off restraint."

In Old Testament times God communicated with the people through visions revealed to His prophets. Sometimes the visions were written down, and sometimes they were not. The Bible mentions "the VISIONS of Iddo the seer" (2 Chr. 9:29). His writings were a source of information for the author of Chronicles regarding the reigns of three kings—Solomon, Rehoboam, and Abijah.

The book of Chronicles also refers to "Zechariah, who had understanding in the VISIONS of God" (2 Chr. 26:5); and to the things that "are written in the VISION of Isaiah the prophet" (2 Chr. 32:32).

Isaiah

Many people do not realize that the great prophet Isaiah received his messages in vision form. But Isaiah himself begins his book with these words: "The VISION (seen by spiritual perception) of Isaiah the son of Amoz, which he *saw* concerning Judah (the kingdom) and Jerusalem (its capital) . . ." (Isa. 1:1).

Through visions God showed him what was going to happen in the days—and even centuries—to come.

Isaiah is considered the foremost of the Old Testament prophets. He has been called "the eagle among the prophets," "the evangelist of the old covenant," and "the prophet of holiness." His writing is lofty in style and conception, and rich in spiritual meaning. He lays particular emphasis on God's love for Israel, and His final dealings with His people in complete restoration under their Messiah forever.

According to Jewish tradition Isaiah was of royal blood, being a first cousin of King Uzziah. He lived in Jerusalem in the center of national life, closely connected with the king and his court. Isaiah's ministry extended over a period of more than forty years. During this time he was an adviser to two kings—*Ahaz* and *Hezekiah*. He was married to a woman who was herself a prophetess, and they had at least two sons.

At one point in his life God made Isaiah a sign and a wonder to his people by requiring him to walk among them for three years "naked and barefoot." This does not mean he was nude. He simply laid aside his outer robe, a sackcloth garment of coarse goat hair, which was the customary attire worn by all the prophets.

This sign was to illustrate a prophecy regarding Egypt and Ethiopia. Judah had trusted in these two countries for assistance against the king of Assyria, instead of trusting in God. True to the prophetic sign, within three years Ethiopia and Egypt were taken into captivity by the Assyrians, and the people were led away "naked and barefoot."

Jerusalem was saved from the same fate only by the help of God. On the night that the enemy—under *King Sennacherib*—encamped round about the city, the angel of the Lord came down and slew 185,000 of the mighty Assyrian army! The sight of all these corpses the next morning caused those that were left alive to flee. Thus was Jerusalem supernaturally delivered.

Isaiah received his call to be a prophet in the year 740 B.C. When he was about twenty years old, he was given a vision of the Lord's glory as He sat enthroned in the heavenly temple. Isaiah tells us:

"In the year that King Uzziah died, (in a VISION) I saw the Lord sitting upon a throne high and lifted up. And the skirts of His train filled the (most holy part of the) temple" (Isa. 6:1).

We learn from John 12:41 that this was a glimpse of the pre-existent Christ in His glory. The apostle John quotes a prophecy from Isaiah. Then he says: *"Isaiah was referring to Jesus* when he made this prediction, for he had seen a vision of the Messiah's glory"* (Living Gospels).

Above the throne stood the seraphim, spirit beings in charge of divine worship and guardianship of the throne. Each of the seraphim had six wings. With one pair they covered their faces, with another they concealed their feet, and with the third pair of wings they flew.

One of the seraphim called out: "Holy, holy, holy, is the Lord of Hosts; the whole earth is full of His glory!" The sound of the angel's voice shook the thresholds of the temple. The holy place was filled with the smoke of God's glory—a symbol of His presence.

The pure praises of the seraphim made Isaiah acknowledge, by contrast, the sins of his own lips. "Woe is me!" he cried out, "For I am a man of unclean lips, and I dwell in the midst of a people of unclean lips. Yet my eyes have seen the King, the Lord of hosts!"

Then one of the heavenly beings flew over to the altar, and with a pair of tongs picked out a burning coal. He touched Isaiah's lips with it, saying, "Now you are cleansed. Your sins are forgiven."

At this point the voice of the Lord was heard asking, "Whom shall I send, and who will go for us?"

"Here am I," replied Isaiah. "Send me."

And the Lord said: "Yes, go. But tell My people this: 'Though you hear My words repeatedly, you won't understand them. Though you watch and watch as I perform My miracles, still you won't know what they mean' " (Isa. 6:9, Living Prophets).

The Lord went on to say that a hardening and a blinding would come upon the rebellious nation of Israel. Isaiah then asked, "How long will it be before they are ready to listen?"

The Lord answered, "Not until their cities are destroyed— without a person left—and the whole country is an utter wasteland, and they are all taken away as slaves to other countries far away, and all the land of Israel lies deserted!

"Yet a tenth—a remnant—will survive. Though Israel is invaded again and again and destroyed, yet Israel will be like a tree cut down, whose stump still lives to grow again" (Isa. 6:13, LP).

In this vision of unforgettable majesty, Isaiah was given his call and commission. He was told what the immediate outcome would be, and also that in the end-time it will only be a remnant of Israel in whom the covenants and promises are realized.

*   *   *

Not all of Isaiah's visions were as exalting and transforming as his first one. In the 21st chapter the prophet says: "A hard and grievous VISION is declared to me." "Living Prophets" tells it most graphically:

"This is God's message concerning Babylon: Disaster is roaring down upon you from the terrible desert, like a whirlwind sweeping from the Negeb.

"I see an awesome VISION: oh, the horror of it all! God is telling me what He is going to do. I see you plundered and destroyed. Elamites and Medes will take part in the siege. Babylon will fall, and the groaning of all the nations she enslaved will end" (Isa. 21:1, 2).

Although this event was some two hundred years in the future, the prophet saw it with the accuracy of history written as it happened. He envisioned the Persian conquerors advancing, mentioning them by name. The suffering he witnessed that would take place in Babylon was frightful. Listen to Isaiah's own words as he describes his reaction to the vision:

"My stomach constricts and burns with pain. Sharp pangs of

horror are upon me, like the pangs of a woman giving birth to a child. I faint when I hear what God is planning. I am terrified, blinded with dismay.

"My mind reels; my heart races; I am gripped by awful fear. All rest at night—so pleasant once—is gone. I lie awake, trembling" (Isa. 21:3, 4).

Then in his mind's eye, he actually seemed to be present at the feast of Belshazzar, king of Babylon. "Look! They are preparing a great banquet! They load the tables with food; they pull up their chairs to eat . . ."

Isaiah saw the people eating and drinking, secure in their reveling. He saw the defilement of the golden vessels taken from God's temple. He watched as the handwriting appeared on the wall. He knew that God's hour had struck! It was time to end the seventy years of captivity and to deliver the chosen people so that their nation might be restored.

Suddenly he heard the words being shouted, "Quick, quick, grab your shields and prepare for battle! You are being attacked!"

The Lord had previously told Isaiah, "When the watchman on the city wall sees a troop of riders, horsemen in pairs on donkeys and on camels, you will know: This is it!" Now the watchman on the wall was shouting, "Look! Here comes a troop of men and chariots, horsemen in pairs!" The deadly foe was at the gates.

In his vision Isaiah heard the watchman cry out what these invaders foretell: "Babylon is fallen, is fallen, and all the idols of Babylon lie broken on the ground!"

The prophet concludes the narration of his vision with these triumphant words:

"O you, my threshed and winnowed one (my own people the Jews who must be trodden down by Babylon), that which I have heard from the Lord of hosts, the God of Israel, I have joyfully announced to you—Babylon is to fall!" (Isa. 21:10).

Remember that all of this witnessed by Isaiah in a vision was not to take place for almost two hundred years. But it was fulfilled exactly as he had seen it, and as the prophet Daniel was later to record it (Dan. 5). The very night of the banquet Belshazzar was killed, and his kingdom taken over by the Medes and Persians.

In another prophecy Isaiah revealed that the prosperous, exultant city of Jerusalem was also to be invaded and to suffer siege and calamity—and this long before the fall of Babylon. The 22nd chapter of Isaiah opens with these words: "The mournful, inspired prediction—a burden to be lifted up—concerning the valley of VISION."

Here Jerusalem is called "the valley of vision" because the prophecy came as Isaiah stood on Zion's hill overlooking the city below. This was another vision of a people engaged in merrymaking, despite the impending danger and death that was threatened by invading armies outside Jerusalem's walls.

Isaiah foresaw that the Assyrians would besiege the city. Many who fled would be captured and slain. The walls of Jerusalem would be breached, and the cry of death echo from the mountainsides. This vision made him look away and weep bitterly . . .

"For it is a day of trouble, and of treading down, and of perplexity by the Lord God of hosts in the valley of VISION, breaking down the walls, and of crying to the mountains" (Isa. 22:5, KJV).

The reason God would permit this to come upon them was that the people of Judah trusted in their weapons of defense and fortified walls to protect them, instead of looking to God and trusting Him for help. Isaiah told them:

"The Lord God of hosts called you to repent, to weep and mourn and shave your heads in sorrow for your sins, and to wear clothes made of sackcloth to show your remorse.

"But instead, you sing and dance and play, and feast and drink. 'Let us eat, drink, and be merry,' you say; 'What's the difference, for tomorrow we die.'

"The Lord of hosts has revealed to me that your unatoned-for sins shall not be purged from you until you are punished. And the punishment will be death" (Isa. 22:12–14, LP).

Isaiah later pronounced a woe upon the drunkards of Ephraim, the ten-tribe northern kingdom of Israel. Ephraim's capital, Samaria, was the glory of Canaan. Built on a hill, Samaria was surrounded by rich valleys and higher hills that were covered over with grain, fruit trees, and vines. But what an ill-use they made of their plenty! They indulged themselves in sensuality; drunkenness in particular was widespread.

Judah and Jerusalem, like Ephraim and Samaria, also had many drunkards. Even the priests and prophets were ensnared in this sin.

"The priest and the prophet reel with strong drink," said Isaiah. "They are confused with wine, they stagger and are gone astray through strong drink. They err in VISION, they stumble in pronouncing judgment" (Isa. 28:7).

Mosaic law obliged the priests to be temperate. Yet they were drunk when engaged in the sacred duties of their office! The prophets were supposed to keep the utmost distance from the sins they reproved in others. Yet many of them had given themselves over to strong drink. No wonder their vision was in error!

Both priest and prophet stumbled in judgment and forgot the law. They reeled and staggered as much mentally as they did physically. They were paving the way to ruin. Isaiah foretold that invasion by Assyria would be their punishment.

A few months after the prophecy was uttered, Ephraim and Samaria were destroyed by the Assyrian king. Judah's judgment was delayed for another hundred years, but it came about as surely as did Ephraim's punishment.

*   *   *

In the 29th chapter, the prophet sees a vision of Jerusalem which is still in the future. It concerns *the battle of Armageddon*, on that great and terrible day when the Lord Jesus Christ returns to this earth.

Isaiah first speaks of the heavy judgment that will be visited upon Jerusalem. "There will be weeping and sorrow; for Jerusalem shall become as her name 'Ariel' means—an altar covered with blood. Enemies will surround the city and build forts around it to destroy it. Her voice will whisper like a ghost from the earth where she lies buried."

Then, suddenly, the picture changes. Jerusalem's enemies will be driven away like chaff before the wind. In an instant the Lord of hosts will come upon them with thunder, earthquake, whirlwind and fire. God is about to deliver His people.

"The multitude of all the nations that fight against Ariel (Jerusalem), even all that fight against her and her stronghold, and that distress her, shall be as a DREAM, a VISION of the night.

"As a hungry man DREAMS of eating, but is still hungry; and as a thirsty man DREAMS of drinking, but is still faint from thirst when he wakes up, so her enemies will DREAM of victorious conquest. But all to no avail" (Isa. 29:7, 8).

Despite the clarity of this prophecy, Isaiah saw that the people were in such a spiritual stupor—so overcome with lethargy, and so lacking in spiritual perception—that God's word was a closed book to them. He told them: "The VISION of all this has become to you like the words of a book that is sealed" (Isa. 29:11).

Religious blindness and empty formalism characterized the condition of the people. God said of them that they paid Him lip service, but their hearts and minds were far from Him. There was no reverence for Him. They just repeated precepts without any thought of their meaning.

The remainder of Isaiah's visions are many and varied. For beauty of style, profundity and breadth of vision, he is without peer. But since our study is based upon the specific scriptural references to dreams and visions, we shall only make a brief summary of the rest of his prophecies.

In them Isaiah predicts the Messiah's first advent and His reception. He tells of the regathering of Israel at the end of the age, and their return to Palestine in unbelief and apostasy. He views the persecution and tribulation they must undergo, followed by the return of their Messiah-King. At this time the remnant that is left will experience bitter repentance and national confession of sin, for they will recognize Him whom they previously rejected and crucified.

Isaiah brilliantly depicts the restoration of Palestine under Christ's millennial reign, and Jerusalem's glory and exaltation as capital of the world. He speaks of the promised blessings for Gentiles in the kingdom. He gives a glimpse beyond the kingdom age to the radiant joy of the new heaven and earth in the eternal state.

His prophecies end with a picture of the worship of the righteous, as contrasted with the torment of the wicked, those who have rebelled against God: "For their worm shall not die, their fire shall not be quenched, and they shall be an abhorrence to all mankind" (Isa. 66:24).

The Bible does not tell us how the aristocratic Isaiah met his death. Tradition has it that he suffered martyrdom by being placed in a hollow log and sawn in half lengthwise. This was done during the persecution of the true servants of God under the evil king Manasseh, son of Hezekiah. It is therefore to Isaiah that Hebrews 11:37 is supposed to refer when it speaks of the prophets, one of whom was "sawn asunder."

Jeremiah

Moving forward in time about a hundred years from Isaiah's day, we meet the second of the major prophets—Jeremiah. The book bearing his name is not called his "vision," as was the book of Isaiah. But we know that many of his revelations from God came visually to him.

Belonging to a priestly family living near Jerusalem, Jeremiah was called to be a prophet when he was a very young man. It was in 626 B.C. that the call came, although the Lord had chosen him long before that. Jeremiah tells us:

"The word of the Lord came to me saying,

"Before I formed you in the womb I knew and approved of you (as My chosen instrument). Before you were born I separated and set you apart, consecrating you; and I appointed you a prophet to the nations" (Jer. 1:4, 5).

Jeremiah protested that he could not speak, for he was only a youth. The Lord replied, "You will go wherever I send you and speak whatever I tell you. And don't be afraid of the people, for I, the Lord, will be with you and see you through."

Then God touched his mouth and said, "Behold, I have put My words in your mouth. Today your work begins, to warn the nations and the kingdoms of the world. In accord with My words spoken through your mouth, I will tear down some and destroy them, and plant others and nurture them and make them strong and great."

Jeremiah's commission was immediately supported by two visions.

"Moreover the word of the Lord came to me, saying, Jeremiah, what do you see? And I said, I see a branch or shoot of an almond tree (the emblem of alertness and activity, blossoming in late winter).

"Then said the Lord to me, You have seen well, for I am alert and active, watching over My word to perform it" (Jer. 1:11, 12).

While this vision would have little meaning for us, it signifiec' much to Jeremiah. The northern kingdom of Israel (Samaria) had fallen to the Assyrians nearly a hundred years before. Since then the Assyrian empire had disintegrated. Now Babylon and Egypt were struggling against each other for leadership of the East. Jeremiah's native Judah, the southern kingdom of Israel, contrived to remain a separate kingdom. But the nation was incorrigibly corrupt.

The apostasy and moral degeneracy of the people was of long-standing. Jeremiah knew that God's judgment upon them would not be forever delayed. Because the almond tree is one of the earliest to show life in the spring, this vision signified that God would very soon execute His purposes and judgments upon Judah.

Jeremiah's prophetic "sight" of this first sign was commended by the Lord. Immediately afterward the word of the Lord came a second time saying: "What do you see?

"And I said, I see a boiling pot, and the face of it is tipped away from the north (its mouth about to pour forth on the south, Judea).

"Then the Lord said to me, Out of the north the evil (which the prophets had foretold as the result of national sin) shall disclose itself and break forth upon all the inhabitants of the land" (Jer. 1:13, 14).

Jeremiah understood that the boiling pot in this vision pictured God's judgment boiling over on Judah for her sin and idolatry. Invasion would come, and it would be from the north. That ruled out Egypt. Babylon was on the east, but they would go around the desert and come down from the north into Palestine.

God then sent Jeremiah out to tell the people all that He commanded him. Though they would attack him for it, God assured him that they would not prevail against him. "For I am with you, says the Lord, to deliver you" (Jer. 1:19).

Jeremiah was a lonely man. The natural aspirations of youth were denied him. God told him not to marry and have children in Jerusalem, for the city would not stand long enough for a family to be brought up in it. The prophet was a gentle person, shy but tenacious, high-strung and emotional. Time and time again he was plunged into the depths of grief and despair.

He was a great soul—abounding in courage, loyalty, and spiritual dignity—yet a tragic figure. Those whom he loved hated him. He unmasked the nation's sins and broadcast its judgment, all the while knowing that it would end in futility. He suffered pain and distress of heart over the calamities that he saw were to come upon Judah.

One of the most unusual visions any prophet ever had was vouchsafed to Jeremiah. He beheld the totally desolate and empty condition of the earth as it was before the days of Adam . . .

This was when the original earth became chaos through the fall of Lucifer. It was then that God brought darkness and the first great universal cataclysm upon the earth to destroy all life. This catastrophic upheaval was far worse than the flood in Noah's day. Noah's flood did not destroy all life, and at that time the heavens had light. There were fruitful places left on the earth, whereas in the judgment brought upon the original earth, nothing remained.

Jeremiah exclaims: "I beheld the earth, and lo, it was without form, and void; and the heavens, and they had no light.

"I beheld the mountains, and lo, they trembled, and all the hills moved lightly to and fro . . . I beheld, and lo, there was no man, and all the birds of the air had fled.

"I looked, and lo, the fruitful land was a desert, and all its cities were laid waste before the Lord's presence, by His fierce anger" (Jer. 4:23–26).

What a graphic picture of the earth under a total curse—desolate, empty, no light, hills and mountains undergoing convulsions—no life of any kind left!

God's purpose in showing Jeremiah the total destruction of

life on this planet was to reveal how the land of Judah would be destroyed in his day, and to make a comparison between the two times. In the original judgment, everything was destroyed. But in the coming judgment, the Lord promised He would not make a full end of the land or of the people.

*   *   *

Jeremiah is particularly noted for his scathing denunciation of the false prophets. These were the professional priests of his day, who used their office to make money. They duped the people of Judah into a state of false optimism. In the 14th chapter, 14th verse, Jeremiah declares:

"Then the Lord said, The prophets are telling lies in My name. I didn't send them, or tell them to speak, or give them any message. They prophesy of VISIONS and revelations they have never seen nor heard. They speak foolishness concocted out of their own lying hearts" (Living Prophets).

There were false prophets in Jeremiah's day, just as there are false clergymen in our day. They were telling the people then: "All is well. Judgment Day will not come. God is love. He sends only peace and blessing."

Sounds very much like the message of many of today's "men of the cloth," doesn't it? Superficial ministers—who do not believe or teach what the Bible says—take only sentences here and there which are to their liking, ignoring everything about repentance for sin, punishment, coming judgment, and God's wrath. *Such religious spokesmen are not sent from God.*

"Therefore, the Lord says, I will punish these lying prophets who have spoken in My name though I did not send them, who say no war shall come nor famine. By war and famine they themselves shall die!" (Jer. 14:15 LP).

As for the people who listen to these false teachers, the Lord added that their bodies would be thrown into the streets, victims of war and famine. "For I will pour out terrible punishment upon them for their sins."

Early in his ministry Jeremiah was forced to leave his home town, which was just three miles outside of Jerusalem, because of a plot against him by his own brethren. The Holy Spirit revealed to him, probably in a vision, that the men of Anathoth planned to kill him.

How well this illustrates the truth of Jesus' statement: "A prophet is not without honor, except in his own country, and among his own kin, and in his own house" (Mk. 6:4).

The treacherous dealing of his neighbors, and especially his own relatives, came as a painful shock to Jeremiah. But that was just the beginning of his troubles. His chief enemies were the faithless and false prophets of Jerusalem, where he went to live after he left the village of his birth.

They were so incensed by his prophecies against Judah that they planned to put him to death in order to silence him. The officiating high priest arrested him, had him beaten with thirty-nine stripes, and made him pass the night in the stocks exposed to the jeers of scoffers at the most public gate of the temple.

This mockery and rebuff caused Jeremiah to feel that he was an utter failure and his labor in vain. He determined to quit speaking the word of the Lord. But then God's word in his heart became like a fire burning in his bones, and he could hold it in no longer. So he continued to prophesy the truth, and to speak out boldly against the false prophets.

In chapter 23, verse 16, he says of them: "They teach you vanity—emptiness, falsity, and futility—and fill you with vain hopes. They speak a VISION of their own minds, and not from the mouth of the Lord."

Many of these wicked men prophesied lies in the name of God by claiming to have received a dream. *God does use dreams to communicate with man, but dreams must be tested to prove whether they are inspired of God.* If they are not, they should be told as just a dream. But if a dream contains God's word, it is to be spoken of as certain truth.

Jeremiah makes this very plain in verses 25-32, chapter 23. God is speaking:

"I have heard what the prophets have said who prophesy lies in My name, saying, I have DREAMED, I have DREAMED VISIONS on my bed at night."

Then the Lord asks, "How long will this continue? If they

are 'prophets,' they are prophets of deceit, inventing everything they say.

"Do they think to cause My people to forget My name by their DREAMS which every man tells to his neighbor, as their fathers forgot My name because of Baal?

"The prophet who has a DREAM, let him tell a DREAM. He who has My word, let him speak My word faithfully. What has straw in common with wheat for nourishment? says the Lord."

God goes on to ask, "Does not My word burn like fire and consume all that cannot endure the test? Is it not like a hammer that smashes to pieces the rock of stubborn resistance?

"So I stand against these 'prophets' who get their messages from each other—these smooth-tongued prophets who say, 'This message is from God!' Their made-up DREAMS are flippant lies that lead My people into sin. I did not send them, and they have no message at all for My people, says the Lord."

After this, God commanded Jeremiah to stand in the court of the temple and speak to the people of all the cities of Judah who came there to worship. He was to tell them that if they would repent, quit their sins, and obey God, the Lord would even yet be merciful to them and withhold His judgment.

But they were insensible to God's offer of pardon, and oblivious to the menace of an invincible enemy. They would not listen to Jeremiah. Instead, the rebellious people joined the priests and rose up against the prophet. They demanded that he be put to death for his predictions against the temple and their beloved Jerusalem. Only by the help of a friend, who got him out of the hands of the mob, did Jeremiah barely escape with his life.

*   *   *

Josiah, Jehoahaz, Jehoiakim, Jehoiachin, and *Zedekiah* were the last five kings of Judah. Jeremiah prophesied under all of them.

In the beginning of the reign of *Jehoiakim*, third of the final rulers, the Lord commanded Jeremiah to make wooden yokes. One of them was to be fastened around his own neck with leather straps. He was to wear this in public as a symbol from God to teach the people submission.

The other yokes he was to send to the kings of six nations, including Judah. These yokes were a sign that all those lands had been given by God Himself to Nebuchadnezzar, king of Babylon. Thus God was warning them to submit themselves to the inevitable yoke of Babylon and serve Nebuchadnezzar. If they would not do this, they would be destroyed.

"So do not listen to your false prophets, your diviners, your DREAMS (whether your own or others'), your soothsayers, your sorcerers, who say to you, You shall not serve the king of Babylon.

"For they prophesy a lie to you, which shall cause you to be removed far from your land. And I will drive you out, and you will perish" (Jer. 27:9, 10).

But the people preferred to listen to the false prophets who swarmed the city, rather than to Jeremiah. The former told them what they wanted to hear.

Later in this same reign of Jehoiakim, Jeremiah was put in prison because of his prophecies. The people believed that they would no longer be troubled by hearing the prophet speak the words of the Lord. But Jeremiah wrote them down upon a scroll. His loyal friend and secretary, Baruch, took them to the temple. There on the fast day a great crowd gathered to worship, and Baruch read the message to many.

This was more than a year after the scroll was begun. Soon afterward the king sent for this lengthy roll and had it read in his hearing. He was sitting in his winter house before an open fire. After three or four pages, the king could stand no more. He took a penknife, cut the roll to pieces, and threw all of it into the fire.

But the word of God came to Jeremiah to rewrite the scroll, this time adding judgment upon judgment!

During the reign of the succeeding king—*Jehoiachin,* fourth of the last rulers of Judah—Jerusalem was besieged. Nebuchadnezzar, king of Babylon, entered the city in 597 B.C. He carried away as captives the best of the craftsmen and citizenry. Jehoiachin himself was deported to Babylon along with the rest. Jeremiah chose to remain behind and keep on with his ministry in Jerusalem.

At first, after the conquest of Jerusalem, Nebuchadnezzer allowed Judah to continue its existence as a vassal state. The successor to the throne of the deposed Jehoiachin was his uncle, renamed *Zedekiah* by the Chaldean king. Zedekiah was a faithless and base man, ruling over the moral dregs of the nation. His officials, and the apostates who remained in Jerusalem to support them, were of a mind to resist Babylon, with Egypt's help. They failed to draw any warning from the fate that had overtaken their brethren.

About this time Jeremiah was given a most descriptive and applicable vision. He tells us: "The Lord showed me (in a VISION) two baskets of figs set before the temple of the Lord.

"One basket had very good figs, like the figs that are first ripe. But the other basket had very bad figs, so bad that they could not be eaten" (Jer. 24:1, 2).

When the Lord asked, "What do you see, Jeremiah?" the prophet replied, "Figs, some very good, and some very bad."

Then the Lord explained that the good figs represented the Jewish exiles who were sent to Babylon. God promised that those who had accepted His judgment would be well-treated and eventually brought back from captivity to their own land. They would understand that it had been God's doing, and they would return to Him with their whole hearts.

"As for the bad figs, which cannot be eaten because they are so bad, surely thus says the Lord, so will I give up Zedekiah the king of Judah, and his princes, and the residue of Jerusalem that remain in this land, and those who dwell in the land of Egypt" (Jer. 24:8).

All who had stubbornly refused to accept God's judgment would be treated like spoiled figs, too bad to use. The Lord went on to say that He would make them repulsive to every nation of the earth. They would be mocked and taunted and cursed wherever He compelled them to go.

God concluded with these words: "I will send massacre and famine and disease among them until they are destroyed from the land of Israel, which I gave to them and to their fathers" (Jer. 24:10, LP).

At the time of the Babylonian conquest of Jerusalem, the temple was plundered by Nebuchadnezzar's soldiers. Some of the sacred vessels of the temple were carried away. The false prophets said that they would be brought back again very soon.

Jeremiah, the true prophet, told them that the vessels would not be brought back for seventy years—until the time of captivity was ended. Furthermore, he said that even those temple vessels which Nebuchadnezzar had not previously taken were going to be carried off.

In a letter to the Jewish exiles in Babylon, Jeremiah advised them to build houses there, plant vineyards, raise children and grandchildren. He told them to pray and work for the peace and prosperity of that land, for only then would they have peace themselves.

Then he warned them again not to trust in the false prophets and mediums that were among them. Even in exile Judah was being led astray by false prophets who predicted an early return from captivity.

Part of the letter stated: "For thus says the Lord of hosts, the God of Israel: Let not your false prophets and your diviners who are in your midst deceive you. Pay no attention and attach no significance to your DREAMS which you DREAM, or to theirs,

"For they prophesy falsely to you in My name. I have not sent them, says the Lord" (Jer. 29:8, 9).

* * *

After he had reigned as king of Judah for several years, Zedekiah compromised himself irrevocably in the eyes of Nebuchadnezzar by entering into treasonable negotiations with Egypt's Pharaoh. As a result, in January, 588 B.C. the Babylonians besieged Jerusalem for the second time.

Jeremiah had warned that this would happen, and he advised surrender. But neither the king nor his officials would listen to what the Lord said through the prophet.

As the siege proceeded, the hostility of Jeremiah's enemies became more intense. When the prophet started to leave the city to go to the land of Benjamin where he had purchased some property, the sentry at the gate had him arrested. He was charged with desertion, flogged, and cast into a dungeon beneath the palace.

Later the king transferred him to a prison in the guard-court. But upon the demand of the princes, the weak king turned Jeremiah over to them to do with as they would. They accused him of being a traitor, and threw him into an unused cistern to die of starvation and exposure. He was lowered into this dreadful pit by ropes, and left to sink in the mire.

But one of the king's slaves, an Ethiopian, heard of the prophet's plight. He pleaded with the king to rescue him. Zedekiah gave the slave thirty men to help get Jeremiah out of the cistern. After his deliverance he remained in the court of the prison where he had previously been confined. He was still there when Nebuchadnezzar captured the city and destroyed the temple in August, 586 B.C., taking the last of its golden vessels back to Babylon.

Zedekiah attempted to flee from Jerusalem, but he was caught and brought before Nebuchadnezzar. There he was made to watch while his sons and all the princes of Judah were killed. Then both of his eyes were gouged out. He was taken in chains to Babylon, and put in prison for the rest of his life.

The people in Jerusalem were taken as prisoners and led in a chain gang to Ramah, about five miles north of the city. Here the captives were gathered and examined. Jeremiah was singled out from the others and released, because his predictions against Judah and Jerusalem had been considered favorable to Nebuchadnezzar.

The prophet was invited to go to Babylon where he was promised excellent treatment. But if he did not want to do this, he was told he was free to go anywhere he wished. Jeremiah chose to remain among the remnant of his people who were to be left to till the land and tend the crops.

Nebuchadnezzar appointed a man named *Gedaliah* as governor over Judah. Jeremiah was to assist him in the task of keeping the peace. But a member of one of the Jewish guerrilla bands, who had fled from Judah to escape the Babylonian armies, assassinated Gedaliah. In addition to murdering the governor and all his officials, including the Babylonian soldiers who were with him, the guerrillas killed a number of other men before making their escape.

The remnant of Israelites, in dire perplexity, besought Jeremiah to ask the Lord what they should do. The answer came that they should remain in the land. But they rejected the word of God and decided to go to Egypt. The Lord warned them if they did this, they would all die in Egypt from sword, famine, and disease. They went, anyway, compelling Jeremiah and Baruch to go with them.

When they settled in the valley of the Nile, they continued the same idolatrous practices that had brought judgment upon them in Judah. Jeremiah sternly warned them against this wickedness. According to Christian tradition, it was because of these warnings and reproofs that Jeremiah met a martyr's death in Egypt, being stoned by his own people. Jewish tradition, however, maintains that he escaped to Babylon and died there. The Bible itself does not tell us of his fate.

As for the Jews who so resented and refused to believe the prophet's words of impending judgment, they were all destroyed —every one of them—in the land of Egypt, just as the Lord had told them they would be.

Lamentations

Jeremiah was one of the greatest of all the prophets, speaking forth God's words faithfully. Yet he met with bitter opposition his entire lifetime. His heart was broken over the sins of his people. From the very beginning he foresaw the tragic end to which the beautiful city of Jerusalem and the magnificent temple were to come.

No wonder that when all the glory that once existed was laid waste, he pours out his sorrow and anguish in his Lamentations. Since this study is concerned with all scriptural references to dreams and visions, we include a few verses from that poetical book, as translated in the Living Series of Bible paraphrases:

"The Lord determined to destroy Jerusalem. He laid out an unalterable line of destruction. Therefore the ramparts and walls fell down before Him.

"Jerusalem's gates are useless. All their locks and bars are broken, for He has crushed them. Her kings and princes are enslaved in far-off lands, without a temple, without a divine law to govern them, or prophetic VISION to guide them.

"The elders of Jerusalem sit upon the ground in silence, clothed in sackcloth. They throw dust upon their heads in sorrow and despair. The virgins of Jerusalem hang their heads in shame.

"I have cried until the tears no longer come. My heart is broken, my spirit poured out, as I see what has happened to my people" (Lam. 2:8–11).

Ezekiel

While Jeremiah was proclaiming the word of the Lord in Jerusalem, another faithful prophet was at work among the early exiles in Babylon. His name was Ezekiel, and he was not only a prophet but a priest as well.

In 597 B.C. when Ezekiel was twenty-five years old, he was carried away to Babylonia. In this early group of captives, just the upper class of people—the flower of the nobility and the best craftsmen in the land—were taken. This was about ten or eleven years before the fall of Jerusalem.

Ezekiel settled in a little village by the river Chebar, about fifty miles from the great city of Babylon. Five years later he received his call as a prophet, and for twenty-two years thereafter he dealt with the discouraged captives to whom God had sent him.

Ezekiel may have been a pupil of the older prophet Jeremiah. At any rate he preached the same message of judgment for sin, the folly of opposing Babylon and seeking help from Egypt. Ezekiel showed that the Lord was justified in sending His people into captivity.

Many prophecies regarding the final restoration of all things—of the nation, the land, the city, and the temple—are included in Ezekiel's messages. He gave to Israel beautiful pictures of the happy life they will enjoy in their ultimate return to Palestine. Then God will gather all His scattered sheep and bring them home to dwell forever in His perfect kingdom.

We do not know if the prophet had any children, but we do know that he was married. His wife died suddenly on the very day that Nebuchadnezzar began his final siege of Jerusalem. Her death was used as a sign to teach Israel that just as surely as God had taken away "the desire of Ezekiel's eyes," so He would take away the desire of their eyes—the beautiful temple, the strength of their nation. Their sons and daughters would be slaughtered by the sword.

God commanded Ezekiel not to weep or show any other sign of mourning over his loss, not even to accept the food brought by consoling friends. Even so would the people of Israel be required to refrain from public mourning over the destruction of Jerusalem.

The Book of Ezekiel opens with a remarkable "visitation from the Most High." It was the first of seven visions of God's glory which were given him. Ezekiel received his call and commission to his prophetic work by means of this vision. It came, as he said:

"As I was among the captives by the river of Chebar, the heavens were opened, and I saw VISIONS of God" (Ezk. 1:1).

In the vision he beheld a whirlwind coming toward him from the north, and a great flaming cloud. In the midst of this was a shining chariot drawn by four cherubim. Each of these living creatures had four faces, two pairs of wings, and what looked like human hands under their wings. A "wheel within a wheel" was beside each one. The rims of the wheels were very high, and they were full of eyes all around.

When the wheels stopped, the wings of the cherubim were let down. Ezekiel saw a crystal floor, or platform, above the heads of these strange beings. On this floor rested a sapphire throne. *Seated on the throne was Almighty God Himself, a figure of brilliant splendor clothed in fiery iridescent radiance.* There was a glowing rainbow round about Him.

This spectacular vision caused Ezekiel to fall prostrate to the ground. He had seen, with his own eyes, the Holy One of Israel —revealed in glory, transported by beings from the celestial realm —coming down to earth to deal in judgment with His apostate people.

Someone may question the very thought of God riding from place to place in anything, let alone a chariot. But in 2 Samuel

22:11 King David, speaking under the inspiration of the Holy Spirit, declares that God came down from heaven . . . "And He rode upon a cherub, and did fly. He was seen upon the wings of the wind."

This same passage is repeated in Psalm 18:10. And in the 68th Psalm we read in the 17th verse: "The chariots of God are twenty thousand, even thousands of angels."

The Bible teaches that God travels from place to place by various means as He chooses. He is not limited to heaven. While His spiritual presence can be in all places at the same time, His spirit body cannot be everywhere present. As for His use of chariots, the scriptures speak in many places of chariots of fire, and chariots drawn by spirit "horses." One of the Psalms tells us that God "makes the clouds His chariot."

John on Patmos, looking into the future, saw heaven opened and Christ coming down to earth as King of kings and Lord of lords. Jesus is pictured riding a white horse—as are all those in His armies. So apparently God *does* choose means of transportation on certain occasions.

The Lord told the prostrate Ezekiel to stand up. The Holy Spirit assisted him to his feet. Then God said, "I am sending you to the nation of Israel, a nation rebelling against Me. They and their fathers have kept on sinning against Me until this very hour. I am sending you to give them My messages. Whether they listen or not, they will at least know they have a prophet among them."

Then Ezekiel saw a hand holding out a scroll with writing on both sides. He unrolled it and observed that it was full of warnings and sorrows and pronouncements of doom. The Lord told him to eat the scroll. This symbolized that he must feed upon and digest the word of God before beginning his ministry. Ezekiel ate it, and it was sweet as honey to the taste. The privilege of being God's messenger brought great joy, though the message itself was one of sadness.

His commission to be God's mouthpiece to the exiles having been completed, the glory of the Lord departed. Ezekiel heard the noise of the wings of the cherubim and the wheels of the chariot as it vanished from sight.

After this second vision of the scroll, the prophet was lifted up by the Spirit and taken from beside the Chebar river back to the colony of Jewish exiles in his own village in Babylonia. Ezekiel sat among them, overwhelmed, for seven days. Then the word of the Lord came to him again. As the appointed watchman for Israel, he was told to pass on to them God's warning: if they did not repent of their wickedness, they would die in their sins. And if Ezekiel did not tell them this, God would require his blood for theirs.

The prophet was then ordered to go out into the valley, and the Lord would talk further with him there. He arose and went. There he saw the glory of the Lord, just as he had in his first vision. He fell to the ground on his face (Ezk. 3:22, 23).

In this vision, his third, Ezekiel was told to imprison himself in his house where he would be stricken dumb. This was so that he could not reprove Israel, except as God opened his mouth to speak through him. There followed instructions regarding a series of signs Ezekiel was to give the people (chaps. 4–6).

These various pantomimes, to be acted out by Ezekiel, were designed to illustrate God's messages. *They were picture-prophecies of the awful conditions that would prevail in Jerusalem during its siege and fall.* The shortage of food and water in the land, and the resultant hunger would drive some of its occupants into cannibalism. Disgrace and defeat would precede the complete destruction of the city. The Lord said that only a remnant would survive to learn the purpose of such terrible chastisements.

As he is delivering a message of doom upon the land of Israel, Ezekiel uses the word "vision" twice. He warns that the day of God's wrath is drawing near. There will be nothing to buy or sell. Even if a merchant lives, his business will be gone. All will be destroyed. Not one of those whose lives were filled with sin will recover.

"The seller shall not return to that which is sold, even were they yet alive. For the VISION of punishment is touching Israel's whole multitude. He shall not come back, neither shall any strengthen himself whose life is in his iniquity" (Ezk. 7:13).

He goes on to say that misfortune and disaster will befall them.

They will long for a vision from the prophet, and for guidance from the law, which was the realm of the priest, and for the counsel of wisdom from the elders. But none will be forthcoming.

"Calamity shall come upon calamity, and rumor shall be upon rumor. They shall seek a VISION of the prophet, and the law and instruction shall cease from the distracted priest, and counsel from the dismayed elders" (Ezk. 7:26).

*   *   *

Ezekiel's fourth vision was most unusual. It occurred a little over a year after his call to be a prophet.

While he was sitting in his own house talking with the elders of Judah, suddenly there appeared before him the likeness of a Man. From His waist down His body was like fire, and from His waist up He was all amber-colored brightness.

"He put forth the form of a hand, and took me by a lock of my head. The Spirit lifted me up between the earth and the heavens, and brought me in the VISIONS of God to Jerusalem,

"To the entrance of the door of the inner court which faces toward the north, where is the seat of the idol-image of jealousy, which provokes to jealousy.

"And behold, there was the glory of the God of Israel (who had loved and chosen them), like the VISION I saw in the plain" (Ezk. 8:3, 4).

Ezekiel was not literally transported to Jerusalem. He was taken there in spirit, while his body remained at home in a trance-like state. In the temple he was shown the terrible idolatry that was being practiced in the very house of the Lord.

First, there was the image of jealousy, a heathen idol so named because of the divine jealousy which it aroused. It was a carved wooden image, probably a replica of the one which originally had been brought into the temple about 650 B.C. by the evil king Manasseh. Later his grandson, good king Josiah, removed this desecration from God's house and burned it. The image had not been there when Ezekiel left Jerusalem. Now he saw it set up in the entrance leading to the holy place!

Next the prophet was taken into one of the hidden chambers

of the gateway. When he became accustomed to the darkness, the sight that met his eyes was shocking. Seventy elders of Israel were carrying on animal worship in secret! They were offering incense to images and to pictures painted on the walls of all kinds of creeping things and unclean beasts.

At the north gate of the temple he was shown another disgraceful scene. There women of Israel sat weeping for Tammuz, a Babylonian god of fertility who was supposed to die annually and subsequently be resurrected. Lascivious and immoral rites were practiced by the women who worshiped this pagan deity.

Ezekiel was then brought into the inner court of the temple. Near the bronze altar about twenty-five men were standing with their backs to the sanctuary of the Lord. They were facing east and worshiping the sun. Their position indicated the greatest contempt for the God of Israel—*Whose glory was at that very moment present in their midst!* Visible to the prophet, it was of course unseen by the apostate Israelites.

Had Ezekiel not witnessed all this for himself, he would never have believed that his people could be committing such despicable acts. Because of all the heinous abominations, God declared that He would deal with these idolaters in wrath. He would show no pity or mercy.

As the vision continued, a divine call went forth for destruction.

Six supernatural beings appeared, each with a sword. With them was one who wore the white linen clothing of a priest and carried a writer's case strapped to his side. These heavenly visitors went into the inner court of the temple and stood beside the bronze altar. Just then the Shekinah glory of the Lord rose from the cherubim where it had rested and stood above the entrance to the temple (Ezk. 9:1–3a).

The man with the writer's case was ordered to walk through the streets of Jerusalem. He was to put a mark on the foreheads of the persons who wept because of the sins they saw around them. The other men were directed by the Lord to follow the linen-clothed scribe through the city. They were to kill everyone whose forehead was not marked.

"Begin right here at the temple," commanded the Lord. And

they began by killing the twenty-five sun-worshipers and the seventy elders engaged in the abhorrent heathen rites in one of the dark chambers of the sanctuary.

When the divine orders had been fulfilled, the man in the linen clothing returned. At the same time the glory of the Lord reappeared, marking Ezekiel's fifth vision of it. Again he saw the throne of beautiful blue sapphire resting over the heads of the cherubim. The temple was filled with the cloud of glory, and the courts were illumined with its brightness (Ezk. 10:1).

The man in linen was told to take a handful of live coals from the flames between the cherubim and scatter them over the idolatry-ridden city. This part of the vision pointed to the burning of Jerusalem as the final stage of her punishment.

Following this, Ezekiel watched the glory of the Lord depart forever from Solomon's magnificent temple. Vivid indeed is the prophet's description of the gradual, majestic departure. First the Shekinah glory left its place above the mercy seat in the holy of holies and moved to the inner court. From there it was slowly borne away on the wings of the cherubim. These were the beings who came in the flaming chariot bearing the throne of God and the Almighty Himself (Ezk. 10:4–22).

The glory passed over the east gate of the temple and rose up from the midst of the city. *It was last seen lingering above the mount of Olives* . . . (Ezk. 11:23).

Afterward the prophet, still by means of the vision, was brought back to Babylon. There he made known to his people all the things he had witnessed. To quote his own words:

"The Spirit lifted me up and brought me in VISION by the Spirit of God into Chaldea, to the exiles. Then the VISION that I had seen went up from me.

"And I told the exiles everything that the Lord had shown me" (Ezk. 11:24, 25).

Ezekiel's audience, however, was deaf to the meaning of the vision he related. So the Lord commanded him to give them, in new symbolic actions, a further picture of the coming fate of Jerusalem, its king, and its people. He was required to act out various signs demonstrating how the people would be driven out of their homes, and how king Zedekiah would be captured, blinded, and imprisoned for the rest of his life. Unbelief in God's true prophets was shown to be the cause of this judgment.

But even these visual portrayals made little impression on the Israelites. Half of them reacted by quoting a common saying that prophecy was no longer fulfilled. So much false prophecy, which *was* of course unfulfilled, had led Israel to doubt all prophecy. The rest of the people believed that Ezekiel's prophecies, though true, referred to a very distant future.

In connection with the first false view, the word of the Lord came:

"Son of man, what is this proverb that you have in the land of Israel, saying, The days drag on, and every VISION comes to nothing and is not fulfilled?" (Ezk. 12:22).

The Lord announced that He would put an end to this proverb. No longer would it be used in Israel. He told Ezekiel to tell them: "The days are at hand, and the fulfillment of every VISION. For there shall be no more any false, empty, and fruitless VISION or flattering divination in the house of Israel" (Ezk. 12:23, 24).

As for their remarks that: "The VISION Ezekiel sees is for many days to come, and he prophesies of the times that are far off" (Ezk. 12:27), the Lord said to tell them there would be no deferment. What Ezekiel had predicted would be performed without delay.

False prophecy accompanied true prophecy in Israel like its shadow. While prophets such as Jeremiah and Ezekiel spoke in God's name a message which they had really received from Him, the false prophets used His name to sanction messages which were merely the product of their own heart and spirit. These messages were smooth and agreeable, but they did not deserve the name of prophecy. They were on the same level as heathen divination.

To all false prophets, God spoke directly, charging them:

"Have you not seen a false VISION, and have you not spoken a lying divination when you say, The Lord says, although I have not spoken?" (Ezk. 13:7).

He went on to say that His wrath will quickly fall upon

Jerusalem and upon "the false prophets of Israel who prophesied deceitfully about Jerusalem, seeing VISIONS of peace for her when there is no peace, says the Lord God" (Ezk. 13:16).

*   *   *

Ezekiel's best-known vision is no doubt that of the valley of dry bones. In a trance, under the influence of God's inspiration, the prophet was transported to a valley full of dry bones. As he prophesied to them, they came together into complete skeletons. These became covered with sinews, flesh, and skin. Then the wind blew upon the inanimate bodies, and they stood up alive!

The dry bones in this vision represent the whole house of Israel. Once they were alive as a nation and enjoyed the grace and favor of God. But they have long been dead because of sin. The prophecy regarding them is that in the future the scattered remains of that dead nation will be brought together. God will put flesh and skin upon them. Through the power of the Holy Spirit He will cause breath to enter those dry bones, and they will live again.

Thus is Israel promised restoration when God gathers them from among the nations where they have been scattered, and brings them back to their own land. Under the Messiah, during the millennium, they will enter once more into the proper relationship with Him.

Many years later—in fact fourteen years after the destruction of Jerusalem—by means of another vision, Ezekiel was again transported to Palestine. Here he witnessed a supernatural and miraculous picture of the great future temple to be built during the kingdom age.

"In the VISIONS of God he brought me into the land of Israel and set me down upon a very high mountain, on the south side of which there was what seemed to be the structure of a city" (Ezk. 40:2).

Entering into the city, Ezekiel saw an angelic being standing beside the temple gate. His face shone like bronze, and he was holding in his hand a measuring tape and a measuring stick.

He said to Ezekiel, "Watch carefully, listen attentively, and take to heart everything I show you, for you have been brought here for that purpose. Then you are to return to the people of Israel and tell them all you have seen."

There followed a lengthy and detailed description of the millennial temple. Then the angel brought Ezekiel to the outer east gate. Here he was granted his sixth vision of the glory of the Lord. *In this vision he saw the Shekinah glory return to the temple, to take up residence in the holy of holies during the coming age.*

The glory of the Lord appeared from the east. The sound of His coming was like the roar of many waters, and the whole earth shone with His radiance.

"The VISION which I saw was like the VISION I had seen when I came to foretell the destruction of the city, and like the VISION I had seen beside the river Chebar (near Babylon). And I fell on my face" (Ezk. 43:3).

The glory of the Lord entered the temple by the gate facing east. Ezekiel was caught up by the Holy Spirit and brought into the inner court. There he beheld the glory of the Lord filling the temple. Then he heard the voice of the Lord speaking to him from within the temple:

"He said to me, Son of man, this is the place of My throne, and the place of the soles of My feet, where I will dwell in the midst of the children of Israel forever.

"And My holy name the house of Israel shall no more profane, neither they nor their kings, by their idolatrous harlotry, nor by the dead bodies and monuments of their kings" (Ezk. 43:7).

The voice from within the temple announced that God would some day dwell forever in the midst of His people. No longer would His sanctuary be defiled as of old by the people's wickedness, or by the nearness of the royal palace and sepulchres.

Ezekiel was then given detailed instructions regarding the altar of burnt offering which is to be built in the future temple. After that he was brought through the inner north passageway to the front of the temple. There he viewed the seventh and last of his visions of the glory of the Lord.

"I looked, and behold, the glory of the Lord filled the house of the Lord. And I fell upon my face" (Ezk. 44:4).

The entire vision closes with a marvelous picture of the river that issues from beneath the sanctuary of the new earthly Jerusalem. Its holy waters will flow down through the city toward the east and into the desert. Then the river will divide and become two great rivers, one flowing into the Dead Sea and the other into the Mediterranean. Wherever its life-giving waters go, they will heal the land.

On either side of the banks of this river are many trees. They are evergreen fruit trees, bearing monthly in abundance. Their leaves will be used for medicinal purposes, for they contain properties that will enable human bodies to live on and on without sickness and disease (Ezk. 47:1–12).

The promised land is to be divided into twelve equal parts for the twelve tribes. The section immediately surrounding the sanctuary will be reserved for the Levites and the priests. East and west of this will be land belonging to the prince of Israel. Adjacent to the holy section to the south of the sanctuary is a strip of land for public use—for homes, pasture, and parks. In the center of this area will be the foursquare city of Jerusalem.

Ezekiel closes his book with these beautiful words expressing the abiding presence of God with His people: "And the name of the city from that day shall be *'The Lord is There'* " (Ezk. 48:35).

As for Ezekiel's personal fate, an uncertain tradition states that he died a martyr's death at the hands of his fellow exiles, who resented the tone of his prophecies.

*   *   *

In this section of our study, we saw where all three men— *Isaiah, Jeremiah,* and *Ezekiel*—received their call, or were initiated into the office of a prophet, by means of a vision. Most of their prophecies were given in vision form.

Occasionally each man was required to act out in his own life the message God wanted to get across to His people. These prophets of old not only saw future events illustrated before their eyes in visions, but they themselves often had to become living illustrations. And none of these assignments was pleasant or easy.

Who hasn't heard the song, *"Dry Bones"*? Or the one that begins: *"Ezekiel saw the wheel, way up in the middle of the air . . ."*? Because of this chapter, we are a little more familiar with the two visions upon which these songs are based.

And we have learned a great deal about a number of other "Visitations from the Most High" as well.

CHAPTER FOUR

Secrets Hidden In Dreams

Daniel is the man who drew back the curtain of the future and unveiled hidden things as no one before him had ever done. He has often been called "the prophet of dreams." Daniel is the last member of the quartet of major "writing prophets" of the Old Testament, as grouped in our English Bible.

Like Isaiah, he was of royal or noble descent. In common with Ezekiel, he was brought as a captive to Babylon, there to spend the rest of his life in exile. Daniel's captivity occurred during Nebuchadnezzar's first invasion of Palestine in 605 B.C. Ezekiel was taken in the second invasion eight years later.

Daniel was a very young man at the time. He and his companions—*Shadrach, Meshach,* and *Abednego*—were princes of Judah. They were handsome, well-educated, intelligent youths, proficient in the sciences, and refined and polished in manners.

All four of them had the good fortune to be installed immediately in the king's palace. They were chosen to be taught the literature and language of the Chaldeans, a group of learned Babylonians who were instructors in the arts and sciences of that day. Supervised by the chief of the palace eunuchs, Daniel and his friends were to undergo a three-year training period to fit them for personal service and attendance upon the king.

Following a custom of the time, Daniel was given the Babylonian name of *Belteshazzar.* From the very beginning he showed himself to be a man who dared to keep a clean heart and body, and God enabled him to find favor in the eyes of his superiors.

The Bible says regarding all four of these young men: "God gave them knowledge and skill in all learning and wisdom." But of Daniel alone the scripture adds: "And Daniel had under-

standing in all VISIONS and DREAMS" (Dan. 1:17). This
means that he was given the supernatural gift of interpretation
of dreams and visions.

Nebuchadnezzar's Dreams

About a year after Daniel was brought to Babylon, the king
had a dream. This was no ordinary dream. It is probably the
most outstanding and prophetically significant dream ever recorded, for it reveals the destiny of the Gentile kingdoms from
Daniel's day to the end of the age.

These were, of course, only the kingdoms that were to come
in contact with the people of Israel from that time until the
Messianic kingdom is set up at the return of the Lord Jesus
Christ. This is the period the Bible calls "the times of the
Gentiles." It is the era when God by-passes His own people, the
Jews, and gives world government into the hands of the Gentiles.

*Notice that the Lord chose a dream as the means of imparting
this important outline of the future.* But why would He give
the dream to a heathen monarch?

The answer is quite evident. Because that part of the future
would be under Gentile rule, it is fitting that God would reveal
it to the first and greatest of the Gentile rulers. The Lord gave
to Israel's prophets many visions that disclosed their future.
So it was that He gave to Gentiles a dream picturing their
history before it happened.

We read in Daniel, chapter two verse one: "In the second year
of the reign of Nebuchadnezzar, Nebuchadnezzar had DREAMS,
by which his spirit was troubled and agitated and his sleep went
from him."

Awaking from sleep, the king realized that he had dreamed a
most impressive dream. If only he could understand its meaning! Then he remembered his magicians, those who claimed
powers of insight into the occult. He decided to test how clever
they were. If they could tel' him the dream, then he could
believe that their interpretation of it would be correct.

"The king commanded to call the magicians and the enchanters
or soothsayers, and the sorcerers and Chaldean diviners, to tell
the king his DREAMS. So they came and stood before the king.

"And the king said to them, I had a DREAM, and my spirit is troubled to know the DREAM.

"Then said the Chaldean diviners to the king in Aramaic (the Syrian language), O king, live forever! Tell your servants the DREAM, and we will show the interpretation.

"The king answered the Chaldeans . . . The decree goes forth from me and I say it with all emphasis, that if you do not make known to me the DREAM with its interpretation, you shall be cut in pieces, and your houses shall be made a dunghill!

"But if you show the DREAM and its interpretation, you shall receive from me gifts and rewards and great honor. So show me the DREAM and the interpretation of it."

"They answered again, Let the king tell his servants the DREAM, and we will show the interpretation of it."

At this Nebuchadnezzar became very angry. He knew that his wise men were just stalling for time. He made it very plain to them:

"If you will not make known to me the DREAM, there is but one sentence for you; for you have prepared lying and corrupt words to speak before me, hoping to delay your execution until the time be changed. Therefore tell me the DREAM, and I shall know that you can tell me the interpretation of it" (Dan. 2:1–9).

The wise men protested that no one on earth could tell another what he had dreamed. What the king required of them was an impossibility. Only the gods, they said, could tell him his dream.

Furious at their inability to produce when they claimed supernatural powers, the king sent out orders to execute *all* the wise men of Babylon. This included Daniel and his three companions.

What could they do? They had to act fast. At this point Daniel displayed great wisdom. He went to see the king personally and promised that if he would grant him time to pray to his God, he would tell the dream and its meaning.

Daniel went home, and there he and his friends held an urgent prayer meeting. They asked God to show them His mercy by revealing to them the dream, so that they would not die with the others. God answered their prayers. That very night He gave the same dream to Daniel that He had given to Nebuchadnezzar.

"Then the secret was revealed to Daniel in a VISION of the night. And Daniel blessed the God of heaven" (Dan. 2:19).

After giving thanks and praise to God for this great favor, Daniel was brought before Nebuchadnezzar. "The king said to Daniel, whose name was Belteshazzar, Are you able to make known to me the DREAM which I have seen and the interpretation of it?

"Daniel replied, No wise man, astrologer, or wizard can tell the king such things. But there is a God in heaven who reveals secrets, and He has made known to king Nebuchadnezzar what it is that shall be in the latter days—at the end of days. Your DREAM and the VISIONS of your head upon your bed are these:

"You dreamed of coming events. He who reveals secrets was speaking to you . . ." (Dan. 2:26–29).

Daniel explained that it was not because he was any wiser than any other living person that he knew the secret of the dream. It was because the one true, living God had showed it to him for the king's benefit.

What Nebuchadnezzar had seen, said Daniel, was a great image. Its head was of gold, the breast and arms of silver, belly and thighs of brass, legs of iron, and feet of iron mingled with clay. As the king looked upon this imposing figure, a stone cut from the mountainside "without hands" fell on the feet and broke them in pieces. The whole image crumbled into fragments and was carried away by the wind. The stone became a great mountain, which filled the entire earth.

Then Daniel said: "This was the DREAM, and we will tell the interpretation of it to the king" (Dan. 2:36).

Daniel said that the head of gold represented Nebuchadnezzar's empire. When it came to an end, another world power would arise. The breast and arms of the statue being made of silver indicated that this second empire would be inferior to Nebuchadnezzar's. After that kingdom fell, a third power—represented by the bronze belly—would rise to rule the world.

Following it would come the fourth kingdom. It would be

strong as iron—smashing, bruising, and conquering. The feet and ten toes of the image, being part iron and part clay, showed that the fifth and last dominion would be divided into ten parts. This kingdom would not hold together, for iron and clay do not mix.

During the period of this empire, the God of heaven will set up a kingdom which shall never be destroyed. A supernatural stone will shatter all the world powers into nothingness. Then this "smiting stone" will become a kingdom which shall stand for ever.

Daniel concluded his interpretation with these emphatic words: "Just as you saw that the stone was cut out of the mountain without hands, and that it broke in pieces the iron, the bronze, the clay, the silver, and the gold, the great God has made known to the king what shall come to pass hereafter.

"The DREAM is certain, and the interpretation of it is sure" (Dan. 2:45).

We of today can understand the meaning of the dream much more clearly than could Daniel. Four of those empires have come and gone since his time—*Babylon, Medo-Persia, Greece,* and *Rome.* The fifth and last world kingdom is now at hand. It is to be formed inside the Old Roman empire territory, and will be a combination of ten separate powers.

The coming of the smiting stone symbolizes Christ's second advent. He will destroy the Gentile world system catastrophically. Then He will set up His own kingdom which will be universal and everlasting.

When Nebuchadnezzar heard Daniel's account of the dream and its interpretation, he fell on his face, acknowledging the greatness of Daniel's God. He appointed Daniel governor of Babylon and chief of the wise men. At Daniel's request his three companions also received posts of honor and authority.

* * *

Years later Nebuchadnezzar had a second dream of prophetical events. He told about it in a proclamation that went out to all nations and peoples under his kingdom. Listen to his own words:

"I, Nebuchadnezzar, was at rest in my house and prospering in my palace.

"I had a DREAM which made me afraid. And the thoughts and imaginations and the VISIONS of my head as I lay upon my bed troubled and agitated me."

Anxious to learn the dream's meaning, the king again called upon his astrologers and soothsayers for an interpretation. This time they ought to be able to give one, not being required to recall the dream itself.

"Therefore I made a decree to bring in all the wise men of Babylon before me, that they might make known to me the interpretation of the DREAM.

"Then the magicians, the enchanters, the Chaldeans, and the astrologers came in. I told them the DREAM, but they could not make known to me the interpretation of it."

The explanations of these sorcerers were most unsatisfactory. Feeling certain that the dream was intended to convey some message of great importance, the king sent for Daniel, who now was known as "master of the magicians."

"At last Daniel came in before me, he who was named Belteshazzar after the name of my god, and in whom is the Spirit of the Holy God. I told the DREAM before him, saying,

"O Belteshazzar, chief of the magicians, because I know that the Spirit of the Holy God is in you, and no secret mystery is a burden or troubles you, tell me the VISIONS of my DREAM that I have seen, and the interpretation of it.

"The VISIONS of my head as I lay on my bed were these . . ." (Dan. 4:4–10).

Nebuchadnezzar went on to describe seeing a lofty and spreading tree which grew as high as heaven. The sight of it reached to the ends of the earth. Its leaves were fresh and green, and its branches were weighed down with fruit. Wild animals rested beneath its shade. Birds sheltered in its branches, and all the world was fed from it.

Then something happened.

"I saw in the VISIONS of my head as I lay on my bed, and behold, a watcher, a holy one, came down from heaven" (Dan. 4:13).

This angel commanded that the tree be cut down, leaving only its stump among the grass in the earth. The stump was to be bound with a band of iron. Then, strangely enough, the holy being in the dream seemed to be addressing a person. He spoke these words:

"Let the dews of heaven drench him, and let him eat grass with the wild animals. Let his heart be changed from a man's to a beast's heart, and let seven times pass over him."

The angel went on to declare that the purpose of this decree, made at the demand of the holy ones, was that all the world might understand that the Most High God rules the kingdoms of mankind. He gives them to whomever He wills, even the lowliest of men.

The king went on to say: "This DREAM I, King Nebuchadnezzar, have seen. And you, O Belteshazzar (Daniel), declare now its interpretation, since all the wise men of my kingdom are not able to make known to me the interpretation. But you are able, for the Spirit of the Holy God is in you" (Dan. 4:18).

Daniel instantly perceived the dream's meaning, but he shrank from voicing it. He sat there stunned and silent for an hour, aghast at its message. Seeing his hesitancy, Nebuchadnezzar pressed him:

"The king said, Belteshazzar, let not the DREAM or its interpretation trouble or alarm you.

"Belteshazzar answered, My Lord may the DREAM be for those who hate you and its message for your enemies" (Dan. 4:18, 19).

Daniel's reply was an attempt to soften the blow. He said he wished the events foreshadowed in the dream would happen to the king's enemies and not to him.

He explained that the tree was Nebuchadnezzar in his greatness. Then, in a simple and straightforward manner, he stated the pronouncement of judgment the dream contained. The king would be cut down and driven from his palace. He would lose his reason and live a beast's life for seven years. At the end of that time, after learning that God rules the kingdoms of men and gives them to whomever He chooses, Nebuchadnezzar would be restored to his throne.

Daniel ended the interpretation with a plea to the king to stop sinning, do what is right, be merciful to the poor, and perhaps even yet God would spare him.

But Nebuchadnezzar did not heed this plea, even though God in His graciousness gave him a full year to repent. During the twelve months which followed the dream, the king forgot all about the counsel he had received.

One day he was strolling on the roof of his royal palace overlooking the river Euphrates as it flowed through the magnificent city of Babylon. He gazed upon the splendid buildings which had been erected under his rule; for he was not only a great warrior, but a builder of note.

According to Herodotus, it was Nebuchadnezzar who constructed the famous "Hanging Gardens," one of the seven wonders of the ancient world. These were a group of five gardens which rose in a series of terraces to a height of 350 feet. Each garden contained trees, shrubs, and flowers of many kinds. It is believed that the king ordered them built to honor his wife who missed her mountain home. At any rate, they bloomed as a living green miracle in the midst of the surrounding desert. The gardens were part of the royal palace.

The king looked out upon the temples and shrines which he had rebuilt and embellished, for he was a very religious man. Scores of temples, for the numerous heathen gods which the people worshiped, filled the city. Babylon was a religious center, as well as a commercial metropolis.

As Nebuchadnezzar's view encompassed all this splendor, he proudly exclaimed, "I, by my own mighty power, have built this beautiful city as my royal residence, and as the capital of my empire!"

But while he was still speaking these words, a voice called down from heaven, "Oh King Nebuchadnezzar, this message is for you. You are no longer ruler of this kingdom. You will be forced out of the palace to live with the animals in the fields and to eat grass like the cows for seven years, until you finally realize that God parcels out the kingdoms of men and gives them to anyone He chooses."

That very same hour this shocking prophecy was fulfilled.

Nebuchadnezzar was chased from his palace. A form of madness took possession of him. He imagined himself a beast, and he did indeed eat grass like the cows. His body was wet with dew. His hair grew as long as eagles' feathers, and his nails became like birds' claws.

The king tells the rest of the story in his own words:

"At the end of seven years I, Nebuchadnezzar, looked up to heaven, and my sanity returned. I praised and worshiped the Most High God and honored Him who lives forever, whose rule is everlasting, His kingdom evermore.

"All the people of the earth are nothing when compared to Him. He does whatever He thinks best among the hosts of heaven, as well as here among the inhabitants of earth. No one can stop Him or challenge Him, saying, 'What do You mean by doing these things?'

"When my mind returned to me, so did my honor and glory and kingdom. My counsellors and officers came back to me and I was re-established as head of my kingdom, with even greater honor than before.

"Now I, Nebuchadnezzar, praise and glorify and honor the King of Heaven, the Judge of all, Whose every act is right and good. For He is able to take those who walk proudly and push them into the dust!" (Dan. 4:34–37, Living Prophecies).

We of today can learn a great deal from this dream given to a heathen monarch 2500 years ago. Claiming all glory to himself and not giving any glory to God was the downfall of Nebuchadnezzar. It was God who had chosen him and given him his kingdom. The Lord had revealed his doom in the first dream of the huge image, but this had not deterred the king's prideful course.

With his own eyes he had seen "the form of One like the Son of God" walking in the midst of the fiery furnace. He had seen Daniel's three companions emerge from the inferno absolutely untouched by it. The witness of this astounding miracle of deliverance had caused Nebuchadnezzar to acknowledge the power of *their* God. He even decreed that henceforth no one speak a word of slander against Him. *But he did not personally accept this great God, nor did he change his own self-exalting and self-centered life.*

God gave him a second dream. Daniel correctly interpreted it,
and added clear words of warning. But even this did not bring
the king to repentance. Then the blow fell.

At the height of his glory, his mind snapped. He remained
insane for seven years. Finally, after the second dream had been
completely fulfilled, Nebuchadnezzar became a different man.
He had learned from bitter experience that God is the Most
High and is sovereign in the earth and the heavens.

It is possible that Nebuchadnezzar was converted to the true
God as a result of this dream. For after he was restored, the king
personally blessed, praised, and honored the living God. He
publicly proclaimed that God's kingdom is an everlasting one,
and that here on earth He alone is supreme, and all His works are
true and all His ways just.

Nebuchadnezzar's life proves the truth of Proverbs 16:18:
"Pride goeth before destruction, and an haughty spirit before a
fall." His life also well illustrates the verses in Job 33:14–17
which say that God speaks once or twice in a dream—to open
men's ears, and seal their instruction, in order that He may
change their course and do away with their pride.

Belshazzar

Years after the death of Nebuchadnezzar, when his grandson
Belshazzar was ruling as crown-prince of Babylon, we find another reference in the scripture to Daniel's ability to interpret
dreams.

The scene was the banquet hall of the king on a certain night
in October, 539 B.C. This was the occasion when Belshazzar
hosted a great feast for a thousand of his lords. The wine flowed
freely, and the guests were noisy and hilarious.

Acting on an impulse, Belshazzar commanded that the golden
and silver vessels which had been taken from the temple at
Jerusalem be brought in. He decided to let his lords, ladies,
and concubines drink from them. These were the sacred vessels
that had been removed from the holy place and the holy of
holies during Nebuchadnezzar's reign.

When they arrived, all of the riotous guests drank from the
sacred cups. Toasts were offered to heathen gods; and idols of

metal, wood, and stone were praised. The atmosphere was filled with coarse laughter, drunkenness, debauchery, and idolatry.

Suddenly, at the height of the reveling, silence fell upon the great banqueting room. All eyes were fastened on a strange apparition. *The fingers of a man's hand appeared and were seen by everyone.* The hand began to write on the plaster of the wall opposite the lampstand!

Terror seized the king. His knees knocked together, and his legs gave way beneath him. What was it that the hand was writing?

In the semi-darkness, lighted only by candles and torches, Belshazzar made out the Aramaic words: "MENE, MENE, TEKEL, UPHARSIN." While he could read the words, he was at a total loss to decipher their significance.

In great fear, he called for his wise men to give an interpretation. The astrologers, Chaldeans, and the soothsayers hurried into the banquet hall. They too could read the words, but could not determine their meaning. On the surface they denoted a series of weights or monetary units. How could this have any relevance to the king?

Belshazzar grew more and more hysterical, and the color faded from his face. He was desperate to learn the import of this mysterious writing. His lords were shaken with astonishment and alarm.

By this time the whole palace was in an uproar. When the queen mother heard what was happening, she rushed into the room. Being the aged widow of Nebuchadnezzar, she recalled that there was a man in the kingdom in whom dwelt the spirit of the holy gods. Her husband had appointed him master of all the magicians, astrologers, Chaldeans, and soothsayers. Urging the king to send for him, she said to Belshazzar:

"An excellent spirit, knowledge, and understanding to interpret DREAMS, clarify riddles, and solve knotty problems were found in this same Daniel, whom the king named Belteshazzar. Let Daniel be called, and he will show the interpretation" (Dan. 5:12).

Daniel, now an old man, came into the hall. Spurning the king's offer of rewards and honors, he nevertheless said he would tell him what the words meant. But first he rebuked Belshazzar for neglecting the lessons of humility taught by Nebuchadnezzar's history and for defiling the sacred vessels taken from God's temple.

"You have lifted yourself up against the Lord of Heaven," Daniel charged. "You have defied and dishonored Him. Therefore the hand was sent from the presence of the Most High God to enscribe this writing."

Then the prophet accurately interpreted the words as a message of doom. He told the frightened monarch: *"The days of the Chaldean empire have been numbered and brought to an end. You have been weighed in the balances and found wanting. Your kingdom will be divided and given to the Medes and Persians."*

And, indeed, that very night the prophecy was fulfilled. Belshazzar was slain, Babylon was captured by the armies of Cyrus the Persian, and shortly thereafter the kingdom was given to Darius the Mede.

So ended the reign of Belshazzar, and the glory of the Chaldean empire.

*　　　*　　　*

The sixth chapter of Daniel tells the story of his being cast into the lion's den for breaking a law forbidding prayer, and of his miraculous deliverance by God. This occurred when the prophet was about ninety years old.

The remainder of the book of Daniel deals with four highly significant visions. Why are they so important? . . . *Because they contain the key to all subsequent Biblical prophecy.* In symbolic form they sketch the history of both Jew and Gentile nations from Daniel's time to the second advent of Christ.

An understanding of these astounding prophetic visions is essential to the proper interpretation of the Olivet discourse of Jesus in the gospels of Matthew, Mark and Luke. The visions also clarify Paul's doctrine of "the man of sin" in 2 Thessalonians. And they are closely and vitally linked with the book of Revelation.

The first two visions of Daniel were received during the reign of Belshazzar. Therefore, we step backward in time from the events of chapters five and six when we come to chapters seven and eight.

Daniel's Four Beast Vision

The seventh chapter of Daniel is considered to be one of the most precious and prominent portions of the "sure word of prophecy." It is worthy of careful study, for it concerns the rise and fall of world empires; the destiny of Antichrist, the last terrible ruler of the times of the Gentiles; the second coming of the Messiah; the judgment throne of God Almighty; and the establishment of Christ's everlasting kingdom.

It begins like this:

"In the first year of Belshazzar, king of Babylon, Daniel had a DREAM and VISIONS of his head as he lay upon his bed. Then he wrote down the DREAM, and told the gist of the matter.

"Daniel said, I saw in my VISION by night, and behold, the four winds of heaven were stirring up the great sea" (Dan. 7:1, 2).

In Daniel's dream he seemed to be standing upon a seashore, as the waves were being lashed to fury by a mighty wind. We recognize that these "four winds in the heavenlies" speak of demonic powers playing a conspicuous role in agitating the governments of the world.

As Daniel watched, out of the storm-tossed waters there came up four huge animals. The first was like a lion, and it had eagle's wings. The second resembled a bear, and it had three ribs between its teeth. The third beast was like a leopard. It had four wings and four heads. The fourth animal was too dreadful to describe, but it was incredibly strong. To quote Daniel's words:

"After this I saw in the night VISIONS, and behold, a fourth beast, terrible, powerful and dreadful, and exceedingly strong; and it had great iron teeth" (Dan. 7:7).

From our vantage point in history, we readily identify the lion-like beast as a fitting symbol of the *Babylonian* empire under Nebuchadnezzar. The bear represented the *Medo-Persian* empire, the ribs in its mouth depicting the remains of those nations it had already devoured.

The leopard symbolized the *Grecian* empire of Alexander the Great, the four heads being his four generals who became his successors. The last beast was the *Roman* empire.

In Daniel's dream, or vision, this latter animal seized the other beasts and stamped upon them with its feet. With overwhelming might, it conquered all the territories of the first beasts—Babylon, Medo-Persia, and Greece. This brutal and vicious creature had ten horns. Since these horns were the last parts of the beast seen by Daniel, they are regarded by Bible scholars as representing ten kingdoms in the latter days when the old Roman empire is to be revived.

Notice that these four beasts symbolize the same world kingdoms that were pictured by the image Nebuchadnezzar saw in his first dream. The ten horns of the last beast correspond to the ten toes of the image. Nebuchadnezzar's picture of world governments presented the *outward* brilliance of their political, economic, and social aspects. Daniel's vision revealed their *inner* nature—selfish, and beastlike in character. Both visions show the end of Gentile world power.

After the ten horns were fully grown, there came up another horn—a little one. Three of the first horns were pulled up by their roots to give it room. This little horn had human eyes and a mouth speaking great things.

We recognize the little horn as symbolizing *Antichrist* who comes in the days of the last kingdom. He will be a human being, and he will utter blasphemies against God. The plucking up of three of the ten horns by their roots depicts Antichrist's overthrow of three of the powers within the ten nation confederacy controlling the Mediterranean Sea. The other nations will submit to him without war.

Daniel continued to relate his dream-vision in these words:

"I watched as thrones were put in place, and *the Ancient of Days*—the Almighty God—sat down to judge. His clothing was white as snow, His hair like whitest wool. He sat upon a fiery throne brought in on flaming wheels.

"A river of fire flowed from before Him. Millions of angels ministered to Him, and hundreds of millions of people stood before Him waiting to be judged. Then the court began its session, and The Books were opened" (Dan. 7:9, 10, Living Prophecies).

This scene is the Old Testament counterpart to the great white throne judgment of Revelation. Here God is called "The Ancient of Days." The throne upon which He is seated is the same one Ezekiel saw brought in by the shining chariot. The Lord's hair and His clothing are pure white. A stream of fire issues from before Him, and innumerable angelic beings attend Him.

In front of the throne are gathered millions of persons about to be judged. Court convenes, and the records are opened.

As the vision passed before Daniel's eyes, he watched until he saw the end of the blasphemous "little horn." He was slain, and his body handed over to be burned. As for the other beasts, or "horns," their kingdoms were taken away from them; but they were allowed to live a short time longer.

Daniel went on to say:

"I saw in the night VISIONS, and behold, on the clouds of heaven came *One like a Son of man.* And He came to the Ancient of Days and was presented before Him.

"And there was given Him, the Messiah, dominion and glory and a kingdom, that all peoples, nations and languages should serve Him. His dominion is an everlasting dominion, which shall not be destroyed" (Dan. 7:13, 14).

Again we of today have an advantage over Daniel in understanding the vision. For we have later prophecies—particularly the Olivet discourse of Jesus, and the Book of Revelation—to add illumination and insight.

The *"One coming on the clouds of heaven to be presented to the Ancient of Days"* is of course the Lord Jesus when He returns to set up His kingdom. He will bring to an end the times of the Gentiles and Gentile world dominion. The destruction of Antichrist is to occur at the time of Christ's second advent, and the judgment of the nations will follow.

The Lord Jesus will receive from God the Father sovereignty, glory, and a kingdom composed of people of all races. They will be His subjects eternally, for His kingdom is an everlasting one that shall never pass away or be destroyed.

Greatly stirred by this thrilling pageant, Daniel was perplexed and troubled as to its meaning. In his account of the vision, he wrote:

"As for me, Daniel, my spirit was grieved and anxious within me, and the VISIONS of my head alarmed and agitated me" (Dan. 7:15).

The prophet went up to one of the many thousands standing beside the judgment throne and asked him for an interpretation of all these things. The man, who perhaps was the angel Gabriel, explained that the four beasts represented four kings who will rule the earth. But in the end the people of the Most High God shall possess the government of the world forever and ever.

Daniel made further inquiry about the fourth beast—the one so brutal and shocking, with its iron teeth and brass claws that tore men apart and stamped others to death with its feet.

He also asked about the ten horns, and the little horn that had destroyed three of the others. Daniel had seen this horn making war against God's people. The little horn with the eyes and the loud bragging mouth was winning, until the Ancient of Days came. Then judgment was given to the saints of God, and after that they possessed the kingdom.

In response to Daniel's questions, the angel explained:

"This fourth animal is the fourth world power that will rule the earth. It will be more brutal than any of the others. It will devour the whole world, destroying everything before it.

"His ten horns are ten kings that will rise out of his empire. Then another king will arise more brutal than the other ten, and will destroy three of them. He will defy the Most High God, and wear down the saints with persecution. He will try to change all laws, morals and customs. God's people will be helpless in his hands for three and one-half years.

"But then the Ancient of Days will come and open His court of justice and take all power from this vicious king, to consume and destroy it until the end.

"Then every nation under heaven, and all their power, shall be given to the people of God. They shall rule all things forever, and all rulers shall serve and obey them" (Dan. 7:23–27, LP).

That was the end of the vision. When Daniel awoke, he was

greatly disturbed, and his face was pale with fright. He did not fully understand the meaning of the vision, even after the angel had interpreted it. He told no one what he had seen, but he kept the matter in his heart.

The Ram, The He-Goat, and The Little Horn

Two years later, about 551 B.C., Daniel had another vision in which God again unveiled the future before him.

"In the third year of the reign of King Belshazzar a VISION appeared to me, to me Daniel, after the one that appeared to me at the first.

"And in the VISION it seemed that I was at Shushan the palace or fortress (in Susa, the capital of Persia), which is in the province of Elam. And I saw in the VISION that I was by the river of Ulai" (Dan. 8:1, 2).

Daniel lifted up his eyes and saw a ram with two horns standing by the river. This animal butted everything out of its way and did as it pleased, until a he-goat suddenly appeared from the west. The he-goat had one tremendous horn between its eyes. In a fury he charged at the ram and broke both its horns, threw the ram to the ground and trampled upon him.

But at the height of the he-goat's power, his horn was broken. In its place came up four others pointing in all directions. Out of one of these sprang a little horn.

This little horn grew very great and behaved arrogantly and wickedly, especially against God's sanctuary. He canceled the daily sacrifices offered morning and evening in the temple. Many people sided with him because of their own apostasy. Righteousness and truth were cast down, and evil prospered . . .

A strange vision indeed! Daniel did not understand it, though he sensed that it was a warning of the rise of some dreadful conspiracy of evil. Then he heard voices:

"I heard a holy one speaking. And another holy one said to the one that spoke, For how long is the VISION concerning the continual offering, the transgression that makes desolate, and the giving over of both the sanctuary and the host of the people to be trampled under foot?" (Dan. 8:13).

To put it plainly, this is what the angel was asking: "How long will it be before the daily sacrifice is restored? How long will the temple be desolate of divine worship, and the sanctuary and God's people be trodden under foot?"

The answer was that the oppressions would last for 2300 days. Then the temple would be cleansed and restored. Some interpret these 2300 days to be 2300 morning and evening sacrifices, or 1150 days, about three and one-half years.

"When I, even I, Daniel, had seen the VISION, I sought to understand it. Then behold, there stood before me one (Gabriel) with the appearance of a man.

"And I heard a man's voice between the banks of the river Ulai, which called and said, Gabriel, make this man Daniel understand the VISION" (Dan. 8:15, 16).

As Daniel was trying to comprehend the meaning of the things he had seen and heard, suddenly he saw a man standing in front of him—at least he looked like a man. Then he heard a voice calling from across the river, "Gabriel, tell Daniel the meaning of his vision!" This voice was probably that of the pre-incarnate Christ.

"So he (Gabriel) came near where I stood. And when he came, I was frightened and fell on my face. But he said to me, Understand, O son of man: for the fulfillment of the VISION belongs to (events that shall occur in) the time of the end" (Dan. 8:17).

Gabriel started toward Daniel, but as he approached, the prophet was too frightened to stand. He fell down, with his face to the ground. The archangel told him that he must understand that the events he had seen in his vision would not take place until the end time.

As Gabriel continued speaking, Daniel remained on the ground. The angel touched him and helped him to his feet. *"I am here,"* Gabriel said, *"to tell you what is going to happen in the last days of the coming time of terror—for what you have seen pertains to that final event in history . . .*

*"*The two horns of the ram which you saw are the kings of Media and Persia. The he-goat is the nation of Greece, and the great horn between his eyes is the first king."

We easily recognize the first king of Greece to be Alexander the Great. He consolidated the whole realm and conquered the world in just thirteen years. The kings of the dual kingdom of Media and Persia are represented by the ram with the two horns.

Twice before Daniel had been informed of the rise of these powers. Medo-Persia was portrayed in Nebuchadnezzar's image under the symbol of the breast and arms of silver. In Daniel's first vision it was a bear with three ribs in its mouth. Greece was symbolized by the brass belly and thighs of the image. Daniel's vision pictured it as a leopard with four wings and four heads.

In Daniel's second vision, the large horn of the he-goat being broken off at the height of its power depicted the sudden death of Alexander. The four other horns that came up pointing in all directions were the four generals who succeeded him, taking over his empire. They formed the countries known today as Greece, Turkey, Syria, and Egypt.

Gabriel said: "Four kingdoms shall arise out of his nation, but not having his (Alexander's) power" (Dan. 8:22).

This part of the vision is now history to us. As for the little horn which sprang up and behaved so arrogantly and wickedly, especially in connection with the temple, it is believed by many that this has reference to the evil ruler Antiochus Epiphanes.

Some see in this "little horn" an example of double reference in Bible prophecy, pointing both to Antiochus Epiphanes and to Antichrist. Antiochus was indeed a type, a foreshadow, of Antichrist, the little horn of Daniel's first vision.

King of Syria from 176 to 164 B.C., Antiochus IV persecuted the Jews with great severity because of their resistance to his attempts to introduce heathen religious observances among them. He robbed the temple, and set up a statue of the Roman god Jupiter (known to the Greeks as Zeus) in the holy of holies. He also pulled down the walls of Jerusalem, commanded the sacrifice of forbidden swine, forbade circumcision, and destroyed all the sacred books that could be found.

Gabriel's interpretation of the vision from that point on is a prophecy which is confined to "the little horn" coming up at the end of human history—Antichrist. The angel's explanation began:

"At the latter end of their kingdom, when the transgressors (the apostate Jews) have reached the fulness of their wickedness (exceeding the limits of God's mercy), a king of fierce countenance, and understanding dark trickery and craftiness, shall stand up" (Dan. 8:23).

This *"king of fierce countenance"* clearly refers to Antichrist. Gabriel revealed that he will be very mighty, shrewd and crafty. His strength will come from satanic power. He will defeat all who oppose him, devastating God's people. A master of deception, he will destroy many by catching them off-guard as they bask in false security.

So great will Antichrist fancy himself to be that he will even take on the Prince of princes (Jesus Christ) in battle. But in doing this, the beast will seal his own doom. He shall be broken by the hand of God, though no human means could overpower him.

The angel Gabriel concluded his message by saying: "The VISION of the evenings and the mornings which has been told you is true. But seal up the VISION, for it has to do with and belongs to the now distant future" (Dan. 8:26).

Gabriel's reference to "the vision of the evenings and the mornings" concerns the daily sacrifices in the temple. Just as they were cut off by Antiochus Epiphanes, so in the future they will again be cut off by Antichrist.

Daniel was instructed to "seal up the vision," for it pertained to a future time and would not be fulfilled until the close of the age.

"And I, Daniel, fainted and was sick certain days. Afterward I rose up and did the king's business. And I wondered at the VISION, but there was no one who understood it or could make it understood" (Dan. 8:27).

So overcome was Daniel by the lengthy vision that he fainted and was ill for days. After he was up and around again, performing his duties for the king, the vision continued to astonish him. Naturally no one was able to understand it.

*   *   *

Before we take up Daniel's third vision, we are going to digress for a brief interval. There are two very interesting stories relating to dreams told about *Cyrus the Persian* and *Alexander the Great*.

Since both of these kings played a prominent role in Daniel's last vision, we include the stories as part of this section.

Cyrus was ruler of both Media and Persia. Actually he took the title *"King of the World,"* for he added almost all Asia Minor to Persia. Two unusual dreams are said to have decided his destiny. They are recorded by the ancient Greek historian, Herodotus.

Cyrus' grandfather was named *Astyages,* and he was king of the Medes. Astyages had a daughter named *Mandane.* One night he dreamed that from her such a stream of water flowed forth that it not only filled his capital, but flooded the whole of Asia. He told this vision to the Magi of his day, who had the gift of interpreting dreams. When they gave him its meaning, he was greatly terrified.

Because of this, when his daughter was of marriageable age, he would not give her to any of the Medes, lest the dream should be fulfilled. Instead he married her to a Persian.

In the first year of this marriage Astyages had another dream. In it he saw a vine grow from the womb of his daughter and over-shadow the whole of Asia. After this vision, which he related to the interpreters, he sent to Persia and had Mandane brought home.

She was pregnant. When the time drew near for the birth of her child, Astyages set a watch over her. He intended to destroy the child immediately, for the Magi had said the dream revealed that the offspring of his daughter would reign over Asia in his stead.

As soon as Cyrus was born, Astyages sent the most faithful man of his household with the orders to take the child to his own home and kill him there. But the servant did not have the heart to carry out this murderous command. He turned Cyrus over to a shepherd who protected him and eventually restored him to his parents.

When Cyrus grew up, he collected a vast army of Persians and deposed his grandfather Astyages as king of Media. It was Cyrus who united the two kingdoms—Media and Persia.

There are other traditions about the birth of Cyrus. One of them maintains that he was the son of Ahasuerus and Queen Esther of the Book of Esther. Ahasuerus being not a name but a title of certain Persian kings, it is possible that he was called Astyages by some, and also that he was the same person called Darius the Mede in Daniel 5:31.

Whether this is true or not, some things regarding Cyrus are matters of record. He was named by God in a prophecy given over 150 years before he was born (Isaiah 44:28). It was he who gave the first decree that the Jews could return to their own land, after the Babylonian captivity, to rebuild their city and temple.

We read of that decree in two places in the Bible: 2 Chronicles 36:23 and Ezra 1:1–3. The latter scripture states:

"Now in the first year of Cyrus king of Persia . . . the Lord stirred up his spirit so that he made a proclamation throughout all his kingdom, and put it also in writing:

"Thus says Cyrus king of Persia, The Lord God of heaven has given me all the kingdoms of the earth, and He has charged me to build Him a house at Jerusalem, in Judah.

"Whoever is among you of all His people, his God be with him, and let him go up to Jerusalem in Judah and rebuild the house of the Lord, the God of Israel, in Jerusalem; He is God."

Cyrus not only released the people of God, but he sent back all the gold and silver vessels of the temple which had been carried off by Nebuchadnezzar. Certainly he was a man divinely appointed and set apart to do a definite work. In 530 B.C. he was slain while on an expedition to the East. His body was returned to Persia and buried in his royal palace.

The pretentious palace of Cyrus the king was built in the form of individual pavilions. Each one lay in the center of a magnificent garden. The whole area was enclosed by a high wall. But all that splendor, like the great Cyrus himself, is long gone and forgotten.

Today if you were to visit that same spot on the southern slope of a hill, among the rough grass of the highlands, you might find the ruins of a small stone building. The steps are still there leading up to what was once the burial chamber of the man who founded the ancient Persian empire, and who was called "King of the World."

Above the entrance to this chamber there could at one time be read the following plea: *"O man, whoever you are and whenever you come—for I know that you will come—I am Cyrus, who gave the Persians their empire. Do not grudge me this patch of earth that covers my body."*

Now, however, the small stone chamber—in which a golden sarcophagus enclosed the mortal remains of the Persian ruler—is empty. So also is the place above the entrance which bore the inscription. Occasionally shepherds with their flocks pass across the wide plateau, where the lion is lord of the chase.

True indeed are the words of the Psalmist: "As for man, his days are as grass. As a flower of the field, so he flourisheth.

"For the wind passeth over it and it is gone; and the place thereof shall know it no more" (Ps. 103:15, 16, KJV).

In connection with Alexander the Great, we have another interesting story linked with dreams. This one is related by Josephus, the well-known Jewish historian.

In the year 333 B.C. Alexander won a major victory over Darius III, last king of the Persians and Medes. His next target was Egypt. On his way there, via a path of victorious conquest, he came to Jerusalem. But surprisingly enough, he did not injure a soul in Palestine. The reason for this was a strange dream.

Just before Alexander left for Palestine, intending to sack Jerusalem, he had a dream in which he saw a man robed in purple and gold. The man invited the king into Asia, and assured him of success in the conquest of it. But the dream also conveyed a warning. Alexander was not to touch this man, his land, or his city.

As the Grecian troops neared Jerusalem, Jaddua the high priest —robed in purple and gold—opened the city's gates and came forth to meet Alexander. He received the ruler with great ceremony. When Alexander saw this man, he did a thing so strange his commander thought he was mad . . .

The fearless and powerful king of Greece dismounted outside the walls of Jerusalem, went up alone and knelt down before the high priest. He had immediately recognized Jaddua as the man of his dream.

Afterward he offered sacrifices in the temple, as the priests of Israel directed him. He was shown the book of the prophecy of Daniel where it predicted that a Grecian would destroy the Persians. Very pleased, Alexander granted the people favors, rested peacefully in the city overnight, and thereafter left Judah unmolested as a religious community.

What Alexander did not know was that Jaddua, the high priest, also had been given a dream of warning. In it he was told to open the city gates, and go out in his purple and gold robes to meet the conqueror. He was to be accompanied by his priests in their habits, and all the people in white.

With two such dreams involved, no wonder the incident had a happy ending!

The Seventy Weeks

A year after the vision of the ram and the he-goat, when he was about ninety years old, Daniel had a third vision.

In studying the prophetical writings of Jeremiah, he discovered that the prophet had expressly foretold that the desolation of Jerusalem would last for seventy years. The Bible says regarding this disclosure that "Daniel understood by books" (Dan. 9:2).

It is interesting to note that even though this great man had been given extraordinary visions, surpassing all that God had previously bestowed on any individual—even though he had experienced miraculous personal deliverance more than once, even though he had the gift of divine interpretation of dreams, and was deemed the wisest man in the kingdom—still he continued to study the scriptures. And he "understood by books."

Don't you think there is a lesson here for us? No matter how much we think we know, or how many gifts of the Spirit we think we possess, or what spiritual experiences we have had, or are having—*we are never to neglect the careful study of God's Word.* Some things He only reveals to those who reverently and faithfully study and re-study the contents of this marvelous Book.

When this particular prophecy of Jeremiah became clear to Daniel, he realized that it had now been almost seventy years since the first captivity. What did he do about it? . . .

In deep prayer, and after fasting long, Daniel confessed the great sin of Israel. He acknowledged that it was their own iniquity that had plunged them into all their troubles. Entreating the Lord to have mercy on His people, he asked that they might be prepared by the grace of God for deliverance from their seventy years of servitude.

"Cause Your face to shine upon Your sanctuary which is desolate," Daniel implored. "Hear, O Lord, and forgive! Do not delay, for Your own sake, O my God, because Your city and Your people are called by Your name" (Dan. 9:17, 19).

While he was still speaking in prayer, Daniel tells us:

"The man Gabriel, whom I had seen in the former VISION, being caused to fly swiftly, came near to me and touched me about the time of the evening sacrifice" (Dan. 9:21).

Gabriel told Daniel that he had come to give him skill and wisdom and understanding. "At the beginning of your prayers," said the angel, "the word went forth, and I have come to tell you, for you are greatly beloved. Therefore consider the matter and understand the VISION" (Dan. 9:23).

We note that Daniel's prayer was immediately answered. The very moment he began to pray, Gabriel was sent to him. Did you ever wonder why one of the highest archangels in heaven was so speedily dispatched to answer this particular prayer of the prophet?

The reason is that he was about to receive a vision of paramount importance. Its message must be communicated with utmost accuracy, not just to the Jews in Babylon, but to generations to come. For God was planning not only the deliverance of Israel from captivity, but a future and infinitely greater deliverance of the whole world from the curse and thralldom of sin.

Daniel was instructed to understand the vision and consider it. But this time Gabriel did not interpret something that had been seen. Instead he gave a direct prophecy concerning Israel and Jerusalem from that day to the end of all Gentile oppression of Jews.

The expiration of the seventy years of captivity was at hand. Now Daniel was to learn of another more glorious release at the end of seventy—not years—but weeks of years.

Gabriel began by announcing:

"Seventy weeks (of years, or 490 years) are decreed upon your people and upon your holy city Jerusalem, to finish and put an end to transgression, to seal up and make full the measure of sin, to purge away and make expiation and reconciliation for sin, and to bring in everlasting righteousness—permanent spiritual and moral rectitude in every area and relation—and to seal up VISION and prophecy and prophet, and to anoint a holy of holies" (Dan. 9:24).

Oh the far-reaching prophecy that is condensed in this one stupendous verse! What is its meaning?

First of all, Gabriel made it plain to Daniel that these seventy weeks of years, or 490 years, are decreed upon "your people (Israel) and your holy city Jerusalem." Therefore, they only concern Israel as a nation at Jerusalem. They do not concern the Gentiles.

Next, the archangel said, six events must take place before this period of seventy weeks of years ends:

1. *"Transgression must be finished."* We know that this will not come until Israel is saved at the return of their Messiah. He will turn ungodliness from them and convert the nation in one day.

2. *"The full measure of sin must be sealed up."* This will only be done at the second advent of Christ when the spirit of repentance is to be poured out upon Israel, and a fountain for sin and uncleanness opened to the nation.

3. *"Reconciliation for sin must be made."* Israel will not be reconciled to God until they accept the blood of Christ as their atonement for sin. This they will do after they have looked upon Him whom they pierced, and mourned bitterly over having caused His crucifixion. When they receive the mercy and forgiveness of God, then in spirit and in truth they will celebrate the day of atonement.

4. *"Everlasting righteousness must be ushered in."* Christ Himself, as King of kings and Lord of lords, will accomplish this when He sets up His kingdom on the earth.

5. *"Vision and prophecy and prophet must be sealed up."* Under the reigning Messiah, the prophecies concerning Israel and Jerusalem and their eternal restoration will all be fulfilled. There will be no more need for prophet or prophetic vision, "for all shall know the Lord from the least unto the greatest of them."

6. Last of all, *"the holy of holies must be anointed."* This means

the cleansing of the city of Jerusalem, and the anointing of the holy of holies in the millennial temple described by Ezekiel.

Obviously, none of these events has as yet taken place.

The angel Gabriel went on to say: "Know therefore and understand that from the going forth of the commandment to restore and to build Jerusalem until the coming of an anointed one, a prince, shall be seven weeks (of years) and sixty-two weeks (of years). It shall be built again with city square and moat, but in troublous times" (Dan. 9:25).

Daniel was not told when the commandment to restore and build Jerusalem would be issued. We of today know that it was in the month of Nisan (March–April), 445 B.C. (Neh. 2:1–8). Gabriel's prophecy revealed that from the time the decree went forth until "the coming of an anointed one, a prince"—or "Messiah the Prince," as the King James version translates it—would be forty-nine years plus four hundred thirty-four years.

In other words, a total of four hundred eighty-three years would elapse between the decree and the entry of the Messiah into Jerusalem.

This prophecy was fulfilled with exactness. The four hundred eighty-three years ended Palm Sunday in the year of Christ's crucifixion. On that day Jesus rode into the holy city, mounted as royalty, and was hailed as God's anointed one. The multitudes received Him, crying out, "Blessed be the King that cometh in the name of the Lord!"

Daniel must have listened to this enthralling prophecy with fascinated interest. To think that God would actually tell him the very year the long-yearned-for Messiah would come into Jerusalem as King of the Jews! How wonderful! Yet Gabriel's next words must have baffled him, coming on the heels of such a thrilling revelation.

"And after the sixty-two weeks (of years) shall an anointed one be cut off or killed, and shall have nothing and no one belonging to (and defending) him" (Dan. 9:26a).

Undoubtedly Daniel did not understand this part of the prophecy. How could he? Who would think that only a few days after acclaiming "an anointed one" as their Messiah, the Jews would "cut Him off" and kill Him? But they did.

When Christ was crucified, indeed He "had nothing and no one defended Him." He was forsaken by all. Israel openly and formally rejected their King. With that rejection which was sealed by His death, the sixty-ninth week came to a full end. The second period of the prophecy was fulfilled. At this point Israel ceased to be a nation in God's program, and the clock of their national life stopped. The destruction of Jerusalem by the armies of Titus in A.D. 70 followed as an inevitable result.

*   *   *

Of the total seventy weeks, or four hundred ninety years, decreed upon Israel and upon Jerusalem for complete fulfillment of the prophecy, Gabriel has so far accounted for sixty-nine weeks, or four hundred eighty-three years. That leaves one week—the seventieth—as yet unexplained.

This final week of seven years will constitute the climax of Jewish history. But between the close of the sixty-ninth week and the beginning of the seventieth, an unreckoned period of time intervenes.

Since the focus of Gabriel's prophecy is limited to Israel and Jerusalem, he merely touches upon certain happenings during that interval. We will discuss them in greater detail presently. But as far as Israel and Jerusalem are concerned, three words sum up these events—destruction, war, and desolations. This is how Gabriel put it:

"The people of the other prince who shall come will destroy the city and the sanctuary. Its end shall come with a flood, and even to the end there shall be war, and desolations are decreed" (Dan. 9:26 b, c).

Here Daniel is given a clear-cut prediction of the destruction of Jerusalem and the temple, which we know occurred in A.D. 70. "The *people* of the other prince who shall come" of course refers to the Romans under their emperor Titus. But "*the prince who shall come*" denotes Antichrist, the world ruler who will appear at the end of the times of the Gentiles. He will come from among the people in one of the ten kingdoms yet to be formed inside the old Roman Empire territory.

The end of Jerusalem and of the temple surely came as a flood that carried Israel away. They were scattered as a nation in A.D. 70, and they have never had a temple in Jerusalem since. Moreover, Gabriel stated, there would be wars and desolation from then on unto the end.

The concluding part of the prophecy began:

"And he shall enter into a strong and firm covenant with the many for one week (seven years)" (Dan. 9:27a).

The "he" refers to the nearest antecedent to this pronoun, which is "the prince who shall come." He, Antichrist, will enter into a covenant with many Jews for a period of seven years. Since the Jews were led away captive after the destruction of Jerusalem, "the prince that shall come" could not possibly confirm a covenant with them until the city was restored as the capital of Israel. Therefore, the concluding part of the prophecy must have a future fulfillment.

Furthermore, the words "and even to the end" (9:26c) previously indicated a period of time not reckoned into the seventy weeks. Thus it is evident that the seventieth week will be the last seven years of this age.

The "week" will begin immediately after the rapture of the church, when Christ comes *for* His own, and they are caught up to meet Him in the air. It will end with the second advent of Christ when He comes *with* all His saints and angels. Then He will sit upon the throne of His glory and judge the nations. Following this, the millennial kingdom will be set up.

Now, what about the interval between the sixty-ninth and seventieth week of Daniel's prophecy?

This period of time is called by Christians "The Church Age." During this "gap period," God has turned from the Jews and Israel as a nation to call out a people for His name among the Gentiles. This age of grace is for the purpose of forming the church, all those who will make up the body of Christ. When the full number is reached, "the times of the Gentiles" will close, and God will again take up dealings with the Jews.

How long the church age is to be no one knows. Predetermined in the eternal program of God, its length is known only to Him.

Already it has lasted almost two thousand years. It began on the day of Pentecost, and it will end with the great "catching up" of the church, the body of Christ.

While the resurrected saints are appearing before the judgment seat of Christ, and later enjoying the marriage supper of the Lamb, the earth will be undergoing the tribulation. The latter half of this seven-year period has been called "the time of Jacob's trouble" by the prophet Jeremiah (30:7), and in the New Testament "the great tribulation" (Rev. 7:14).

Prior to the beginning of the tribulation, Israel will be restored in Palestine. A sanctuary will have been built, and temple worship reinstated. Even after Antichrist comes on the world scene, for a time the Jews will stand in favor with him. He makes a seven-year covenant with them, and all seems to be well.

But then, suddenly, the covenant is broken. Worship for the Jews ceases, and the time of *the great tribulation* ensues.

Gabriel's prophecy of the seventieth week concludes with these words:

"In the midst of the week he shall cause all the sacrifices and the offerings to cease (for the remaining three and one-half years). And upon the wing or pinnacle of abominations shall come one who makes desolate; until the full determined end is poured out on the desolator" (Dan. 9:27 b, c).

This tells us that when Antichrist breaks his covenant with Israel in the middle of the seventieth week, he will enter and take over Palestine. The Jewish temple will be made his capital. He will first do away with all Jewish sacrifices. Then he will set himself and his image in the temple to be worshiped as God.

Jesus referred to this desecration when He said: "When you see the appalling sacrilege spoken of by the prophet Daniel standing in the holy place, (let the reader take notice and ponder and consider and heed this), then let those who are in Judea flee to the mountains" (Matt. 24:15, 16).

The faithful remnant of Israel who refuse to worship the beast will have to flee into the mountains. There they will be cared for until the three and one-half years are ended. When this time of severe and unprecedented persecution is over, God will break the yoke of Antichrist off the neck of Israel.

The heavens will open as Christ returns to earth in power and great glory. Antichrist will be defeated at the battle of Armageddon and cast alive into the lake of fire. Then indeed "the full determined end will be poured out on the desolator." That will terminate forever Gentile domination over the Jews.

With the establishment of the Messianic kingdom, the throne of David will again be occupied by a prince of Israel. The last king of David's line—Zedekiah—died in chains in Babylon after he was taken there in 586 B.C. The prophet Ezekiel predicted that Judah's last king would be removed, his crown taken off, and that Israel would be "overturned, overturned, and overturned." The crown would not be restored "until He whose right it is would come"—meaning, of course, the Messiah.

At Christ's first coming, Israel in mockery crowned her Messiah with thorns. But when He returns in glory as King of kings and Lord of lords, He will wear a golden crown. In fact, Revelation 19:12 states that "on His head are many kingly crowns."

Then—at last—Israel will receive Him with open arms and grateful hearts. Under His personal reign, they will once again have their own kingdom, a kingdom of righteousness and peace which shall have no end.

Daniel's Vision of Christ

Five years after the vision of the seventy weeks, Daniel was given a fourth and final vision. It is related in the last three chapters of the book bearing his name, and these chapters encompass one tremendous prophecy.

"In the third year of Cyrus king of Persia a word was revealed to Daniel, who was called Belteshazzar. The word was true, and it referred to great tribulation, conflict and wretchedness. And he understood the word and had understanding of the VISION" (Dan. 10:1).

The vision came to Daniel after he had been "mourning" (fasting and praying) for three full weeks. On this particular day he was walking beside the bank of the Tigris River . . .

Suddenly he lifted up his eyes and looked, and behold—he saw a man clothed in linen garments, with a belt of purest gold around his waist. He had glowing, lustrous skin; and from his face came blinding flashes like lightning. His eyes were pools of fire. His feet shone like polished brass, and his voice was like the roaring of a vast multitude of people.

Daniel was with some companions, but he says: "I alone saw the VISION (of this heavenly being), for the men that were with me did not see the VISION, but a great trembling fell upon them, so that they fled to hide themselves.

"I was left alone and saw this great VISION, and no strength was left in me" (Dan. 10:7, 8). The experience was so overpowering that Daniel grew pale and weak with fright.

Some believe that this heavenly being was the angel Gabriel, but he is never thus described in any other part of the Bible. The person Daniel saw was none other than the Son of God, Christ the Messiah, in His pre-incarnate existence as the second person of the Trinity. The vision is in almost every detail like John's description of the exalted Christ in the first chapter of Revelation.

When Daniel heard the sound of Christ's voice, he fell in a deep sleep with his face upon the ground. Then a hand touched him and set him upon his hands and knees. An angel said to him:

"O Daniel, you greatly beloved man, understand the words that I speak to you, and stand upright, for to you I am now sent" (Dan. 10:11). When these words had been spoken, Daniel stood to his feet trembling.

Note that the angel stated that he was "sent" by another to make a revelation known to Daniel. In exactly the same way Gabriel was instructed to interpret the three previous visions that were given to the prophet. Therefore, no doubt, the interpreting angel in this case was again Gabriel.

The angel went on to tell Daniel that his request had been heard in heaven. The answer was dispatched the first day he began to fast before the Lord and pray for understanding regarding his people. That very day Gabriel was sent to meet him. But for three weeks he was blocked by the mighty evil spirit who overrules the kingdom of Persia.

Here is an example of an answer to prayer being delayed because of warfare in the heavenlies. Indeed "we are not wrestling with flesh and blood—contending only with physical opponents—" as Paul tells us in Ephesians 6:12 "but against despotisms, against the powers, against (the master spirits who are) the world rulers of this present darkness, against the spirit forces of wickedness in the heavenly (supernatural) sphere."

Behind the enactment of human history, earthly governments are operated by unseen evil spirits or demons. Satan is the power behind this world system. He has a host of fallen angels. Of these, certain trusted ones are responsible to him for carrying out his will in the governments of men.

Remember that the devil is recognized in scripture as being *"the god of this world"* (2 Cor. 4:4). Jesus called Satan *"the prince of this world."* The word "prince" means "chief ruler, first in rank or power."

But God also has His trusted angels. They carry out His will concerning what He has purposed to take place in the kingdoms of this world. Hence there are wars between these two groups of angels in the heavenlies.

Such a conflict occurred in connection with Gabriel's being sent to answer Daniel's prayer. The "prince of the kingdom of Persia" was the evil spirit working in and through the government of Cyrus (not Cyrus himself) to hinder him in his good intention to repatriate the Jews.

The satanic ruler of Persia came against Gabriel. But Michael, one of the chief officers of the heavenly army and the guardian angel of the Jews, came to Gabriel's assistance.

The battle was serious. Satan knew that Gabriel was bringing a very important prophecy to Daniel regarding what was to happen to Israel in the future. Certainly the devil did not want this to be made known, for it would reveal his own defeat in the latter days. Through Daniel, men for ages to come would learn of Satan's doom.

Don't think for a moment that the devil is unaware of the ultimate restoration of Israel in their promised land. He knows that when the times of the Gentiles end, his rule of this world will be terminated. He and his demons will be imprisoned, and the perfect government of Christ during the kingdom age will follow.

For that reason, as the untiring enemy of God, Satan did all in his power to stop Gabriel from bringing this prophecy to Daniel. But with Michael's help, Gabriel was enabled to break through.

"Now I have come," the angel told Daniel, "to make you understand what is to befall your people in the latter days. For the VISION is for many days yet to come" (Dan. 10:14).

As Gabriel began his message, Daniel kept his face to the ground, unable to utter a word. He was stricken dumb by the import of the revelations. Gabriel had to touch his lips before he could speak. Then the prophet cried out:

"O my lord, by reason of the VISION sorrows and pains have come upon me, and I retain no strength. For how can my lord's servant (who am so feeble) talk with this my lord?" (Dan. 10:16, 17).

Gabriel touched him again—making the third touch from heaven—and Daniel felt his strength return. *He listened as the angel unfolded one of the most phenomenal prophecies in all the Bible . . .*

*   *   *

First the angel Gabriel said that when he finished what he had to reveal, he would have to return to fight with the hostile evil spirit, the prince of Persia. And after that, the satanic ruler of Greece would come. (This prince is the one who later caused Alexander the Great to become so successful.) God has to defeat the satanic rulers of certain realms before the succeeding kingdom can be ushered in to fulfill His prophetic word. The evil forces constantly seek to hinder such fulfillment.

After Gabriel told Daniel this, there followed from the mouth of the angel a lengthy prediction of future historical events concerning Israel and the holy land. It was subsequently so perfectly fulfilled that modern critics say it must have been written after it happened. But, of course, that was not the case.

The prophecy began with a description of the reigns of the first Persian kings, up to the conquests of Alexander the Great and the subdivision of his empire. Next followed an account of the various episodes in the history of the Greek kingdoms of Syria and Egypt, "the kings of the north and south" respectively. The Jews were deeply involved in those wars.

"In those times," Gabriel said, "there shall many stand up against the king of the south (Egypt). Also the robbers of thy people shall exalt themselves to establish the VISION; but they shall fall" (Dan. 11:14, KJV).

The vision to which Gabriel referred is that of the ram, the he-goat, and the little horn—Daniel's second vision.

About 198 B.C. Antiochus the Great, king of Syria, and Philip of Macedonia united in battle against Egypt, and they took possession of Palestine. "The robbers of thy people" were the Jews who rejected their religion and sided with Syria. By aiding the establishment of Syrian power in Palestine, they indirectly helped to fulfill the vision concerning "the little horn." We remember that the little horn sprang up out of Syria.

Gabriel spoke of him as he went on to predict the coming of "a vile person" who would obtain the kingdom of Syria by flatteries (11:21). This was the infamous Antiochus Ephiphanes. By crafty and deceitful means he emerged victorious in a war with Egypt, and had himself crowned king of that land. Soon his mighty empire controlled the entire eastern end of the Mediterranean.

Antiochus then came against Jerusalem, sacking it and butchering tens of thousands of Jews. Gabriel prophesied of his plunder and desecration of the temple—his taking away of the daily sacrifices, placing a pagan god in the sanctuary, and offering a swine upon the altar. The angel foretold the rebellion of the Maccabees and their successful exploits for Israel.

Then the prophecy took a different turn.

Gabriel predicted the coming of a final "king," of whom Antiochus Ephiphanes was but a type. This king is none other than Antichrist of the very end times. Gabriel said of him:

"This king shall do according to his will. He shall exalt himself and magnify himself above every god, and shall speak astonishing things against the God of gods, and shall prosper till the indignation be accomplished. For that which is determined (by God) shall be done" (Dan. 11:36).

The *"king"* of this prophecy is the same one who is called *"the prince who shall come"* in the vision of the seventy weeks. He is also *"the little horn"* in the vision of the four beasts, and *"the king of fierce countenance"* in the vision of the ram and the he-goat.

In the New Testament he is designated by Paul as *"the man of sin* . . . who opposes and exalts himself proudly and insolently above all that is called God or that is worshiped, taking his seat in the temple of God, proclaiming that he himself is God." John calls him *"Antichrist"* in his epistles, and *"the beast"* in the book of Revelation.

This king's power, throne, and authority will come from Satan. He will make war on Jews and Christians alike, and multitudes will be killed by him. The false prophet, whom John also calls a "beast" (Rev. 13:11–15), is to be his religious leader.

At the beginning of the latter half of the tribulation period, Antichrist will set up his capital in the Jewish temple in Jerusalem. He will have great power and success. It will be just as Gabriel predicted: "He shall prosper till the indignation be accomplished." While Antichrist reigns, he will be invincible. Human opposition cannot destroy him. Only the outpouring of God's wrath (indignation) will bring his doom.

This will come in the battle of Armageddon at the second advent of Christ. Antichrist will be cast alive into the lake of fire, along with the false prophet. After the millennium, Satan himself will be thrown into the same place with them.

In conclusion, Gabriel imparted to Daniel some important details regarding the end times . . .

He said that Michael, the guardian angel of Israel, will arise to deliver all those whose names are found written "in the book." This is the Book of Life, in which the names of all the righteous are recorded.

The deliverance to which Gabriel referred has several facets. For some there will be deliverance from physical death. In the early part of the tribulation, one hundred forty-four thousand Israelites will be "sealed" on their foreheads by an angel to protect them from the trumpet judgments (Rev. 7:1–8). Then, midway in the tribulation period, the fleeing remnant of Israel will be delivered from the wrath of Satan, who has just been cast down to the earth (Rev. 12:13–17).

For the righteous dead there will be deliverance through resurrection. Gabriel spoke of this when he said: "Many of those who sleep in the dust of the earth shall awake, some to everlasting life" (Dan. 12:2a). As for the unrighteous dead, they will "awake to shame and everlasting contempt." Their resurrection, however, will be a thousand years later when all the wicked dead are raised and come before the great white throne judgment (Rev. 20:5, 11–15).

Daniel was then told to close up the words and seal the book until the time of the end, for the prophecy would not be understood until that day.

"Then many shall run to and fro and search anxiously (through the book)," said Gabriel, "and knowledge (of God's purposes as revealed by His prophets) shall be increased and become great" (Dan. 12:4).

The Book of Daniel was written to the Jewish people, and they will not understand it—its truths will not be open to them—until the seventieth week begins. When their hearts turn to the Lord, the veil will be removed from their minds. At last they will have an understanding of these prophecies. There will be great excitement when they find out that Jesus was their Messiah, and is soon coming to reign. They will run to and fro giving forth the knowledge of the word of God.

As Gabriel finished speaking, Daniel looked up and saw that there were now three heavenly beings present . . .

Gabriel was on one side of the brink of the river. (Remember that the vision began as Daniel was walking along the bank of the Tigris River). On the opposite shore was another angel, probably Michael. In addition to these two, there was the same divine Person Daniel had seen at the very beginning of the vision, Christ Himself—the "man clothed in linen." He was standing upon the waters of the river.

One of the angels asked Him, "How long shall it be to the end of these terrors—these suffering, trying days that are to pass over the people of Israel?"

In answer Christ lifted both hands unto heaven and swore by Him that liveth forever that it would be for "a time, times, and a half." This is reckoned to be the three and one-half year period of the great tribulation—the time of Jacob's trouble. "And when they have made an end of shattering and crushing the power of the holy people," added Christ, "all these things shall be finished" (Dan. 12:7b).

Daniel heard His words, but did not understand what they meant. He asked, "O my Lord, what shall follow then?"

In reply Christ said to him, "What I have said is not to be understood until the time of the end. Many shall be purified by great trials and persecutions. But the wicked shall continue in their wickedness, and none of them will understand. Only those who are willing to learn will know what it means."

Then the Lord told him that there would be two additional periods of time following the end of the three and one-half years. First, there will be a period of thirty days. Some believe this is to be for the judgment of the nations. Others think it is to allow necessary time for cleansing the land after the tribulation is over.

The second period of time will include another forty-five days. This may be for the actual setting up of Christ's kingdom.

We do not know how long it will take for the millennial temple to be built; the resurrected saints, as the new rulers of the earth, to be sent out to every part of the world; government offices of the civil kingdom of heaven on earth to be established, and new laws published. But all this will be done before the millennial reign in its fulness begins.

In speaking of these additional time periods, the Lord told Daniel: "Blessed, happy, fortunate, spiritually prosperous, and to be envied is he who waits expectantly and earnestly—who endures without wavering beyond the period of tribulation—and comes to the 1335th day!" (Dan. 12:12).

On that day—at long last—the kingdom of heaven will come on earth. To all the "sheep nations" the glorious proclamation will go out: *"Come ye blessed of My Father, inherit the kingdom prepared for you from the foundation of the world!"*

As the vision closed, Christ pronounced a final benediction upon His beloved servant Daniel: "Go now to the end of your life and your rest," said the Lord. "For you will be resurrected with the other saints, and have your part in all the wonderful things at the end of the days."

On those comforting words of assurance, the book of Daniel concludes.

As to an actual record of Daniel's death, we have no certain evidence. Rabbinical tradition says that he returned to Jerusalem among the exiles freed by the royal edict of Cyrus. But it is also believed that when he died, he was entombed in Susa, the capital city of the Persian kings—the very place where he witnessed the second of his amazing visions.

* * *

Incomparable indeed are the dreams and visions recorded by Daniel. Without an understanding of them, one cannot truly understand the Book of Revelation. Nothing is more exciting than to look into the future, and that is just what we did in this chapter.

In studying the two dreams God gave to a heathen king, and the four visions He gave to Daniel the prophet, we saw how these dreams and visions were inter-related. The events they foretold were even presented in chronological arrangement. But the thrilling part was to discover—with the help of the angel Gabriel, and the eternal Christ Himself—the secrets hidden in those dreams and visions!

Our knowledge and understanding of God and His precious Word does not end here. We are ready to meet some more fabulous people and learn about their visions. Although they are called "The Minor Prophets," it is only in *the size of their books* that these prophets are minor. Their messages are of "major" importance, and most Christians need to know them better.

CHAPTER FIVE

"The Lord Said To Me . . ."

The prophet of old was not a man who—for one reason or another—decided to go into the ministry; then managed to get himself ordained by some organization; and after that began to preach sermons.

The true prophet was personally called, and specifically commissioned, by the Lord Himself. He was a man of God who stood in the counsel of the Lord, and who spoke forth the literal word of God. "The word of the Lord came" to him. This means that God was the author of the words that he spoke. God simply took the prophet and made him His mouthpiece to the people.

How did he receive the message which the Lord gave him?

Frequently it was by dreams and visions. That is why the prophet was first called a *"seer"*—one who foresees events. But the prophet also received messages by direct experience. We read in I Samuel 9:15: *"Now the Lord had told Samuel in his ear . . ."* Samuel actually heard God speak to him with an audible voice, in the same way he would hear any other voice.

No wonder the prophet could speak with such authority and certainty. He knew that what God said to him was true and would come to pass. He could be sure that what he beheld in a vision would be accomplished, for it came from heaven and not from men.

A variety of prophets were sent by God, that they might strengthen the hands of one another. Each of them sought to stem the tide of evil, and to call the people back to holiness and the righteousness of the law. Their messages were often filled with warnings and with pronouncements of judgment upon sin. To the faithful they voiced encouragements and promises concerning the

future. Their predictions were absolutely accurate, for exact fulfillment has always been one of the proofs of genuine God-given
prophetic utterance.

All of the prophets repeated again and again the familiar
phrases: "The word of the Lord came to me . . . The Lord said
to me . . . Hear the word of the Lord . . . Thus saith the
Lord . . ."

We shall meet some of these men whom God chose and commissioned to act as His spokesmen, and we'll find out what the
Lord revealed to them in visions.

Are the visions God gave them really important? Indeed they
are.

The visions of Daniel and Ezekiel are so spectacular that they
tend to overshadow the visions of lesser known prophets in the
Old Testament. Some Christians are not even aware of the fact
that other prophets had visions. Yet many of them are tremen-
dously meaningful—as, for example, the eight very unusual visions of Zechariah.

We will have to wait until we come to Zechariah before delving
into these, since we will take the prophets in their Biblical sequence. Thus Hosea is the first person we meet. This Old Testament writer is quoted no less than thirty times in the gospels and
epistles. His is a love story that went wrong . . .

Hosea

Hosea lived in the northern kingdom of Israel during the latter
700's B.C. He was not trained in a "school of the prophets," but
was just a layman called by the Lord. Early in life God commanded him to marry a woman who was a harlot.

"The Lord said to Hosea, 'Go and marry a girl who is a prostitute, so that some of her children will be born to you from other
men. This will illustrate the way My people have been untrue to
Me, committing open adultery against Me by worshiping other
gods.'

"So Hosea married Gomer . . . and she conceived and bore
him a son" (Hos. 1:1, 2, Living Prophecies).

After bearing him two more children, to whom the Lord gave
symbolic names, she deserted him for her lovers. The marriage

was for a time dissolved. Later God told Hosea to go and find Gomer and buy her back from her current paramour. Taking a bag of money and some barley, he "redeemed" her for less than the price of a common slave. He made a contract with her to abide with him many days and not to play the harlot with any other man.

Despite his personal domestic tragedy, Hosea saw in Gomer's unfaithfulness to him a parable of Israel's unfaithfulness to God. In his own love and tenderness, he saw the reflection of God's love for Israel. And in his forgiveness and continued efforts for his wife's salvation, he saw a parallel to God's loving-kindness and tender mercy toward the faithless nation. God was seeking to win Israel back, even as Hosea was Gomer.

But in both cases, a painful discipline was necessary. Although Hosea bought his wife back, she was not to live with him as his wife. She must sit as a widow in sorrow and chastisement until the day when he would take her to himself, after her cleansing.

So it will be with Israel. She must be a long time without a king or prince, without an altar, temple, or priests. But in the end time her Messiah will return, and Israel will come trembling and submissive to her Lord and to His blessings.

The sum of Hosea's message to Israel was that God loved her despite her sin. When she returns to Him in repentance, He will forgive and heal her. And one day He will gather her again under her Messiah into His abiding presence forever.

The reason Hosea is included in this study of dreams and visions is not because of any particular vision. It is because his marriage to Gomer is in itself a vision—a vision proclaiming God's great love for shameful and unworthy sinners. Certainly it illustrates very beautifully the Lord's redeeming grace that "buys them back" after they have gone after other loves.

Also Hosea is included in our study because of these lines in chapter 12, verses 9 and 10. The words are addressed to wayward Israel:

"I who am the Lord your God . . . have spoken to you by the prophets, and I have multiplied VISIONS for you, and have appealed to you through parables acted out by the prophets . . ."

"Yet they would not listen or give heed to any of these. Therefore judgment was inevitable. As Hosea stated: "In my VISION, I have seen the sons of Israel doomed" (Hos. 9:13, LP).

Those who imagine that the God of the Old Testament is only a God of justice and wrath would do well to study the book of Hosea attentively. Tenderness is as much an attribute of God as it is the keynote of Hosea's prophecy. Listen to these poignant words that the Lord speaks to His people:

"O Israel, how well I remember those first delightful days when I led you through the wilderness! How refreshing was your love! How satisfying, like the early figs of summer in their first season!

"But then you deserted Me for Baal-peor, to give yourselves to other gods, and soon you were as foul as they . . ." (Hos. 9:10, LP).

"When Israel was a child, I loved him as a son and brought him out of Egypt . . . I trained him from infancy; I taught him to walk, I held him in My arms. But he doesn't know or even care that it was I who raised him . . .

"Oh, how can I give you up, My Ephraim? How can I let you go?" (Hos. 11:1, 3, 8, LP).

Hosea's message of mercy mingled with judgment, ending with a promise of future restoration and reunion, reminds us of certain words spoken by Jesus. Just before departing from the temple at Jerusalem, the Lord Jesus voiced His last public pronouncement. Here where they had rejected Him and scorned His love, refused to be convinced by His mighty miracles, and were even now about to take His life—here He made a final heart-rending plea to the people He had come to save:

"O Jerusalem, Jerusalem, thou that killest the prophets, and stonest them which are sent unto thee, how often would I have gathered thy children together, even as a hen gathereth her chickens under her wings, and ye would not!

"Behold, your house is left unto you desolate.

"For I say unto you, ye shall not see me henceforth, till ye shall say, 'Blessed is he that cometh in the name of the Lord' " (Matt. 23: 37–39, KJV).

Then in the same majestic, regretful way that the Shekinah glory left Solomon's temple of long ago, so the Saviour—the Glory of Israel—departed forever from this temple . . .

Hosea's ministry was a long one. During his lifetime, Israel—composed of the ten tribes of the northern kingdom—was in rapid decline. Usurpers quickly succeeded one another on the throne by assassinating the ruling monarch. The people worshiped pagan gods. They paid no attention to Hosea's warnings that such apostasy would bring judgment.

About the middle of his ministry, a great part of Israel was carried away by the Assyrians. With the fall of their capital city of Samaria in 722 B.C. the kingdom of Israel came to an end.

Hosea lived to see many of his prophecies fulfilled. Still to be realized are his glorious promises of pardoning grace and future restoration, when his people come back to the Lord in repentance and in faithfulness.

Joel

The second prophet to whom we are introduced is Joel. While Hosea prophesied to Israel (the northern kingdom), Joel's ministry was to Judah (the southern kingdom). He appeared on the scene before Hosea, probably about 800 B.C.

Joel is the man who gives for the first time in the Bible the great prophetic concept of *"the day of the Lord."* This is not a twenty-four hour day, but a long period of time. It begins with the tribulation, includes Christ's return in glory, and continues through the millenium. It ends with the purification of the heavens and earth by fire—just before the new heaven and new earth are established forever.

The little book bearing Joel's name is one of the briefest, and yet one of the most disturbing and heart-searching, of the Old Testament. In it he warns Israel of the suffering she is to experience because of her backslidings. But his prophecies also assure her of God's blessings afterward, when she comes to repentance and obedience to His will.

In telling about a plague of successive swarms of locusts and the utter devastation left behind them, Joel prophetically points to something in the future which will be far more terrible. The locusts prefigure a destruction of frightening dimensions that will come from Almighty God, as the day of the Lord's judgment approaches.

The great battle of Armageddon is graphically foretold by the prophet. He describes the scene as the Lord's supernatural army appears to put down the enemies that surround Israel, threatening to destroy her:

"It is a day of darkness and gloom, of black clouds and thick darkness. What a mighty army! It covers the mountains like night! How great, how powerful these 'people' are! The likes of them have not been seen before, and never will again throughout the generations of the world!

"Fire goes before them and follows them on every side! . . . No weapon can stop them . . . The earth quakes before them and the heavens tremble. The sun and moon are obscured and the stars are hid.

"The Lord leads them with a shout. This is His mighty army, and they follow His orders. The day of the judgment of the Lord is an awesome, terrible thing. Who can endure it?" (Joel 2:2, 3, 8, 10, 11, LP).

God promises military deliverance for Israel:

"I will remove these armies from the north and send them far away. I will turn them back into the parched wastelands where they will die. Half shall be driven into the Dead Sea and the rest into the Mediterranean, and then their rotting stench will rise upon the land. The Lord has done a mighty miracle for you" (Joel 2:20, LP).

Joel is best known for his prophecy of the outpouring of the Holy Spirit. The apostle Peter quoted from it more than eight hundred years later in his famous sermon on the day of Pentecost. Partial fulfillment of this wonderful prophecy occurred at that time. But complete fulfillment will be realized during the latter part of the tribulation, when there is a great spiritual revival in Israel.

"And afterward I will pour out My Spirit upon all flesh. Your sons and your daughters shall prophesy, your old men shall DREAM DREAMS, your young men shall see VISIONS" (Joel 2:28).

Joel makes it clear that dreams and visions are charismatic gifts of God. *They are included with prophecy as promised gifts of the Holy Spirit.*

The scripture goes on to say that there will be signs and wonders in the heavens and on the earth—blood and fire and pillars of smoke. The sun will be turned into darkness and the moon to blood before the great and terrible day of the Lord shall come.

The chapter ends on this hopeful note: "Everyone who calls upon the name of the Lord will be saved. Even in Jerusalem some will escape, just as the Lord has promised; for He has chosen some to survive."

Joel also gives a picture of the time of judgment when the Lord settles the score with the nations. Those that have persecuted Israel must be judged before restoration can begin. God said through Joel:

"I will gather the armies of the world into the Valley Where Jehovah Judges and punish them there for harming My people, for scattering My inheritance among the nations and dividing up My land . . .

"Collect the nations. Bring them to the Valley of Jehoshaphat; for there I will sit to pronounce judgment on them all."

As the prophecy continues, the judgment of the nations blends with Armageddon: "Now let the sickle do its work; the harvest is ripe and waiting. Tread the wine press, for it is full to overflowing with the wickedness of these men.

"Multitudes, multitudes waiting in the valley of decision! Waiting for the verdict of their doom. For the day of the Lord is near, in the Valley of Judgment . . .

"The Lord shouts from His temple in Jerusalem, and the earth and sky begin to shake. But to His people Israel, the Lord will be very gentle. He is their Refuge and Strength."

At last unbelieving Israel receives her Messiah, and Joel closes his prophecies with these promises from God:

"Then you shall know that I am the Lord your God . . . Jerusalem shall be Mine forever . . . Sweet wine will drip from the mountains, and the hills shall flow with milk . . . Israel will prosper, and Jerusalem will thrive as generations pass.

"For I will avenge the blood of My people; I will not clear their oppressors of guilt. For My home is in Jerusalem with My people" (Joel 3:2, 12–21, LP).

Amos

The third prophet we are to meet said of himself:

"I am not really one of the prophets. I do not come from a family of prophets. I am just a herdsman and fruit picker.

"But the Lord took me from caring for the flocks and told me, 'Go and prophesy to My people Israel' " (Amos 7:14, 15, LP).

This man's name was Amos, and he lived near Bethlehem in the time of Hosea—the 700's B.C. Amos was not brought up in the class from which prophets usually came, nor was he trained in the prophetic schools. Yet this humble shepherd of meager education became one of the greatest writers of all time. He received his training straight from God on the wild uplands of Judah.

His opening words reveal that the instruction was given in the form of visions, for he says he "saw" them:

"The words of Amos, who was among the herdmen of Tekoa, which he *saw* concerning Israel in the days of Uzziah king of Judah, and in the days of Jeroboam the son of Joash king of Israel" (Amos 1:1, KJV).

The theme of Amos' prophecies was God's judgment upon various nations, Gentiles and Jews alike, because of their sins and rebellion against Him. In particular, however, he made it clear to Israel that—even though they were chosen and blessed as God's people—they would not escape His judgment. Pointing out the backslidings of the nation, the prophet stated in detail God's case against them.

The Lord sent Amos to the northern kingdom of Israel during the reign of their last great king, Jeroboam II, about 760 B.C. It was an age of economic boom, with luxurious living, moral corruption, and rampant idolatry. All twelve tribes of Israel were at that time facing complete destruction if they did not amend their ways. But regardless of warnings of approaching calamity and judgment, Israel continued in apostasy and unbridled love of pleasure.

Finally it was necessary for God to keep His word concerning their destruction.

Amos, in addition to denouncing openly the social injustice

of the wealthy citizens of Samaria and Bethel, told Israel of coming judgment in five visions (chapters 7–9). Four of these visions were introduced by the words: "Thus hath the Lord God *showed* unto me . . ." What did Amos mean by "God showed me"?

In explanation, we point out that there are two senses in which the word "vision" is used in Hebrew prophecy. In the first sense, a state of mind closely akin to that of a dreamer is meant. The prophet falls into a kind of ecstasy, and has no control over the pictures which pass before his mind. Balaam is a good example of this, for we recall that the Bible said of him: "he saw the vision of the Almighty, falling down, and having his eyes open."

The second sense of the word means that the subject matter of the preaching is divinely inspired, but the prophet's own mind and will play an important part in throwing the matter into the form of a picture. The visions of Amos belong to the latter class.

Each of his five visions is one in which judgment is set forth under a symbol. In the first vision the prophet saw green fields. Then God showed him a vast swarm of locusts, which He was planning to use to destroy the main crop that sprang up after the first mowing. (The initial part of the crop went as taxes to the king.)

Amos implored "O Lord God, forgive, I pray You!" The Lord relented and did not fulfill the vision. "It shall not take place," He said (7:1–3).

In the second vision (7:4–6) God showed the prophet a great fire He had prepared to punish Israel. It was so terrible as to consume the waters and devour the entire land. Again Amos fervently prayed for mercy. God answered and said, "This also shall not be."

In the third vision (7:7–9) Amos saw the Lord standing beside a wall, with a plumbline in His hand. The measuring revealed how far out of line Israel was. They were so warped by sin and idolatry as to be past correction. This time Amos had not the heart even to pray. Israel's judgment was certain. "I will not again pass by them," said the Lord. The door of mercy was shut.

Then God showed Amos a fourth vision (8:1–3). He saw a

basket full of ripe fruit, so ripe that it was soon to perish. The Lord revealed the sad parallel that the people of Israel, like the basket of overripe fruit, were rotting at the heart. The guilty nation was "ripe" for judgment, and God would not defer their punishment any longer.

The last vision began with these words: *"I saw the Lord standing at the altar . . ."* (Amos 9:1).

This particular altar was not the one in the temple at Jerusalem. It was the altar at Bethel, the chief sanctuary of the northern kingdom. Built there by Jeroboam I, it was an idolatrous imitation of God's true altar in Jerusalem. Here in this rival temple false priests ministered, and golden calves and hideous pagan deities were worshiped.

No wonder the great mass of the people assembled there for worship were to meet with destruction—like the Philistines in the house of their god, when the mighty Samson brought the pillars of that temple down, and the roof crashed upon the bodies of all those therein!

Now the Lord was standing at the altar of burnt offerings in the outer court to prohibit further sacrifice. The order for destruction was given. God gave the command to smash the tops of the pillars, and shake the temple until the pillars crumbled and the roof crashed down upon the people below.

"The remainder of them I will slay with the sword," said the Lord. "Though they run, they will not escape. They will all be killed."

God went on to say, "I will root up Israel, that sinful nation, and scatter her across the world. Yet I have promised that this rooting out will not be permanent. Israel shall be sifted by the other nations as grain is sifted in a sieve, but not one true kernel will be lost."

While Amos' visions ended with judgment, his book closes with the picture of a bright future for God's chosen people. The whole promised land will once more be a united kingdom under the throne of David. This will happen after the second advent of Christ.

"Then, at that time," said the Lord through Amos, "I will rebuild the City of David, and return it to its former glory . . .

"I will restore the fortunes of My people Israel, and they shall rebuild their ruined cities, and live in them again. They shall plant vineyards and gardens, and eat their crops and drink their wine.

"I will firmly plant them there upon the land that I have given them. They shall not be pulled up again, says the Lord your God" (Amos 9:14, 15, LP).

Obadiah

The next prophet whose acquaintance we are to make is Obadiah. His is the shortest book in the Old Testament, having only a single chapter of twenty-one verses. The prophecy it contains was given by means of a vision, for the book opens with these words:

"The VISION of Obadiah. Thus saith the Lord God . . ."

Nothing is known of Obadiah himself, not even what century he lived. It could have been anywhere from before 800 B.C. to after 600 B.C. His main message is God's judgment upon the land of Edom because of her pride, cruel hatred, and inhumanity to Israel.

Who were the Edomites?

These people were descendants of Esau, brother of Jacob. There had been bitter enmity between Edom and Israel from the time Edom refused to let the children of Israel, under Moses' leadership, pass through their land on the way to Canaan. Ever after that Edom always gave aid to the enemies of God's people. They gloated over Israel's calamities, and even helped her enemies plunder, capture, and murder her people. (Incidentally, the wicked Herods of the New Testament were of general Edomite stock.)

Edom's treasure was enormous wealth from iron and copper mines and caravan trade. She was also noted for her wise men —Eliphaz, the friend of Job, being one of them.

Obadiah, in condemning Edom, points to those who dwelt in the clefts of the rock: "You are proud because you live in those high, inaccessible cliffs. 'Who can ever reach us way up here!' you boast. Don't fool yourselves!

"Though you soar as high as eagles, and build your nest among the stars, I will bring you plummeting down, says the Lord . . .

"Every nook and cranny will be searched and robbed, and every treasure found and taken . . . In that day not one wise man will be left in all of Edom! says the Lord. For I will fill the wise men of Edom with stupidity" (Obad. 3, 4, 6, 8, LP).

Obadiah's mention of "those who dwelt in the clefts of the rock" has reference to *Petra,* Edom's capital. Petra is the Greek translation of *"Sela,"* as it is called in the Old Testament. The city is hewn out of rock, high in the mountains of what is now Jordan.

Today Petra is known as the silent city of the forgotten past, the rose-red city, half as old as time. It is called the rose-red city because of its amazing color—all shades of red sandstone. Located about one hundred twenty miles southeast of Jerusalem, midway between the Dead Sea and the Gulf of Aqaba, it still exerts a magic spell upon the minds of those who have been there.

Petra has only one approach, and that is through a deep rock cleft six thousand feet long. It is surrounded by high cliffs, pierced by narrow ravines. These ravines form places of defense where one man can hold out against an army. That is why it has always been considered an impregnable stronghold.

Many temples and tombs are cut into the rock. Since the Moslems conquered the city in the 600's A.D., the Arabs have kept modern transportation from Petra, and it remains as preserved as it was in ancient times.

From the very beginning Edomites and Israelites have been two different people in manners, customs, and religion. Edomites were idolaters, and their history is one of wars with Jews. Under King David they were completely defeated and made subject to Israel for about one hundred fifty years. After the Babylonian captivity the Maccabees compelled them to embrace the Jewish religion or leave their country. From then on they were ruled by Israel. In the millennium their territory will again be under Israel.

Obadiah pronounces Edom's doom in these words:

"For the day of the Lord is near upon all nations. As you have done (Edom), it shall be done to you. Your dealing will return upon your own head . . . And there shall be no survivor of the house of Esau, for the Lord has spoken it" (Ob. 15, 18).

This came to pass about A.D. 70–73 when the Romans captured Jerusaem and then Masada. Known by then as Idumeans, the last of them sided with the Jewish defenders of Masada and died there rather than be taken captive by the Roman army. The Edomites lost their existence as a nation and, as such, perished forever from the face of the earth.

As for Jacob's descendants, the closing verses of Obadiah promise: "The house of Jacob shall possess their own (former) possessions . . ." During the millennium Israel will re-occupy not only her own land, but also Philistia and Edom. (See Isa. 11:14).

Israel is to rejoice in the holy reign of the Messiah. "For deliverers will come to Jerusalem and rule all Edom. And the Lord shall be king!" (Ob. 17, 21, LP).

Micah

Of the twelve minor prophets, Jonah is next in sequence. But since we have no mention of visions in connection with him, we will go on to Micah.

His messages came to him in the form of visions, for the scriptures states: "The word of the Lord that came to Micah . . . which he *saw* . . ." (Mic. 1:1). When God's word came to the prophet, a vision of divine revelation was given. He saw the things which he foretold as if they had already been accomplished.

The term "country preacher" would be applicable to Micah. He lived in the days of Isaiah (700's B.C.). But while his contemporary belonged to the ruling class in Jerusalem, Micah was one of the oppressed peasantry in Judah. Isaiah voiced the word of God to kings. Micah addressed the common people in the little villages around Jerusalem.

Perhaps that is why God chose him to prophesy the birthplace of the Messiah. Little Bethlehem, onc of the smallest of the towns of Judah, was named by Micah 700 years before Christ was actually born there.

"But you, Bethlehem Ephratah, you are little to be among the clans of Judah. Yet out of you shall One come forth for Me who is to be Ruler in Israel; whose goings forth have been from of old, from ancient days—eternity" (Mic. 5:2).

It was this passage of scripture that the scribes quoted to King Herod when the wise men from the East came to enquire, "Where is he that is born King of the Jews?" In the same verse the coming Messiah is declared to be God—an eternal Being who is alive from everlasting ages past.

Although he lived in rural surroundings, Micah was familiar with the corruptions of city life in Israel and Judah. He foretold that the splendid and prosperous city of Samaria, which was the capital of the northern kingdom, would become a heap of rubble. This occurred in 722 B.C. when the Assyrians destroyed the city. Micah declared that its fall was due to its sins of idolatry and oppression.

The prophet foresaw a like fate coming upon the southern kingdom of Judah. Because of this, and as a sign that the impending invasion would be followed by captivity, Micah announced: "Therefore I will wail and howl, I will go stripped and naked" (Mic. 1:8). Overwhelmed with grief and filled with deep anxiety, Micah walked barefoot and without his outer garments, in the guise of a captive, to illustrate his sorrow and shame.

Don't think for a moment that the prophets of old *enjoyed* making God's pronouncements of judgment. They did not speak out of ill-will, but out of a heart that mourned and lamented the punishment that must come upon their people.

Micah predicted that the judgment of enemy invasion would come right up to the very gates of Jerusalem. This was exactly what happened in 701 B.C. when Sennacherib's army took all the walled cities of Palestine and laid siege to Jerusalem itself. Only a miraculous divine intervention saved the city.

Like Amos and Isaiah, Micah denounced the wealthy landowners in Israel who took advantage of the poor. He condemned the corruption rampant among the religious leaders of his day, and the gross miscarriages of justice perpetrated by those dedicated to upholding the law. The fact that all of this was carried on in an atmosphere of religiosity proved for Micah to be the crowning insult.

It is in connection with his denunciation of the apostate clergy that Micah uses the word "vision":

"You false prophets! You who lead His people astray . . . This is God's message to you: The night will close about you and cut off all your VISIONS. Darkness will cover you, with never a word from God. The sun will go down upon you and your day will end.

"Then at last you will cover your faces in shame, and admit that your messages were not from God" (Mic. 3:5-7, LP).

Micah, the true prophet, filled with power and with the Spirit of God, fearlessly exposed the false clergymen of his day. He declared because they had kept others in the dark, God will bring them into the dark. There they will be silenced and shamed forever. In the end they will be forced to admit that they never had any real calling, and that they did not preach a true message from God. They will be seen for what they are— imposters, sensual, using their office simply to make a living and to advance their own personal interests.

God has ordained two offices of man—the office of government, and the office of the ministry. When either of these is corrupted, and their divine purpose perverted, the Lord is very severe with those who abuse them—and justly so.

The false prophets of Micah's time flattered and deceived the people for mercenary gain. They huckstered their solemn office to please sinners, telling them they were perfectly all right, when actually they were within a step of ruin.

Regrettably, these unworthy ministers have many a counterpart in our religious world today!

The most familiar scripture passage from the entire BOOK of Micah is this one:

"He hath showed thee, O man, what is good. And what doth the Lord require of thee, but to do justly, and to love mercy, and to walk humbly with thy God?" (Mic. 6:8, KJV).

Too often this verse is quoted as a complete definition of all that God expects of His people. However, a careful reading of the context in which the verse is found makes it plain that it refers to *ethical conduct,* not to what God requires *spiritually.*

The people to whom Micah was speaking had forgotten God. When they were faced with this, they inquired of the prophet, "How can we please the Lord? Shall we come before Him with burnt offerings?"

Micah replied that they could not win God's favor by sacrifices such as the heathen offered to their gods. The Lord does not want their wine and oil and children. He wants their *obedience.*

This truth is as applicable to us today as it was to the people of Judah. The saving grace of God cannot be earned by pretentious offerings, or by elaborate forms of worship. Humility, mercy, and justice should be the way of life of the person who wants to be well-pleasing to God. But in addition to righteous conduct, there must be *a real personal experience of God in the life.*

Above all, as Jesus stated, we must love and worship God "in spirit and in truth. For the Father seeketh such to worship him" (Jn. 4:23). "In spirit" means with the whole regenerated personality—including soul, mind, emotions, and desires. And "in truth" means in harmony with full revealed truth according to the Word of God—not in accordance with some doctrine or teaching of man, or in the empty ceremonies of man-made organizations.

We must have a life-changing, personal experience with the Lord. If our religion is only a creed, a beautiful church building with its particular rituals, and our position as a member of that church—it is nothing!

Micah predicted Israel's future restoration in the kingdom of the Messiah. He foretold the great events of the latter days when God's covenant with Abraham will be fulfilled. Like Isaiah, and in almost the same words, he spoke of the time when the house of the Lord shall be established in the top of mount Zion, and all nations shall seek it. War will cease, and the Lord shall reign in Jerusalem forever.

The closing verses of Micah are read each year by Jewish worshipers in the afternoon service on the day of atonement. They are indeed beautiful:

"Who is a God like You, Who forgives iniquity and passes over the transgression of the remnant of His heritage? He retains not His anger for ever, because He delights in mercy and loving-kindness.

"He will again have compassion on us. He will subdue and tread under foot our iniquities. You will cast all our sins into the depths of the sea.

"You will show Your faithfulness and perform the sure promise to Jacob, and loving-kindness and mercy to Abraham, as You have sworn to our fathers from the days of old" (Mic. 7:18–20).

Nahum

Nahum, our next prophet, lived in the 600's B.C. He immediately acknowledges the supernatural character of his message by identifying his prophecy as "The book of the VISION of Nahum."

Nahum's central theme is *"Judgment on Nineveh."* As such, it is really a sequel to the book of Jonah. When the earlier prophet announced the destruction of Nineveh, the people—from the king on down—repented, and the city was spared. But in less than 150 years they had deliberately returned to their sins, cruelties, and idolatry. Nineveh had her chance. Therefore, the message of Nahum is a statement of certain and final doom.

Nineveh was one of the oldest and largest cities of the world up to that day, the foundation of which went back before 4000 B.C. according to archeologists. Later on Nimrod marched northward, captured and rebuilt it as part of his kingdom (Gen. 10:11, ASV). By Nahum's time, Nineveh was the capital of the Assyrian empire. Situated on the bank of the Tigris River, about two hundred thirty miles north of modern Baghdad, she was once a glorious sight to behold . . .

The magnificent palaces of her kings were adorned with silver and gold and elaborate furnishings. Much larger than Babylon, greater Nineveh had many suburbs. The metropolitan area measured from sixty to eighty miles in circumference. The walled inner city had fifteen gates in it.

Would God destroy such a great city with all its inhabitants? Yes, He would. And He did just that. For with all her wealth and all her beauty, Nineveh was a wicked, rebellious and apostate city. She was full of tyranny and cruelty—a bloody city that made war against many. Countless were her slain. Robbery, drunkenness, plunder, murder, lies, deceit, the leading of nations into idolatry and people into witchcraft—her evil was continuous.

Tradition tells us that upon the city that was considered unconquerable, heavy and constant rain began to fall. The Tigris River rose higher and higher. Finally it undermined the city walls, and even washed away part of them. Through these breaks, the besieging Medes and Babylonians entered.

Too late the king of Nineveh tried to rally his drunken nobles to defense. When he saw there was no hope of escape, he built a large funeral pyre in the palace. There he burned his concubines, his eunuchs, and himself. The queen escaped the burning, but she and her maidens were taken captive by the invaders.

Nahum predicts the story well. With the utter destruction of Nineveh in 612 B.C., providentially engineered by the God whom Assyria had despised, the dominion of the Assyrian empire was ended. And through this, we recognize anew the Lord's sovereignty over the destinies and actions of all nations. The great city of Nineveh was left to fall into a heap of desolate ruin. Today it is a pasturing-place for flocks of sheep.

God is slow to anger, says the prophet, but He is great in power. When He determines to take vengeance on His enemies, there is no doubt that He is able to carry out His purpose.

In the past after many warnings and pronouncements of judgment on individuals and nations, He sent earthquakes, fire from heaven, famines and plagues. So in the future His wrath will again be poured out. The God who did not spare Nineveh has not changed.

Yet the "false prophets" of our day go on teaching: "God is love—the loving Father of all mankind. He wouldn't hurt His children. He wouldn't send anyone to hell. There is no such place, anyway. We are all on our way to heaven, just taking different roads to get there . . ."

This watered-down, namby-pamby, completely unscriptural

concept of deity is hardly what Nahum proclaimed. Listen to a few of his words:

"The Lord avenges, and He is full of wrath . . . He will by no means clear the guilty. The mountains tremble and quake before Him and the hills melt away. The earth is upheaved at His presence; yes, the world and all that dwell in it.

"Who can stand before His indignation? And who can stand up and endure the fierceness of His anger? His wrath is poured out like fire, and the rocks are broken asunder by Him" (Nah. 1:3, 5, 6).

So deeply and effectively did God bury Nineveh that every trace of her existence disappeared for 2000 years. Not until the 1840's did archeologists begin to unearth the mounds covering her ruins, and to confirm the Biblical account of her history.

Habakkuk

Of all the prophets, the next one alone seemed more concerned about God's holiness and justice being vindicated than about Israel escaping punishment. His opening words begin:

"The burden which Habakkuk the prophet did *see* . . ." thus signifying that his message came visually. Of the man himself, we know nothing other than the fact that he lived in Judah in the 600's B.C. Possibly he was a priest or a member of the Levitical choir.

Habakkuk's prophecy is presented in the form of a conversation between himself and God. The prophet begins by voicing a desperate cry, "O Lord, *how long* will You go on tolerating the sin, oppression, injustice, and wickedness of Your people? *Why do You allow* such awful crimes as are being committed in Judah to continue?"

God replies that a terrible day of retribution is coming upon Judah. The instrument of divine judgment will be a new force He is raising on the world scene, the Chaldeans, a cruel and violent nation. "They will march across the world and conquer it," says the Lord.

The Chaldeans were originally a tribe of Semites living between Babylon and the Persian gulf. In the 700's B.C. they overpowered Babylonia. The two great kingdoms of the Babylonians and Chaldeans were then united. Because of this, the names Chaldean and Babylonian are closely associated, and sometimes mixed in usage.

But if God is holy, questions Habakkuk, how can He use a nation more wicked than His own people as a rod of punishment? Surely He cannot condone the inhumanity and idolatry of the Chaldeans, whose atrocities are worse than the evils they are sent to punish!

"How long," he asks the Lord, "is this waste of human life and brutality to go unchecked by Your righteous intervention?"

The prophet then goes to a watchtower to await God's answer. It comes through a vision. The Lord regards the vision as important enough to command Habbakkuk to write it down, for it is of permanent value.

"The Lord answered me, and said, Write the VISION, and engrave it so plainly upon tablets that everyone who passes may be able to read (it easily and quickly) as he hastens by.

"For the VISION is yet for an appointed time, and it hastens to the end (fulfillment). It will not deceive or disappoint. Though it tarry, wait (earnestly) for it; because it will surely come. It will not be behindhand on its appointed day" (Hab. 2:2, 3).

This answer of the Lord is true for all time. That is why He instructed Habakkuk to write it down. God made it clear that the things He planned would not happen right away. But slowly, steadily, surely, the time would come when the vision would be fulfilled. It would come to pass on its appointed day. *A sovereign God will deal with the wicked in His own time and way.*

Habakkuk's prophetic vision also gives a glimpse of the second coming of Christ. This is indicated by the fact that these same words are quoted in Hebrews 10:37 using the word "he" instead of "it": "For yet a little while, and *he* that shall come will come, and will not tarry."

No wonder God wanted this written down for all to see!

In the vision God goes on to explain that the pride of the Chaldeans would be their downfall. Their love of wine and wealth, combined with their cruelty, would betray them. Nevertheless Judah needed punishment for her iniquities, and the Chaldeans were to be used to correct them. After that Chaldea's turn for judgment would come, and then she would be utterly blotted out. As for God's people, they will yet enjoy a glorious future and a kingdom where the Lord Himself will rule.

Two marvelous verses of scripture are included in this prophecy. The first is the one that made such an impact on Martin Luther. In fact it started him out on his great crusade which brought about the Reformation.

The scripture consists of only six words—but they are power-packed: *"The just shall live by faith."* This verse is found in Habakkuk 2:4 and is quoted three times in the New Testament —in Romans, Galatians, and Hebrews.

The other scripture beautifully states God's ultimate purpose in creation: *"For the earth shall be filled with the knowledge of the glory of the Lord, as the waters cover the sea"* (Hab. 2:14).

Following the vision, Habakkuk makes a prayer to God for national revival to come to Israel. The prayer is cast in the form of a poem or psalm (Chapter 3). It speaks of trust in God, and in the certainty of the Lord working out His own purposes according to plan.

In this prayer Habakkuk relates a vision, which we interpret to be that of the Lord Jesus Christ returning to earth at His second advent . . .

The prophet describes seeing God move across the deserts from Mount Sinai, His brilliant splendor filling the earth and sky. From His hands flash rays of light. He veils His awesome power, as He stops for a moment to gaze at the earth. Then He shakes the nations, scattering the mountains and leveling the hills.

The sun and moon begin to fade, obscured by the brilliance from His arrows and the flashing of His glittering spear. He marches across the land in righteous anger, and tramples down the nations in His wrath.

He goes forth to save His chosen people. He destroys with their own weapons the wicked who have come like a whirlwind, thinking Israel will be an easy prey. The Lord's horsemen march across the sea. The mighty waters pile high . . .

God's words in this vision have quite an effect on Habakkuk.

Listen to the way he reacts: "I heard, and my whole inner self trembled, my lips quivered at the sound. Rottenness entered into my bones, and under me—down to my feet—I trembled" (Hab. 3:16).

We can see by this that Habakkuk did not take lightly the word of the Lord. All the prophets received God's every word with reverence and awe, and we would do well to do the same. The scriptures tell us that the Lord will regard the man who trembles at His word:

"Thus saith the Lord . . . To this man will I look, even to him that is poor and of a contrite spirit, and trembleth at my word" (Isa. 66:2, KJV).

It is interesting to note that the Quakers were so named because their founder, George Fox, once quoted this passage from Isaiah. Fox told a magistrate that men should literally "tremble at the word of the Lord." Whereupon the justice called his group *"The Quakers."*

Have you ever been so moved by the word of God that you quivered and shook as you read it?

Habakkuk, having seen the greatness of God, closes his book with a positive statement of consecration. He declares that no matter what happens: "I will rejoice in the Lord, I will exult in the (victorious) God of my salvation!" (Hab. 3:18).

Zechariah

Because this book is primarily concerned with all scriptural references to dreams and visions, we must pass over the prophets *Zephaniah* and *Haggai*. There is no allusion to either dreams or visions in their prophecies.

In speaking of their revelations, both of them state: "The word of the Lord came unto me, saying . . ." Perhaps God made His message known to them purely in an audible way, apart from any visions. But this, of course, we do not know.

In the case of the last prophet in the Old Testament, *Malachi*, he simply says: "The burden of the word of the Lord to Israel by Malachi . . . thus saith the Lord . . ."

We note, in passing, that of all the prophets, only three spoke after the exile in Babylon. They were Haggai, Zechariah, and Malachi. We conclude this section of our study with the greatest of these—Zechariah.

This prophet was a strong and wise leader of people who were very weak during his time. Zechariah began to prophesy in 520 B.C. It is believed that he was born in Babylon as one of the Jewish captives. He was the grandson of Iddo, who is mentioned in the book of Nehemiah as the head of one of the priestly families that returned from the exile.

Zechariah's ministry was in Jerusalem. Along with the older prophet Haggai, with whom he was associated, he urged the people to rebuild the temple. The Jews had begun to do this when they first returned to their own land, but enthusiasm for work on the house of the Lord soon waned. No progress was made beyond laying the foundations. The work remained unfinished for fifteen years. During this time each person was more interested in building his own private house.

What a contrast was this little remnant of a people with what had once been the powerful nation of Israel! Even now they were only in their promised land because a foreign monarch had permitted them to return. Judah was a Persian province, under Zerubbabel their appointed governor.

But Haggai and Zechariah encouraged them to believe that they would be a free nation again. In glowing pictures they predicted the restoration of their kingdom under the Messiah. They promised that their future would be far more glorious than the past had ever been. Their efforts were most successful. Under their inspiration and enthusiasm, the temple was completed, and in 516 B.C. it was dedicated.

The Book of Zechariah is Messianic and apocalyptic in message. Because of this, he foretells both advents of the Saviour more than any other prophet, with the exception of Isaiah. He unfolds his divine tidings in a series of visions, the rich imagery of which must have made a powerful appeal to the Oriental mind.

The visions were given at a time of growing impatience on the part of the returned exiles. They could perceive no sign of God's presence, or of His interest in their labors and difficulties. The people began to lose faith in the Lord. Thus these visions came just at the right moment. They not only revealed the marvelous providence of God in the present—as well as His never-failing love for His people—but they brought a bright hope for the future.

All eight of Zechariah's visions were received on the same night in February, 519 B.C. (Zech. 1:7). This was three months after he preached his first sermon in which he called the people to repentance (1:1–6).

The opening vision beautifully assured scattered and downtrodden Israel that God knew every detail of their circumstances. His messengers were ever on the alert, bringing communications to their King from all parts of the earth.

Reading from "Living Prophecies," Zechariah tells us that the word of the Lord came to him:

"In a VISION in the night. I saw a man sitting on a red horse that was standing among the myrtle trees beside a river. Behind him were other horses, red and bay and white, each with its rider.

"An angel stood beside me, and I asked him, 'Sir, what are all those horses for?'

" 'I'll tell you,' he replied.

"Then the rider on the red horse—he was the Angel of the Lord—answered me, 'The Lord has sent them to patrol the earth for Him.'

"Then the other riders reported to the Angel of the Lord, 'We have patrolled the whole earth, and everywhere there is prosperity and peace' " (Zech. 1:8–11).

There were two angels in this vision who spoke to Zechariah. One stood beside him acting as an interpreter, and the other was in the midst of the myrtle trees. *This latter Angel was none other than the second person of the Godhead, the pre-incarnate Christ.* The red horse He rode appropriately denoted the redemption of His first advent, and the warfare of His second advent.

The myrtle trees symbolized Israel as God's covenant people. The other riders were angelic agents of God's great host. They were sent forth to accomplish various missions, and to ascertain conditions on the earth.

Upon hearing their report, the Angel of the Lord prayed this prayer: "O Lord of Hosts, for seventy years Your anger has raged against Jerusalem and the cities of Judah. How long will it be until You again show mercy to them?"

God Himself answered the Angel, speaking words of comfort and assurance. He said that he cared very much what happened to Judah and Jerusalem, and that He was angry with the heathen nations sitting around securely at ease. Because they had afflicted His people far beyond what was necessary, the Lord then announced:

"Therefore I have returned to Jerusalem filled with mercy. My temple will be rebuilt, says the Lord of Hosts, and so will all Jerusalem.

"Say it again: the Lord of Hosts declares that the cities of Israel will again overflow with prosperity. The Lord will again comfort Jerusalem, and bless her, and live in her" (Zech. 1:16, 17, LP).

Another vision immediately followed the first one, and it likewise guaranteed the preservation of Israel.

In the second vision Zechariah saw four animal horns. He asked the interpreting angel, "What are these?" The reply came that they represented four world powers that have scattered Judah, Israel, and Jerusalem. The only four Gentile powers who have scattered (and will yet scatter) Judah, Israel, and Jerusalem are: *Assyria, Babylon, Rome,* and *the future empire of Antichrist.* Therefore, we thus identify them.

Assyria and Babylon had already dispersed Israel before the time of the vision. In A.D. 70 Rome destroyed Jerusalem and drove out the Jews. They are to be driven out of their land one more time. In the middle of the tribulation period, Antichrist will force the faithful remnant of Israel out of Palestine—perhaps into the wilderness of modern Jordan.

Then the Lord showed Zechariah four "carpenters," or blacksmiths.

"What have these men come to do?" the prophet asked.

The angel replied, "They have come to take hold of the four horns that scattered Judah so terribly, and to pound them on the anvil and throw them away" (Zech. 1:21).

The meaning here is quite plain. The carpenters, or "smiths," were empowered to cut off these horns, for severe judgment was decreed on those nations who ravaged and persecuted God's people. We of today know that three of those powers have already been destroyed. Even so, the last of the Gentile powers to scatter Israel will be utterly cast down.

In Zechariah's third vision he saw a man with a measuring stick in his hand. This surveyor is the same divine personage as the red-horse rider of the first vision—Christ Himself.

When the prophet asked him where he was going, the man told him, "To measure Jerusalem. I want to see whether it is big enough for all the people."

Then the interpreting angel who was talking with Zechariah went over to meet another angel coming toward him.

"Go tell this young man," said the other angel, "that Jerusalem will some day be so full of people that she won't have room enough for all! Many will live outside the city walls, with all their many cattle—and yet they will be safe.

"For the Lord Himself will be a wall of fire protecting them and all Jerusalem. He will be the glory of the city" (Zech. 2:4, 5, LP).

This promise of prosperous expansion and divine protection for Jerusalem refers to the millennium. Then Christ will be the glory in the midst of her, ruling personally and visibly on earth.

In the remainder of Zechariah's vision, the Lord addressed Israel directly. He summoned those still remaining in Babylon to leave there, because judgment was about to fall upon that city. This was a prophetic statement pertaining to the immediate present. The Lord then closed His remarks with a prediction for the future.

He told Jerusalem to rejoice, for the day will come when He will dwell there. At that time many nations will be converted to the Lord, and they too shall be His people. Christ's habitation on earth during the millennium is to be the temple in rebuilt earthly Jerusalem. But His real home will be the new Jerusalem, which is then still in heaven.

The fourth vision of Zechariah is perhaps the most fascinating of all. We read from Living Prophecies:

"Then the angel showed me (in my VISION) Joshua the high priest standing before the Angel of the Lord. And Satan was there too, at the Angel's right hand, accusing Joshua of many things" (Zech. 3:1).

This Joshua is, of course, not Joshua the leader of Israel in the conquest of Canaan. He is the high priest who returned with the Jews from their recent Babylonian captivity. As such, he was prominently associated with Zerubbabel in the erection of the second temple. Zechariah no doubt knew him well.

The "Angel of the Lord" is again the second person of the Trinity. Satan is standing at His right hand, which is the position of a plaintiff in Jewish law courts. He is demanding that the heaviest sentence of the law be executed upon this representative of the people of Israel.

Suddenly the voice of God is heard ringing through the Court of Heaven:

"I reject your accusations, Satan. Yes, I the lord, for I have decided to be merciful to Jerusalem—I rebuke you. I have decreed mercy to Joshua and his nation. They are like a burning stick pulled out of the fire" (Zech. 3:2).

Satan is effectually reprimanded by the Lord on the basis of God's sovereign grace, despite Israel's sin.

As Joshua stands before the Angel of the Lord, he is clothed in "filthy garments." These symbolize sin and unfitness in the presence of God, signifying the nation's past idolatry and neglect of the worship of God. The Angel instructs that the filthy garments be removed and Joshua clothed with proper attire. Heavenly raiment fit for that holy place is given him. The high priest's mitre is placed upon his head.

The sin-stained garments are put forever out of sight, as Joshua is pardoned and purified by divine mercy. Nothing more is heard of Satan, the accuser. He cannot remain in the presence of sovereign grace with its forgiving, cleansing, and transforming power.

What a beautiful parallel with the atoning work of our Saviour! He removes the filthy rags of our corrupt nature, and clothes us anew with the robe of His own righteousness. Clad in garments that have been made white in the blood of the Lamb, we are presented faultless before the presence of God.

The Angel of the Lord then speaks very solemnly to Joshua, saying:

"The Lord of Hosts declares: 'If you will follow the paths I set for you and do all I tell you to, then I will put you in charge of My temple, to keep it holy. And I will let you walk in and out of My presence with these angels.

"Listen to me, oh Joshua the high priest, and all you other priests. You are illustrations of the good things to come. Don't you see?—Joshua represents My Servant The Branch whom I will send" (Zech. 3:7, 8).

This is a great Messianic promise. Joshua and his fellow-priests are a sign of the Lord's favor, which will culminate in the appearance of God's servant, The Branch. "The Branch" was a recognized title of the Messiah. In both Jeremiah and Isaiah's prophecies, the Messiah is designated as being a branch of the Lord and a branch of David the king.

The Lord continues speaking:

"He will be the Foundation Stone of the temple that Joshua is standing beside. And I will engrave this inscription on it seven times: *I will remove the sins of this land in a single day.*"

The vision concludes with this kingdom blessing:

"And after that, the Lord of Hosts declares, you will all live in peace and prosperity. Each of you will own a home of your own where you can invite your neighbors" (Zech. 3:9, 10).

The single day in which the sins of the land will be removed will be the day of Christ's visible return to earth. Then "all Israel shall be saved, and ungodliness turned from Jacob." The surviving Jews will look upon Him whom they pierced and rejected the first time He came. After bitter mourning and repentance, they will receive Him. They will cry out, "Blessed is He that cometh in the name of the Lord"—just as Jesus Himself prophesied. A nation will be converted and "born in a day."

Zechariah's fifth vision contains one of the most familiar verses of all scripture. You will easily recognize it when we come to it.

Apparently the prophet had fallen asleep after the last tremendous vision, for he says that the angel who had interpreted the previous visions woke him.

"And he said to me, What do you see? I said, I see a lampstand all of gold, with its bowl for oil on the top of it. Seven lamps are on it. There are seven pipes to each of the seven lamps which are upon the top of the lampstand.

"And there are two olive trees by it. One is upon the right side of the bowl, and the other is upon the left side of it (feeding it continuously with oil)" (Zech. 4:2, 3).

Zechariah asked the angel, "What does this mean?"

He was told that the addition of the bowl to the candlestick, causing it to yield a ceaseless supply of oil from the olive trees, is the word of the Lord to Zerubbabel. That word is saying: *"Not by might, nor by power, but by My Spirit, says the Lord of Hosts"* (Zech. 4:6).

This is, of course, the familiar passage of scripture to which we alluded. But the context in which it is found is not so familiar to the average Christian.

In the vision the seven-branched golden lampstand symbolized Israel as God's witness to the pagan nations around her. For Christians it typifies Christ as the true Light of the world. Into the bowl atop the candlestick, oil was continually dropping from two olive trees. From this bowl, seven pipes diffused the oil to the seven lamps. Oil is the symbol of the Holy Spirit. Consequently, this part of the vision showed that the true source of Israel's power was not their own number (which was few), nor their human effort (which was weak), but the Spirit's anointing.

Likewise, we as Christians do not accomplish anything worthwhile for God merely in our own strength, or by our own ability, but only by the power of the Holy Spirit.

The purpose of the vision was obviously to encourage Joshua and Zerubbabel in their task of restoring the temple and the nation of Judah after the recent exile of seventy years. Its symbolism let them know that God would help them carry on the work, not by external forces, but by His own Spirit.

All the difficulties and oppositions that lay in the way would be removed, even those that seemed insurmountable. This is made very clear in the verse that follows:

"For who are you, O great mountain (of human obstacles)? Before Zerubbabel . . . you shall become a plain (a mere mole hill)! And he shall bring forth the finishing gable stone of the new temple with loud shoutings of the people, crying, Grace, grace to it!" (Zech. 4:7).

The great mountain was an apt symbol of Darius I, who made a decree that work on the temple should cease. But the angel said that this opposition was to disappear like a mountain being removed or becoming a plain. The temple would be completed, and the headstone laid with shoutings of "May God bless it!"

The seven lamps were explained to be the eyes of the Lord watching over the whole earth continually. Zechariah then asked the interpreting angel about the two olive trees on each side of the lampstand, and the two olive branches by which the golden oil is emptied out. He was simply told that they represent the two anointed men who stand before the God of all the earth.

In this particular vision the two *branches* represented Zerubbabel as civil ruler, and Joshua as high priest. Most Bible scholars believe that the *olive trees* portray the office of king and priest respectively. These are the two positions of authority in which human instruments are anointed by God to assist in the administration of the earth.

Both of these offices are united in Christ. They will be fully and perfectly fulfilled when He returns as King-Priest to assume ownership and control of the earth. And it is from Christ that the (oil) Holy Spirit proceeds.

So far Zechariah's five visions have all promised many blessings to the people—God's watchful care, His vindication against their enemies, Jerusalem expanded and protected in millennial glory, the conversion, cleansing and restoration of Israel as a high-priestly nation . . .

But these blessings would be worthless if evil still remained.

Wickedness, however, will be removed from the land, as Zechariah's next two visions showed.

The prophet's sixth vision was very brief and to the point. He looked up and saw a scroll flying through the air. It appeared to be about 30 feet long and 15 feet wide. The angel explained what it contained:

"This scroll," he told me, "represents the words of God's curse going out over the entire land. It says that all who steal and lie have been judged and sentenced to death."

"I am sending this curse into the home of every thief and everyone who swears falsely by My name," says the Lord of Hosts. "And My curse shall remain upon his home and completely destroy it" (Zech. 5:3, 4, LP).

The flying scroll signified that evil-doers will be punished, and their sins will bring consuming judgment upon their homes. The curse went out over the face of the whole land. All mankind is liable to the judgment of God. His righteous wrath is proclaimed against all sinners, but particularly against those who steal and those who lie in the name of the Lord.

In his seventh vision, Zechariah viewed something else traveling through the sky. This was a bushel basket—which, when its heavy lead cover was lifted off, revealed a woman sitting inside!

The interpreting angel told Zechariah that the basket was filled with the sin that prevailed everywhere throughout the land. "The woman represents wickedness," he said. He pushed her back into the basket and clamped down the heavy lid.

Then the prophet saw two women flying toward him with wings like those of a stork. They took the bushel basket and flew off with it, high in the sky.

"Where are they taking her?" Zechariah asked the angel.

"To Babylon," he replied, "where she belongs, and where she will stay."

Babylon is the symbol of world idolatry and wickedness. Its name was derived from "Babel," one of the chief ancient cities ruled by Nimrod. The infamous "tower of Babel," built about three hundred years after the flood, was located there. Just as Babylon was the site of the first great rebellion against God following Noah's day, so it will be the site of the last great rebellion in the closing days of this age.

The Bible predicts that Babylon will be rebuilt in the future (Rev. 14:8; 16:19; 18:1–24). It will again become the commercial, political, and religious center of the East. Antichrist will make it his capital and reign from there during his rise to power. In the middle of the seven-year tribulation period he will leave Babylon to make Jerusalem his headquarters. There he will rule during his three and one-half years of control over the nations.

"Babylon as a mystery" is the name the Book of Revelation gives to the ecclesiastical systems of man (Rev. 17:5). All of these apostate religions will link together after the rapture of the true church. The prevailing world religion will be a revival of the old Babylonian religion. This was a mixture of sorcery, witchcraft, enchantments, astrology—in other words, "spiritism"—which things are an abomination in the sight of God.

Zechariah's vision depicts the removal of all religious and commercial wickedness from the earth. The bushel basket denotes ungodly commercialism. The woman symbolizes the religions of the satanic world system. Her complicity in the evils of commercialism imprisons her.

At Christ's second advent, both of these systems will be destroyed, so that they can deceive God's people no more.

The prophet's final vision, his eighth, provides a fitting conclusion to this series of highly significant messages presented in visual form. *It pictures judgment upon the nations, preparatory to Christ's millennial reign.*

Zechariah says: "Again I lifted up my eyes and saw, and behold, four chariots came out from between two mountains. The mountains were of firm, immovable bronze" (Zech. 6:1).

These immovable bronze mountains depict the firm decrees of God. From the midst of them came four chariots. The first chariot had red horses, the second black horses, the third white ones, and the fourth was drawn by dappled horses.

Zechariah asked the angel who talked with him what these chariots were. He was informed that they were the four heavenly agents who execute judgment upon the earth. These holy angels are the ministers of God's providence, which moves as swiftly as chariots.

The different colors of the horses portray the various judgments. Red signifies war and bloodshed; black, famine and starvation; white, victory and conquest; and dappled means death.

It is noteworthy that the first of Zechariah's eight visions showed God's universal providence in mercy, with messengers coming *to Him* from all parts of the earth. The last vision revealed God's universal providence in judgment, with chariots going forth *from Him* into all the earth.

The chariot pulled by the black horses was directed to go north (to Babylonia). The one with the white horses was to follow, and the dappled-greys were to go south (to Egypt). The red horses were impatient to be off, that they might patrol the earth. The Lord dismissed them.

"Then He summoned me, and said to me, Behold, these that go toward the north country have quieted My Spirit of wrath and have caused it to rest in the north country" (Zech. 6:8).

By this, God meant that His wrath had been appeased by being poured out upon the north country. They were the enemies of Israel who had overstepped their commission in punishing Israel, and who had also fulfilled their own time for retribution.

This closing vision assured Israel that judgment would be administered upon their enemies. Furthermore, angelic agents would continue to patrol the earth, watching and protecting God's people. In the operation of divine providence, the Lord's purposes will be performed as He has appointed them.

With the ending of the eight visions, there followed an actual historical event—Joshua's coronation—for which the visions were preparatory. This constituted the summation and climax of the visions.

The Lord instructed Zechariah to have certain Jewish metalsmiths make crowns of silver and gold. One of them was to be placed on the head of Joshua, the high priest. The other crown was to go in the temple as a memorial of the faithfulness of God in restoring the kingdom and priesthood to Israel through their Messiah.

The Lord said that Joshua represents the Man who will come, whose name is *The Branch*. He will build the true temple of the Lord. This, of course, will be at Christ's second advent when He takes over the kingdoms of the world.

"To Him belongs the royal title. He will rule both as King and as Priest, with perfect harmony between the two!" (Zech. 6:13, LP).

Not only will Christ build the temple, but He will bear the glory, and rule upon His eternal throne as a King-Priest. This will be the throne of David. The kingdom will be that of David, re-established and elevated to eternal glory and power. The kingship and priesthood of Israel will be combined in Christ, and there will be no enmity between the two offices as when two men filled them.

We see now that all eight visions pointed to the kingdom restored to Israel under her Messiah King-Priest.

Although Zechariah relates no further visions, he makes mention of dreams and visions in two other places. In chapter 10 he is speaking about the material and spiritual blessings that the Lord will shower down upon His people in the millennium. He says how foolish it would be to ask idols for anything like that.

"For the idols have spoken vanity, and the diviners have seen a lie, and have told false DREAMS; they comfort in vain" (Zech. 10:2, KJV).

The diviners were the prophets whose visions were a cheat and a sham. They told false dreams, which were not from God. The people received nothing in the past from their idols, said Zechariah, and they will get nothing in the future. There is no comfort in promises that don't come true. Because of believing these men instead of believing the word of God, Judah and Israel were led astray. They wandered like lost sheep, with no shepherd to protect them.

In chapter 13 the Lord is saying that when Israel accepts the cross "in that day"—the day of her national conversion—"there shall be a fountain opened to the house of David and to the inhabitants of Jerusalem for sin and for uncleanness." In that day the Lord will cut off the names of all idols from the land. They shall no more be remembered. The false prophets and the unclean spirit will be removed from the land also.

"If any one again appears falsely as a prophet, then his father and his mother who bore him shall say to him, You shall not live, for you speak lies in the name of the Lord. And his father and his mother who bore him shall thrust him through when he prophesies.

"And in that day the false prophets shall every one be ashamed of his VISION when he prophesies. Nor will he wear a hairy or rough garment to deceive,

"But he will deny his identity and say, I am no prophet. I am a tiller of the ground, for I have been made a bond servant from my youth" (Zech. 13:3–5).

In the millennium if any man dares to prophesy by an unclean spirit, his parents will be the first to accuse him. He will be executed without mercy, in keeping with the law demanding death for idolaters. No one will boast then of his prophetic gift. Nor will anyone wear the rough camel skin garments of the ancient prophets, in an attempt to fool people.

False prophecy will at last be brought to an end. The pseudo-prophet will have to confess that he is not a true prophet, but is only a farmer, and that is all he has ever been.

In that day Israel will be purged of all idolatry and crass materialism. The religious leaders of Christ-denying Judaism will cast aside their outer trappings, and be so ashamed of their former errors that they will confess they never were "prophets" at all. When Jerusalem looks upon the One whom her people pierced, she will repent with true sorrow. The fountain that cleanses from sin will be opened to her, and the blessings and judgments of God's kingdom will follow.

Oh what a day when the Lord Jesus Christ will be King over all the earth!

Zechariah closes his marvelous book with more details about the day of the Lord. He speaks of the battle of Armageddon, the physical changes that will take place in Palestine when Jerusalem is restored, particularly the river of life-giving waters flowing out from the sanctuary. He predicts judgment on any nation that refuses to send representatives to come and worship the Lord of Hosts, and to celebrate the feast of tabernacles.

His final words have to do with the holy character of the millennial kingdom. Everything in Jerusalem will be specially consecrated to God. The word "holiness" itself will be on the bells of the horses, and on every pot in the city. Sacrifices will be continued as a memorial to the work of Christ on the cross.

And in that day there will never be a godless or unclean person in the house of the Lord!

No wonder Zechariah's prophecy is called the Book of Revelation of the Old Testament. It is full of promises of the coming Messiah—first as the lowly One, riding upon a humble beast—and then as mighty Sovereign, when He comes in all His glory to reign as King over all the world.

"And His dominion shall be from sea even to sea, and from the river even to the ends of the earth" (Zech. 9:10).

*   *   *

We have finished the many wonderful dreams and visions in the Old Testament. Now we are going to adventure into the New Testament. But before we do, some reader may be wondering, "What do all these promises for Israel have to do with me? I'm not a Jew. I'm a Christian, and I expect to go to heaven when I die. I don't care to return to this earth and live in Palestine, no matter how nice it's fixed up!"

When we come to the great visions in the Book of Revelation, we will thoroughly present what the Bible teaches about the future dwelling place of the Christian. However, for now, a brief explanation is in order.

It is true that there are distinctions between Israel and the church, the body of Christ. The latter is a "called-out assembly" with special relationship to Jesus. We are redeemed by His precious blood, and at the rapture we are to go to heaven to be with Him.

But we will not stay there. At the second advent, Christ returns to the earth and all His saints with Him.

It is equally true that the promises made to Abraham, and the prophecies that were given to him and to his seed down through the generations, are earthly promises to an earthly people. Israel means the Jews who are the physical descendants of Abraham through Isaac and Jacob. God separated them from the rest of mankind and entered into covenant relationship with them.

Israel was promised a nation, a land, and a citizenship in Canaan. Furthermore, the Lord spoke these words through the prophet Nathan in reference to David: "I will establish the throne of his kingdom forever" (2 Sam. 7:13). In fact, God made the promise to David three-fold: his house, his kingdom, and his throne would each be eternal.

When, and how, will all these promises be fulfilled?

The answer is "in the millennium under the reign of Christ the Messiah." Then Israel will enjoy great material blessing in their promised land. They will "no more be pulled up out of their land which I have given them, saith the Lord thy God." The house, kingdom, and throne of David are to be restored in Jerusalem, from whence Israel will have universal dominion over the nations.

But since Christ Himself is going to be the King-Priest of Israel, dwelling visibly and bodily in the temple in the holy city for a thousand years, don't we Christians who expect to be with Him have some connection with the promises to Israel?

Indeed we have. Remember that Jesus said to His disciples in Matthew 19:28: "Truly I say to you, in the new age—the Messianic rebirth of the world—when the Son of man shall sit down on the throne of His glory, you (who have become My disciples, sided with My party, and followed Me) will also sit on twelve thrones and judge the twelve tribes of Israel."

Here we see the place of the twelve apostles in the eternal kingdom. They will each rule over one of the tribes of Israel under David their king. In Luke 22:29, 30, Jesus again speaks to His disciples of the kingdom He will set up on the earth at His second advent:

"As My Father has appointed a kingdom and conferred it on Me, so do I confer on you (the privilege and decree)

"That you may eat and drink at My table in My kingdom, and sit on thrones, judging the twelve tribes of Israel."

Christ, David, and the twelve apostles are not going to be the only ones reigning on the earth. All resurrected saints—Jewish and Christian—will have some part in the kingdom.

"Blessed and holy is he that hath part in the first resurrection. On such the second death hath no power, but they shall be priests of God and of Christ, and shall reign with him a thousand years" (Rev. 20:6, KJV).

An elaboration of this promise is recorded in Revelation 5:10 . . .

John, in vision, witnessed the Lamb on His throne, and the twenty-four elders falling down before Him with harps and golden bowls of incense in their hands. They sang a new song, "Thou art worthy." The words of that song speak of those who have been redeemed by His blood as being "out of every kindred, and tongue, and people, and nation." They weren't just "white Protestants" in other words.

And they sang: "You have made them a kingdom (royal race) and priests to our God, and they shall reign (as kings) over the earth!"

We would do well at this point to remember that Paul said there is neither Jew nor Greek in Christ Jesus, but they are all one. "Know and understand that it is (really) the people (who live) by faith who are (the true) sons of Abraham" (Gal. 3:7).

"If you belong to Christ (are in Him, who is Abraham's Seed), then you are Abraham's offspring and (spiritual) heirs according to promise" (Gal. 3:29).

The believer in Christ, through faith in Him, inherits the promises given to Abraham. Being Christ's, we are Abraham's seed. Consequently we are entitled to the great blessings and privileges of the promise.

We must remember also that in all prophecy there is both a literal and a spiritual application. Bible prophecy regarding Israel is to be taken literally for them, but its spiritual meaning may also be applied to the church.

So we see that we Christians *do* have a very real connection with Israel and the Old Testament promises. We who are of faith are blessed and justified with Abraham. The gulf between Jews and Gentiles has been bridged by Christ and the gospel. All are Abraham's spiritual seed; all are heirs by promise. *Kinship to*

Abraham in the spiritual sense is determined by faith like his, not lineal descent from him.

Yes, most assuredly, the Old Testament does have relevance for us.

One day in the dispensation of the fulness of times, the mystery that was hid for ages will be manifest. Jews and Christians —Israel and the church—all things which are in heaven and which are on earth will be gathered together in one in Christ. And He will *be* all, and *in* all, forevermore.

Hallelujah, what a Saviour!

Enlightened and enriched by this background from the Hebrew scriptures, we are much better prepared to understand and appreciate the dreams and visions in the New Testament.

CHAPTER SIX

Breakthrough From The Beyond

Did you know that the Bible records six dreams in the New Testament, and all of them are found in the gospel of Matthew? Each dream marked an important breakthrough from the beyond, designed to communicate divine knowledge, instruction, or warning.

Four of those dreams were given to one person. That man was none other than Joseph, the husband of Mary the mother of our Lord. We remember that the man who was called "the dreamer" in the Old Testament was also named Joseph.

Joseph

In the opening words of Matthew's gospel, Christ the Messiah —the Anointed—is announced as the son (descendant) of David, the son (descendant) of Abraham. This statement links Jesus with the two great covenants God made with David and with Abraham.

The genealogy of Jesus is then given through Joseph, because he was a legal heir to the throne of David by reason of his lineage. Joseph was *the legal father* of Jesus, though of course not His actual father. But if Mary had not been the lawful wife of Joseph, Jesus' royal claim would have been rejected from the outset. For it was through the father—not the mother—that the crown rights descended.

Jesus was also "the son of David" through His mother's line. She was a descendant of David through his son *Nathan*. Joseph's family had come through David's son *Solomon*. This was the "kingly line." But there was a curse on it, while there was no curse on the other line.

So we see that Jesus was truly descended from the royal family, both on His mother's side and on His legal father's side.

Since the Jews took no account of women in genealogies, Joseph in Luke's gospel is called "the son of Heli" instead of the son of Jacob, who "begat" him according to Matthew. Joseph was the legal son of Heli, his father-in-law, and naturally took the place of Mary in the genealogy. Probably Heli had no son of his own to receive the family birthright, so he may even have adopted Joseph to be his legal heir.

At the time of Jesus' birth there was no Jewish king of Israel. There had been no king on David's throne since 587 B.C. when Zedekiah, the very last king of Judah, was deposed and taken captive to Babylon. Herod the Great, an Idumean, was but a puppet king under Rome's domination. Palestine had been under the control of Rome since 63 B.C. The Jews had some political liberty, but were required to pay a yearly tax to the Roman government.

As for their religious life, the Jews adhered rigorously to their forms of worship, but the Romans had the right to appoint and remove their high priest. Consequently the office was often obtained by deception, bribery, and even murder. Though the priesthood became more and more corrupt, the priests still possessed great power. But they used it for their own selfish purposes. They paid scrupulous attention to the ceremonies of religion, all the while making oppressive financial demands on the people.

Just as there was *no true king* and *no true priest* at the time of Jesus' birth, so there was *no prophet* of God either. From the days of Malachi to the beginning of New Testament times, no prophet spoke or wrote. These were four hundred years of prophetic silence.

Thus the time was ripe for a deliverer to come to Israel, and for the voice of God to be heard again in the land.

It was at this point that God saw fit to send forth His Son. Clothed in the garb of humanity, He came to be prophet, priest and king—all three—to His people, in addition to being the Saviour of the world.

The facts regarding Jesus' birth are made very plain in Matthew's gospel. We read in chapter one verse 18:

"Now the birth of Jesus Christ took place under these circumstances: When His mother Mary had been promised in marriage to Joseph, before they came together she was found to be pregnant (through the power) of the Holy Spirit."

Luke's gospel goes into greater detail regarding the matter. He tells of the angel Gabriel's visit to the virgin Mary in the city of Nazareth. The startling announcement was made to her that she would conceive in her womb through the power of the Holy Ghost.

"The Holy Spirit will come upon you," said Gabriel, "and the power of the Most High will overshadow you (as a shining cloud)" (Lk. 1:35a).

By a creative act of God, conception was to take place in the womb of the virgin. God would unite Himself with a miraculously generated human body. That this union of deity and humanity was to produce an absolutely holy nature is made clear by Gabriel's next words:

"And so the holy (pure, sinless) Thing which shall be born of you will be called the Son of God" (Lk. 1:35b).

Uniquely unclassifiable, the angel could only term the child to be conceived in this supernatural way *"that holy Thing."* But when He was born, His name was to be called Jesus.

"He will be great (eminent)" Gabriel told Mary, "and will be called the Son of the Most High. The Lord God will give to Him the throne of His forefather David,

"And He will reign over the house of Jacob throughout the ages. And of His reign there will be no end" (Lk. 1:32, 33).

Matthew simply says that Mary "was found to be with child of the Holy Ghost." He goes on to say that Joseph, her betrothed, being a just and upright man, did not want to expose Mary to public shame and death because of this pregnancy. He knew that he was not the father of her unborn child, but people would not believe what really happened. They would attribute her condition to adultery; and according to Jewish law, the penalty for this was stoning.

We aren't told whether Joseph believed Mary's account of the angel's visit or not, but we can certainly understand why he was in a quandary as to what he should do. Even if he did not believe ill of the woman he loved, the fact remained that she was pregnant—and not by him.

What was the honorable course of action for him to take? More important, in the sight of God, what was the right thing for him to do?

Joseph contemplated divorcing Mary quietly and secretly. In those days betrothal was a legal contract almost equivalent to marriage, and it could not be broken off without a formal divorce. Joseph could do this without giving a reason. A Jewish husband could divorce his wife, if she did not please him, simply by giving her a bill of divorce in the presence of witnesses. It was not necessary to specify the cause.

Being the gentle, good, and devout man that he was, Joseph made no hasty or rash decision. There is no record of anger or censure toward Mary. He quietly deliberated the matter; and one night as he lay asleep, God gave him the answer in a dream.

"As he was thinking this over, behold, an angel of the Lord appeared to him in a DREAM, saying, Joseph, descendant of David, do not be afraid to take Mary (as) your wife. For that which is conceived in her is of (from, out of) the Holy Spirit.

"She will bear a Son, and you shall call His name Jesus (in Hebrew means Saviour). For He will save His people from their sins (that is, prevent their failing and missing the true end and scope of life, which is God)" (Matt. 1:20, 21).

The angel of the Lord who visited Joseph in this dream was no doubt Gabriel, the same one who had come to Mary. In her case he appeared in person, while to Joseph he appeared in a dream. Have you ever wondered why God sent Gabriel in actual visible form to Mary when she was wide-awake, yet He chose to have the angel visit Joseph in a dream while he was sound asleep?

Perhaps it was because of the tremendous importance of the message to Mary, and in order to give her a chance to ask questions of Gabriel (which she did). At any rate, it was a real angel-to-person contact. As for Joseph, it is possible that the composed condition of sleep best enabled him to receive the divine message.

Did you ever stop to think what might have happened if Mary had said, "Good heavens, I can't believe such a thing is possible! Imagine a virgin like me getting pregnant by the Holy Ghost. It's against all laws of nature. It's scientifically incredible. And besides, I certainly don't want to subject myself to the shame and disgrace of such a thing. Joseph would never believe me, and that means I would be stoned to death! No thank you, Gabriel. I just couldn't take it."

Or what if she had reacted in the opposite fashion and declared, "Oh what a compliment! God singled *me* out from all other women on earth. And He sent you, an archangel, to me! Just think—I am 'highly favored of the Lord.' He is with me, and I am blessed above all other women. *I'm* going to be the mother of the long-awaited Messiah! Wait till my friends hear about this!"

Mary did not voice either of these sentiments. Instead she replied simply: "Behold I am the handmaiden of the Lord. Let it be done to me according to what you have said" (Lk. 1:38).

In perfect submission to the will of God, Mary did not torment herself afterward with worry over what people might think, or how she could prove the divine origin of this conception. Conscious only of her own innocence, she calmly and trustingly committed herself to the Lord.

When she went to visit her cousin Elizabeth (who was soon to become the mother of John the Baptist), in an outburst of joy and reverence, Mary exclaimed: "My soul magnifies and extols the Lord! My spirit rejoices in God my Savior;

"For He has looked upon the low station and humiliation of His handmaiden . . . He who is almighty has done great things for me, and holy is His name" (Lk. 1:46–49).

In thanksgiving and in praise she awaited the birth of the blessed Messiah, who was to be His own mother's Saviour, as well as the Redeemer of the world.

Getting back to Joseph and his dilemma, we must again recognize the fact that God regarded a dream as a worthy means of communication. In this instance it was essential that the means accomplish the end. Joseph must be personally convinced through a direct message from God that Mary had told him the exact truth, and furthermore that he should go ahead with the wedding.

Is this what happened? Yes, indeed, for we read in verses 24 and 25 of Matthew's first chapter:

"Then Joseph being aroused from his sleep, did as the angel of the Lord had commanded him. He took (her to his side as) his wife,

"But he had no union with her as her husband until she had borne her first-born Son, and he called His name Jesus."

So impressive was the dream that it awakened Joseph from his slumber. There was no question in his mind but that its source was divine. In prompt obedience, he did as the angel had bidden him and solemnized the marriage. Although Mary was his legal wife, he had no marital relations with her until after the birth of her child. And when her son was born, Joseph called His name Jesus, according to the angelic direction given him.

The Wise Men

Jesus was born in Bethlehem in the days of Herod the king.

Now Herod was not a king in the true meaning of the word. The emperor of Rome had appointed him governor of Judea, and the Roman senate later gave him the title *"king of the Jews"* in 40 B.C. Although he lavishly expended money on the reconstruction of the Jerusalem temple, he was not a Jew by religion, and he built temples to pagan deities elsewhere.

The Jews over whom he ruled hated Herod, mainly for two reasons. He was of despised Edomite blood; and he had displaced by murder the last of the high-priestly kings from the family of the Maccabees, Jewish heroes. Herod had married into this family by taking as one of his ten wives the granddaughter of a former high priest. But he had her killed too.

Herod had many children, and much of his life was spent in putting down plots of his various sons to get possession of the throne. Notoriously jealous and insanely insecure, any rumor of a rival king instantly roused the aged tyrant's worst fears. When he heard that wise men from the East had come to Jerusalem inquiring "Where is he that is born King of the Jews?" he was greatly alarmed.

These wise men, or Magi, were religious astrologers from Persia or Arabia. They studied prophecies, explained omens, interpreted dreams, and practiced divination. In their own country they had seen an extraordinary star in the heavens, one that had never been seen before. This star was not the result of a conjunction of planets, nor an exploding nova, but was a totally supernatural astronomical phenomenon. It seemed to hover over the land of Palestine.

Having observed such a remarkable star, and being familiar with the Jewish expectation of a great king to be born to their people, these learned men followed the star into the land of Judea. When they arrived in Jerusalem, they announced that they had come to worship the king whose star had been seen in the east.

Practically everyone pictures these wise men as kings, three in number. Our Christmas music always includes the carol about the Magi: "We Three Kings of Orient Are." *But the Bible doesn't say there were three of them, or that they were kings.* Where then did we get that idea?

The fact that they brought three gifts—gold, frankincense and myrrh—led to the assumption they were a trio. Their expensive gifts were worthy for a king to give. But Christian tradition has regarded them as kings because of this prophetic passage in a Messianic psalm:

"The kings of Tarshish and of the isles shall bring presents. The kings of Sheba and Seba shall offer gifts.

"Yea, all kings shall fall down before him. All nations shall serve him" (Ps. 72:10, 11).

Herod learned of the visit of the wise men to Jerusalem, and that they had come in search of a recently born "King of the Jews." He first called in all the chief priests and scribes and demanded to know where the expected Messiah-King should be born. They told him it would be in Bethlehem. Their knowledge was based on the prophecy in Micah (5:2), which we noted in the previous chapter of this book.

Summoning the wise men, Herod then sent them to Bethlehem. He instructed them to search diligently for the young child. When they found him, they were to let him know, so that he might come and worship him also. Of course Herod had no intention of doing this. Murder was in his mind, not worship. Therefore, God who reads the thoughts and intents of the heart, kept the wise men from returning to Jerusalem.

The star they had previously seen in the east again guided the Magi. It went before them until it came and stood over the place where the young child was.

Here again tradition, especially the typical Sunday School pageant, gives us an erroneous picture. The wise men are invariably shown joining the shepherds in the stable at Bethlehem on the night of the Saviour's birth. A careful reading of the scriptures, however, clearly indicates that this was not what happened.

When the wise men found Jesus, the Bible calls Him *"the young child"* who was *"in the house."* This is in contrast with *"the babe lying in a manger"*, which is the way He is described at the time of the shepherds' visit.

It would seem that as soon as the tax enrollment was over, and the crowds attending it had dispersed, Joseph and Mary obtained a house in Bethlehem. They would have had no difficulty doing so then, and very likely they intended to settle there permanently.

No doubt it was from Bethlehem, a distance of only five miles from Jerusalem, that the infant Jesus was taken to the temple for dedication. In keeping with Jewish law, forty days after His birth, Mary and Joseph brought Him into the temple to present Him to the Lord. They also came to offer sacrifices conforming to Mosaic requirements.

It was after this that the Magi visited Jesus. He must have been over a year old by this time. Otherwise Herod would never have ordered the slaughter of all male children two years old and under, "according to the time when he had diligently enquired of the wise men."

When the Magi saw the young child with Mary His mother, they fell down and worshiped Him. To drop to one's knees when paying homage to a monarch was customary. But in addition to respect, these men offered religious worship to the child before whom they knelt. Eastern custom also required that royalty be approached with a gift. The Magi presented to Jesus the most costly products of the countries in which they lived—gold, frankincense, and myrrh.

With the object of their long journey at last accomplished, they prepared to return to Jerusalem and inform Herod of their finding. But "being warned of God in a DREAM that they should not return to Herod, they departed into their own country another way" (Matt. 2:12, KJV).

Thus we are told of the second dream in the New Testament. It seems particularly appropriate that a dream was the method of divine revelation to the Magi, since they were interpreters of dreams. Obedient to the dream, they avoided Jerusalem and set out for home by another route.

More Dreams for Joseph

Following their departure, the Bible tells of another warning received in like manner. This is our third dream, and it was given to Joseph. Apparently Gabriel, the same angel who had appeared to him in his first dream, was again the messenger.

"Now after they had gone, behold, an angel of the Lord appeared to Joseph in a DREAM and said, Get up! (Tenderly) take unto you the young child and his mother, and flee to Egypt, and remain there till I tell you (otherwise). For Herod intends to search for the child in order to destroy him" (Matt. 2:13).

Did you notice the phrase "remain there till I tell you otherwise", which was included with the command to flee to Egypt? In these words Joseph was given a promise of continued care and guidance. He could expect to hear from God again. But until fresh orders were forthcoming, he was simply to do as he was told.

As he had done after the first dream, Joseph was quick to obey the instructions imparted in this one. He knew the dream was from the Lord, and so he and the little family set out on their journey. They traveled by night for greater security.

Egypt was a place of refuge easily reached from Bethlehem. It was outside the dominion of Herod and contained a population of at least a million Jews, who were more wealthy and enlightened than those of Palestine. God directed Joseph, Mary and Jesus to a safe place among their own kindred.

Today, if you were to travel the road from Bethlehem to Cairo, you would come into the quiet little village of Mataria on the right bank of the Nile. Rising from among the fields of sugar cane is the dome of the Church of the Holy Family. In a nearby garden stands the great decayed trunk of a sycamore tree. It is called *"The Tree of the Holy Virgin."* In its center— so legend tells us—Mary and the child Jesus hid from their pursuers during their flight from Palestine.

This garden is also famous for its balsam bushes, which are not found anywhere else in Egypt. The historian Josephus relates a very interesting story explaining how they got there . . .

After the murder of Caesar, Cleopatra—the ambitious Queen of Egypt—several times visited the land of Judea and Jerusalem. Through her wiles she was able to obtain from Herod the whole of the seacoast of Palestine with all its cities. Mark Antony presented them to his mistress as her personal property.

She also acquired some very valuable plants that were contained in large fragrant gardens in the city of Jericho on the Jordan. These were reared from seeds which the Queen of Sheba is supposed to have brought as a present to King Solomon. Cleopatra took cuttings of the balsam bushes home with her. She instructed that they be planted in the temple gardens at Heliopolis. This famous city is the "On" of the Bible, the place where Joseph of Old Testament times was married to Asenath, daughter of the high priest of that city.

Under the care of skilled Jewish gardeners, these rare and precious shrubs flourished on the Nile. Here in the garden of Mataria, just outside the city of Heliopolis, Joseph of New Testament times—with Mary and Jesus—are said to have found refuge. What an historic spot it is!

Josephus also tells us much about Herod, the one who caused this flight into Egypt. The writer calls him the most cruel tyrant who ever ascended the throne. But Josephus does not mention the massacre of the innocents at Bethlehem and in all the surrounding coasts, which Herod ordered when he found that the wise men had mocked him and thwarted his plot to kill the infant Jesus.

However, this slaughter fits in perfectly with the revolting character of the man of whom it is said: "He ruled like a wild beast."

Five days before his death in 4 B.C., Herod had his son Antipater assassinated. On his deathbed Herod made a will designating three of his younger sons as his successors.

Archelaus was to rule in Judea and Samaria. *Antipas* was to be tetrarch of Galilee and Perea, the land east of the Jordan. *Philip* was bequeathed the north-eastern territories. Antipas is the Herod who imprisoned and executed John the Baptist, and to whom Jesus was sent by Pilate for judgment. Jesus once described him as "that fox."

It was in connection with two Herods—Herod the Great, and his son Archelaus—that the fourth and fifth dreams recorded in the New Testament were given.

Again Joseph was the recipient. The fourth dream came during the sojourn in Egypt, and it revealed the death of the first Herod.

"When Herod died, behold, an angel of the Lord appeared in a DREAM to Joseph in Egypt, and said,

"Rise. (Tenderly) take unto you the child and his mother, and go to the land of Israel, for those who sought the child's life are dead" (Matt. 2:19, 20).

Having been obedient to God's commands, which were twice before imparted to him in dreams, Joseph again complied with divine instruction. He and Mary and the young child left Egypt for the land of Israel.

But on their way they heard that Archelaus was reigning in Judea, and that he was as wicked and cruel as his father . . .

His first act had been to send troops to Jerusalem, where three thousand people were butchered on one day alone. The courts of the temple were strewn with corpses. This was in retaliation for the Jews' demand that atonement be made for the horrible murder of two of their well-known scholars. The elder Herod had burned these learned men alive because they took down the golden Roman eagle from the gateway of the temple. Previous to this, Herod the Great had put to death countless priests and Pharisees, and completely exterminated many noble Jewish families.

Revolt had begun in Jerusalem. The turmoil and unrest spread through the country like wildfire.

Bloody clashes ensued. The royal palaces of Judea were plundered and set ablaze. The governor of Syria hastened to the scene with a powerful Roman army, strengthened with troops from Beirut and Arabia. As soon as the marching columns appeared in sight of Jerusalem, the rebels fled. They were pursued and captured in droves, and two thousand men were crucified.

News of this terrifying situation reached the ears of the little family returning from Egypt. No wonder Joseph was afraid to go into Judea. The Lord had told him to go to the land of Israel, but where in that land would it be safe?

Once again God spoke to Joseph by means of a dream. The scripture says: "And being divinely warned in a DREAM, he withdrew to the region of Galilee" (Matt. 2:22b).

It is interesting to note that God led Joseph step by step. He could have included these instructions to go to Galilee in the former dream—or disclosed the whole picture from beginning to end in the dream before that. He chose instead to reveal His will by degrees. Even so, we at times must wait upon the leading of the Lord in our lives. But if we obey each direction as it comes, we may confidently expect that further guidance will be given us as we go along.

"And he (Joseph) came and dwelt in a city called Nazareth: that it might be fulfilled which was spoken by the prophets, He shall be called a Nazarene" (Matt. 2:23, KJV).

This scripture probably has reference to Isaiah 11:1 where the Messiah is spoken of as "a Branch (netzer) out of the stem of Jesse." The prophets Jeremiah and Zechariah also used the term "Branch" as a Messianic title.

So it came about that Nazareth was the town in which Jesus spent His childhood and youth. Located in Galilee, it was part of the territory ruled by Antipas. Although he was extremely pleasure-loving, he was known to be more humane than his brother Archelaus.

The town was a peaceful place situated in a high valley surrounded by hills. Its scenic beauty caused St. Jerome to call Nazareth *"The Flower of Galilee."* Groves of date palms, fig trees, and pomegranates clothed the encircling hills in many shades of green. The fields were full of wheat and barley. Vineyards were laden with delicious grapes, and all along the countryside grew an abundance of brightly colored flowers.

In the village were the open-air workshops of various craftsmen. It was here that Joseph had his carpenter's shop. One of the little houses, with their clay walls clustered together, belonged to the family of Jesus. His mother went to the well at the foot of a hill where a spring supplied plentiful water. She brought her filled jar home, skillfully balancing it on her head. This well is still in use today, and it is appropriately called *"Mary's Well."*

Nazareth was the lovely setting which provided Jesus with so many of His parables—of sowing and harvesting, of the wheat and the tares, of the mustard seed, the vineyard, and the lilies of the field.

Because of its altitude of 1200 feet, with some of its hills rising to 1600 feet, Nazareth commanded an impressive view. To the northeast one could see majestic, snow-capped Mount Hermon. On the west Mount Carmel and the blue Mediterranean were visible. To the south lay the Plain of Esdraelon, and on the east rose the hemispherical slopes of Mount Tabor.

Here in Nazareth Jesus lived for almost thirty years. He received the regular training of a Jewish lad in home and synagogue. With His family He went annually to Jerusalem to attend the three great feasts of Passover, Pentecost, and Tabernacles.

It was in the synagogue at Nazareth where He read the Messianic scripture from Isaiah, and then proclaimed that He was the fulfillment of the prophecy it contained (Luke 4:16–21). To the ears of the entire congregation, this was startling, and His words amazing!

But they were highly offended when He classed Himself with

Elijah and Elisha, whom they considered to be the greatest of prophets. And when He intimated that God would show further favor to the Gentiles, whom they despised—this was too much!

In wrath they thrust Him out of the city. Leading Him to the brow of the hill on which Nazareth was built, they attempted to cast Him down headlong. But Jesus passed out of their midst and went His way.

Later He came among them once more, and preached in their synagogue on the sabbath day (Matt. 13:54–58). They could not deny that He spoke with exceptional wisdom. They had heard about the many miraculous works He had done in other places. But they had known Him ever since He was a child. He used to be one of the town's carpenters. His family still lived there, and they knew them too.

Scornfully they inquired about His education. Where did He get all this knowledge, and the power to do these mighty things? Who did He think He was?

Filled with unbelief and contempt, they rejected Him for the second time. Jesus said to them, "A prophet is not without honor, save in his own country, and in his own house."

After healing a few of their sick, He left—*never to return to Nazareth again.*

Claudia

The sixth and last dream recorded in the New Testament is the only one in the Bible in which a woman is the dreamer.

Her name was Claudia Procula, and she was the wife of Pontius Pilate, Roman procurator of Judea. She is said to have been inclined to Judaism, or even to have been a proselyte, and afterwards to have become a Christian. In the Greek Church she is canonized.

We know much more about Pilate than we do about his wife. He is described by Josephus as an extortioner, a tyrant, a blood sucker, and a corruptible character. Another historian, Philo of Alexandria, writes of him: "He was cruel, and his hard heart knew no compassion. His day in Judea was a reign of bribery and violence, robbery, oppression, misery, executions without fair trial, and infinite brutality."

Pilate was appointed Roman procurator of Judea in A.D. 26. He held the office for ten years. His usual residence was at Caesarea, but each year he went to Jerusalem to keep order at the time of the national feasts. The wives of provincial governors were permitted to accompany their husbands. That is how Claudia happened to be in the holy city at the time of Jesus' arrest, trial, and crucifixion.

Pilate had complete power of life and death over the people who lived in Judea, Samaria, and part of Idumea—unless they were Roman citizens. He appointed the high priests and controlled the temple and its funds. The very vestments of the high priests were in his custody and were released only for festivals.

That he hated the Jews was made unmistakably plain to them again and again. His first action on taking office was to antagonize the Jews by hanging up golden shields bearing the emperor's name in Herod's palace in the middle of Jerusalem. Previous procurators had avoided using such standards in the holy city. The Jews appealed to Rome to enforce the rights that had been guaranteed them as a religious community. Emperor Tiberius ordered the removal of the shields.

Josephus and Eusebius allege a further grievance of the Jews against Pilate. He was charged with misappropriating funds from the temple treasury. The money was used to build an aqueduct for the purpose of conveying water to the city from a spring some twenty-five miles away. The Jews demonstrated against this when Pilate came up to Jerusalem. He sent his troops against them, and a large number were slain.

About this time Jesus was informed of another outrage committed by Pilate. Some men from Galilee had been murdered in the courts of the temple while they were killing the animals they had brought as sacrificial offerings. The blood of these Galileans "Pilate had mingled with their sacrifices."

When Jesus was told of this heinous act, His reply was startling. He said to the people who brought him the news:

"Do you think that those Galileans were greater sinners than all the other Galileans, because they have suffered in this way?

"I tell you, No. But unless you repent—(that is) change your mind for the better and heartily amend your ways, with abhorrence of your past sins—you will all likewise perish and be lost (eternally)."

He repeated this statement after referring to a similar instance:

"Or those eighteen on whom the tower in Siloam fell and killed them, do you think that they were more guilty offenders than all the others who dwelt in Jerusalem? I tell you, No. But unless you repent . . . you will all likewise perish" (Lk. 13:2–5). (It is possible that the tower which collapsed was in some way connected with building Pilate's aqueduct, and the men who were killed were workmen on that project.)

Notice that Jesus did not use these incidents to foster rebellion against authority, cruel and unjust though it was. His emphasis was on the necessity of personal repentance, and of making peace with God in time. Death can come suddenly and unexpectedly, and therefore it is vitally important that everyone be ready. In addition, He cautioned His hearers not to judge men's sins by their sufferings in this world.

So much for background events connected with Pontius Pilate. It is his wife's very disturbing dream with which we are chiefly concerned.

This dream occurred on the same night that Jesus was betrayed. Claudia must have retired about the time Christ and His disciples entered the Garden of Gethsemane. As she was drifting off to sleep, just a short distance away Jesus was kneeling on the ground, in deep prayer to His Father. He was preparing to drink the bitter cup of humiliation and agony in which the sinless Lamb of God would take upon Himself the sins of fallen mankind.

Perhaps Claudia saw in her dream the unfolding of the shameful events in this incomparable tragedy. It is possible that she witnessed the kiss of betrayal by Judas Iscariot, as the Roman soldiers and Jewish priests gathered around Jesus. She may have seen them lay hold on Him and bind His hands, and hurry Him away into the city . . .

His captors took Him first to the palace of *Annas,* the former high priest. Annas in actuality shared the power of that office with his son-in-law, *Caiaphas.* Christ was to be tried formally before the Sanhedrin, the highest tribunal of the Jews, but

Annas was given the privilege of conducting a preliminary investigation before the official trial (John 18:13).

The object of this examination was to induce Jesus to incriminate Himself, the available evidence against Him being weak. Annas tried to entrap Jesus into the admission that He had founded a secret society. Jesus repudiated the suggestion, and refused to be drawn into making any statements likely to implicate His disciples. At this point one of the officers slapped Jesus in the face with the palm of his hand.

Annas ordered Jesus to be taken to Caiaphas, the incumbent high priest and president of the Sanhedrin. Here in the adjoining apartments of Caiaphas, the priests, scribes and elders were assembled. Caiaphas questioned Jesus under oath, *"Are you the Christ, the Son of God?"* Jesus answered, *"I am."* (In the King James Version: "Ye say that I am" Lk. 22:70.) Then, as proof of His Messiahship, He added that they would one day see Him sitting on the right hand of God, and coming in the clouds of heaven.

This declaration was a positive and unmistakable assertion by Jesus that He was the Messiah. He identified Himself with the well-known Messianic prophecy in Daniel:

"I saw on the clouds of heaven One like a Son of Man. He came to the Ancient of Days and was presented before Him. And there was given him, the Messiah, dominion and glory and a kingdom, that all peoples, nations and languages should serve him" (Dan. 7:13, 14).

Upon hearing these words, the high priest rent his clothes and charged Jesus with blasphemy. Caiaphas asked the council for their opinion. They answered that Jesus was guilty of death. Some spat in His face and struck at Him. Others slapped Him.

In the early hours of the morning, Jesus—still bound—was led away to Pilate. Under Roman rule, the Sanhedrin could not execute the death sentence. They could only pass judgment, to be ratified by the Roman authority.

At the Praetorium, official residence of Pilate, he and his wife Claudia were sound asleep. The governor was roused from his bed and hastily summoned to another part of the palace. This was the open-air judgment hall in which Pilate held court.

Here stood the prisoner Jesus, surrounded by soldiers and a crowd of spectators.

Just outside the entrance were the members of the Sanhedrin, priests and elders. They would not come into the hall. It would defile them to enter a Gentile house not purged from the presence of leaven in prospect of the Passover.

The Jews began at once to voice their charges. They accused Jesus of sedition, of withholding tribute from Caesar, and of claiming to be a king. They knew that the charge of blasphemy on which the Sanhedrin condemned Him would have no weight with Pilate.

Pilate asked Jesus, "Are you the King of the Jews?"

Jesus answered, "My kingdom is not of this world."

Pilate replied, "Then you are a king?"

"Yes," said Jesus. "I was born for that purpose. I came to bring truth to the world. All who love the truth are my followers."

"What is truth?" Pilate exclaimed.

Then he went out again to the people and told them, "He is not guilty of any crime." Pilate recognized that the accused man was the object of hatred that had been stirred up by the Pharisees. That alone was sufficient reason for this tyrannical enemy of the Jews to reject their demand and to acquit Jesus. But in addition, Pilate personally found no fault in Him.

The mob reacted in rage to the governor's pronouncement. They loudly denounced him and threatened him with the censure of his superiors. The priests and elders angrily shouted, "He (Jesus) has caused riots against the government everywhere he has gone, from Galilee to Jerusalem!"

"Is he then a Galilean?" Pilate asked.

When they told him yes, Pilate said to take Him to Herod. Galilee was under Herod Antipas' jurisdiction, and he was in Jerusalem for the Passover. By this maneuver Pilate thought to shift the responsibility of the trial from himself to Herod.

The soldiers hurried Jesus to the judgment hall of Herod, the man whose hands were stained with the blood of John the Baptist. Herod asked Jesus question after question, but there was no reply. The chief priests and other religious leaders stood by shouting their accusations.

Irritated by Jesus' silence, and because He would do no miracle to satisfy Herod's curiosity, the evil ruler and his soldiers began to taunt and ridicule Jesus. In an attempt to mock His claim to be a king, Herod arrayed Him in a gorgeous robe, the kind worn by candidates for office in Rome. Then Jesus was sent back to Pilate.

When the Jews returned with their prisoner, Pilate called the chief priests, the elders and the people together. He reminded them he had already examined Jesus and found Him innocent of any crime. He told them that they had brought complaints against Him, but they had not been able to prove a single charge. He had sent Jesus to Herod, the tetrarch of Galilee, one of their own nation. But he also had found in Him nothing worthy of death.

"I will therefore chastise him," Pilate announced, thinking that scourging Jesus would pacify the mob. "Then I will release him."

It was the governor's custom to release one Jewish prisoner each year during the Passover celebration, which itself commemorates a deliverance. The prisoner to be freed could be anyone the Jews wanted. This year there was a particularly notorious criminal in jail named Barabbas. Pilate asked the crowd, "Which shall I release to you—Barabbas, or Jesus which is called Christ?"

Just then, as Pilate sat down on the judgment seat, a message was brought to him from his wife Claudia. Its contents read:

"Have nothing to do with that just and upright Man, for I have had a painful experience because of Him today in a DREAM" (Matt. 27:19).

We have no way of knowing what was in that dream of Pilate's wife, but it must have been a vivid experience. It frightened and troubled her. No doubt it could have been considered a nightmare. In the dream Claudia was given evidence that Jesus was a righteous man—innocent of any wrong-doing —but she also saw things that caused her much suffering.

Perhaps, in her dream, she witnessed the terrible scourging Jesus was soon to undergo. A scourge was a Roman implement for severe bodily punishment. It was a whip composed of about a dozen leather cords, which had jagged pieces of bone or metal at each end to make the blows more painful. The victim was tied to a post and flogged on the bare back. Each blow would cut the flesh in several places. The law permitted that up to forty stripes could be administered. So hideous was the punishment that the victim often fainted, and some died under it.

Possibly Claudia saw in her dream the soldiers plaiting a crown of thorns and putting it on Jesus' head . . . draping a purple robe around Him, and then saluting Him, *"Hail, King of the Jews!"* before striking Him with their hands.

She may have heard the frenzied cries of the bloodthirsty crowd shouting, *"Crucify him, crucify him!"* Perhaps she saw Him hanging on the cross, blood flowing down from His head, His hands and His feet. She may even have been given a glimpse of Him coming in the clouds of glory, with all His mighty angels—the Lord of heaven and earth revealed in flaming fire.

Whatever it was that Claudia saw and experienced in her dream, she awoke with a cry of horror. Realizing that her husband was at that very moment ready to pass judgment upon this holy Man, she hastily wrote a message of warning and had a servant take it at once to Pilate.

If ever a man should have listened to his wife and acted upon her advice, this was the time. But Pilate was afraid of the people. At this point they were so inflamed by the priests and rulers that they behaved like wild beasts. The pressure was too great for his weak character.

He gave in to their demand that he release Barabbas, and he ordered that Jesus be scourged.

When this terrible punishment was over, Jesus—with bleeding brow and lacerated back, His countenance marred with pain—was brought before the Jews. Pilate said to them, *"Behold the man!"* The words were gently and sympathetically spoken, intended to move the crowd to compassion. Pilate hoped that the spectacle of Christ's suffering would cause the people to let Him go.

But when the chief priests and officers saw Him, they raised the awful cry, "Crucify him, crucify him!"

Three times Pilate had told the people that he found no fault in Jesus, but they would not listen. "By our laws," they screamed, "he ought to die because he called himself the Son of God."

When Pilate heard this, he became more frightened than ever. He remembered the warning and the dream of his wife. Perhaps this man *was* some kind of a god in human form. He took Jesus back into the palace again and asked Him, "Where did you come from?"

Jesus gave no answer.

"Don't you realize that I have power to release you or to crucify you?" demanded Pilate.

Then Jesus said, "You would have no power at all over me unless it were given to you from above. Therefore the one who delivered me to you has the greater sin."

He was referring to Caiaphas, the high priest. The latter was much more guilty than Pilate, for the Roman governor was only acting in the performance of his duty. Pilate did not know the real issues at stake in the rejection and condemnation of Jesus. Caiaphas knew He was the Messiah, and yet deliberately sought to kill Him.

After this last conversation with Jesus, Pilate was more anxious than ever to release Him. But the Jewish leaders shrieked, "If you let this man go, you are no friend of Caesar's! Anyone who declares himself a king is a rebel against Caesar."

And so, afraid of this threat to report him to Rome for acquitting a treasonous rebel, Pilate gave in to the will of the mob. But before he did, he took water and washed his hands in front of the multitude. He said to them, "I am innocent of the blood of this good man. The responsibility is yours."

In blind and vindictive rage the people yelled back, *"His blood be on us, and on our children!"*

Then Pilate released Barabbas, and delivered Jesus to be crucified.

The Saviour was taken out of the city, carrying His cross, to the place known as "The Skull." It is called in Hebrew *"Golgo-*

tha", and in Greek *"Calvary."* There Jesus was nailed to the cross, which was set up between the crosses of two thieves.

Over the head of every victim of crucifixion was inscribed his particular offense. Pilate posted a sign above the cross of Christ reading: JESUS OF NAZARETH, THE KING OF THE JEWS. This was mockery, not an allegation of any crime. The sign was written in Hebrew, Latin, and Greek—the three common languages in Palestine. Thus Pilate, instead of accusing Jesus as a malefactor, proclaimed Him as a King, and that three times.

The chief priests objected to this title. They regarded it as an insult to the Jews, because it insinuated that the fitting ruler for such a nation was a condemned criminal. They asked Pilate to change the inscription from "The King of the Jews" to "He said, 'I am King of the Jews'".

But Pilate, who thoroughly despised the jealous and crafty priests and rulers, was obstinate. He replied coldly, "What I have written, I have written."

The Bible contains two more references to Pilate after the crucifixion. Both are in connection with Christ's burial . . .

A rich man from Arimathea named Joseph, one of Jesus' followers, went to Pilate and asked for the body. This was a very bold and brave thing to do, for the regular procedure required that Christ be buried with the other criminals. Whether the fact that Joseph was a member of the Sanhedrin influenced Pilate's decision we do not know, but the governor issued an order to release the body.

The next day at the close of the Passover, the chief priests and Pharisees requested Pilate to seal the tomb until the third day. They feared that Christ's disciples might steal the body and then tell everyone He came back to life. Pilate told them to take a guard of four soldiers and make the tomb absolutely secure.

This is the last we hear of Pontius Pilate in the scriptures. But history tells us a little more about him.

A few years after the death of Christ, Pilate finally overreached himself in his cruelty to the Jewish people. A group of Samaritans had assembled at Mount Gerizim in response to a person who promised to show them the ark of the covenant. This individual claimed that the ark and other sacred vessels had been hidden there. A great multitude came to the mountain. Pilate surrounded and captured them, executing many.

A Samaritan delegation protested this slaughter to the governor of Syria, and he ordered Pilate to answer the accusation of the Jews before the emperor. Pilate was on his journey to Rome to face these charges when the emperor died.

We are not told the outcome of the trial. But one legend says that as a result of it, Pilate was sent to Gaul as an exile; and that he committed suicide there. According to another story, Pilate's body was thrown first into the Tiber River, then into the Rhone. Neither river would receive it. Finally the body was plunged into a lake near Lucerne, Switzerland. This legend probably rose because a mountain near this lake is called Mount Pilatus. The ghost of Pilate is said to haunt the region to this day.

Pilate was made a saint by the Abyssinian Church, because it was believed that he was converted to Christianity and died a martyr. And so, strangely enough, both Pilate and his wife Claudia were canonized by eccelesiastical authority.

What stupendous events surrounded the only dream the scriptures record as having been given to a woman!

Various References to Dreams and Visions

No other actual dreams are spoken of in the New Testament. Dreams in general, as well as visions, are mentioned by the apostle Peter in his sermon on the day of Pentecost. He quoted from the prophet Joel:

"And it shall come to pass in the last days, God declares, that I will pour out of My Spirit upon all mankind. Your sons and your daughters shall prophesy—telling forth the divine counsels—and your young men shall see VISIONS (that is, divinely granted appearances), and your old men shall DREAM (divinely suggested) DREAMS" (Acts 2:17).

Here we have a scripture which unequivocally links dreams and visions with prophecy as part of the charismatic gifts of the Holy Spirit.

Most Christians, when they speak of the gifts of the Spirit, will name them as: the word of wisdom, the word of knowledge, faith, the gifts of healing, the working of miracles, prophecy, discerning of spirits, various kinds of tongues, and the interpretation of tongues. But the Spirit is not limited to these nine. God Himself has stated that divinely given dreams and visions will be included in the outpouring of His Spirit "in the last days."

Dreams and visions are not only a means of revelation from God, but they are spiritual gifts administered by the Holy Spirit as He wills. Therefore, we of today are promised that God will still direct certain individuals and impart knowledge and wisdom through dreams and visions, just as He has done from the time of Abraham. In fact, in the latter days more of mankind than ever before will be the recipients of these divinely granted messages.

The word "dreamers" is used by Jude, one of the brothers of Jesus, in his letter to Christians.

Jude is speaking of the lusts and sins of certain ones who had turned away from the faith. He compares their state of unbelief to that of the disobedient Israelites who died in the wilderness. He likens their rebellion to that of the angels who fell from their heavenly estate, and their lasciviousness to that of the people of Sodom and Gomorrha. Then he states:

"Likewise also these filthy DREAMERS defile the flesh, despise dominion, and speak evil of dignities" (Jude 8, KJV).

Jude called them "filthy dreamers" because they were spiritually asleep, and in their delusion they had opened the door to all manner of filthiness. They were false teachers who perverted the faith. Their lives were immoral, they degraded their bodies, and laughed at those in authority over them, even scoffing at the glorious ones—the angels from heaven.

While the New Testament contains no other references to dreams, it has much to say about visions.

We find the word "vision" first used in the gospel of Matthew. Jesus Himself voices it at the conclusion of a most glorious occasion. Do you know what that significant event was?

In case you haven't already guessed, it was:

The Transfiguration

During the last year of Christ's ministry, He departed from Galilee where His many miracles had brought Him tremendous popularity among the people. His fame reached its peak in the feeding of the five thousand. This clear proof of His Messiahship made the masses decide to crown Him King.

But Jesus refused to be crowned as an earthly Messiah. For this reason, the crowds—and even many of His wider circle of disciples—left Him. He withdrew then, with the twelve, to the northern part of Palestine. They came to the beautiful region of Caesarea Philippi, located at the foot of majestic Mount Hermon.

Knowing that His public ministry on earth was hastening to a close, and the sacrificial part of it about to begin, Jesus sought solitude with His little band of disciples. He must prepare them for what awaited Him in Jerusalem.

Before speaking of the sufferings and death that lay ahead, Jesus gave them an opportunity to confess their faith in Him, that they might be strengthened for the coming trials. He asked them a crucial question: "Who do you say that I am?"

By divine revelation, Peter declared: *"You are the Christ, the Son of the Living God!"*

This was a clear and express confession of His deity. Immediately afterward Jesus began to show His disciples that He must go to Jerusalem and suffer many things at the hands of the elders, high priests, and scribes—and be killed. The Lord knew that if the disciples were not well-grounded in the recognition that He was the Son of God, this would greatly shake their faith.

Up to this point they had mistakenly believed that Christ's kingdom was soon to be established—with all external honor, pomp, and power. But instead of this, He told them that suffering, shame and death awaited their Master. However, He plainly said that He would be raised from the dead on the third day, and that victory would ultimately be His.

Jesus told them: "The Son of man is going to come in the glory of His Father, with His angels . . ."

Then He added a remarkable statement: "Truly, I tell you, there are some standing here who will not taste of death before they see the Son of man coming in (into) His kingdom" (Matt. 16:27, 28).

This promise is now about to be fulfilled.

A week has passed since Peter's confession and the prediction that followed it. Jesus calls three of the disciples—Peter, James, and John—away from the others. They are the most spiritually perceptive of the group, and therefore closest to the Lord. He leads them across the fields and far up a rugged path on the side of Mount Hermon. This mountain, whose snow-capped top rises to a height of nine thousand feet, is the highest in all the region of Palestine.

It is evening, and they have spent the day traveling and listening to Jesus. As darkness gathers around them, they prepare to rest for the night. Jesus steps a little apart from them and begins to pray. At first the disciples join Him in prayer. But after a time weariness overcomes them, and they fall asleep.

Jesus had tried to explain to them about His second advent and the kingdom He will establish at that time. But they did not comprehend His words. Therefore His prayer is that they might be given a manifestation of this glorious future event. He desires that His Messiahship be shown to them not just through deeds, as it has heretofore, but in a more personal way.

He asks that a glimpse of His kingdom be revealed to their human eyes, and that they be given supernatural sight to behold it. Jesus prays that the disciples might see for themselves His full deity, as a preview of the glory He will have in His millennial kingdom. The remembrance of this may sustain their hearts in the hour of His humiliation and agony, and of their own sorrow and fear.

Peter's confession of Him as the Son of the Living God will then be divinely confirmed. All of them will know beyond any shadow of doubt Who He is. They will understand that His ignominious death is a part of the great plan of redemption.

As Christ is praying, suddenly the heavens open, and holy radiance descends upon Him. Arising from His position of prayer, Jesus stands to His feet. The glory of the Godhead bursts through His veil of flesh and merges with the brightness coming from above. The brilliance of the light awakens the disciples.

"Now Peter and those with him were weighed down with sleep. But when they fully awoke, they saw His glory (splendor and majesty and brightness) . . ." (Lk. 9:32).

"And His appearance underwent a change in their presence. His face shone clear and bright like the sun, and His clothing became white as light" (Matt. 17:2).

In awe and amazement they gaze upon the transfigured form of their Master. Against the blackness of the night, the face of Christ—shining like the sun in noon-day strength—is inexpressibly resplendent. His garments are radiant. They are dazzling white with a glory which seems to come from within.

Later Peter is to write of this scene: "We were eye-witnesses of His majesty." And John is to say: "We beheld His glory, the glory as of the only begotten of the Father."

As the disciples become able to bear the wondrous light, they discover that Jesus is not alone. "Behold, two men were conversing with Him—Moses and Elijah, who appeared in splendor and brightness. They were speaking of His exit (from life), which He was about to bring to realization at Jerusalem" (Lk. 9:30, 31).

Moses and Elijah appear—the former representing the Law, and the latter the prophets. Christ is seen in the midst of them as greater than both. Moses had been dead about 1300 years; and Elijah, who never died, was taken up into heaven almost 900 years before. Yet here they are, fully conscious, wearing clothes, and talking with Jesus.

The subject of their conversation is the exodus which Jesus is to accomplish at Jerusalem. This means not simply His physical departure, but the spiritual aspects of His death on the cross, and the resurrection to follow it. Christ's "going-out" is to be the means of redemption for His people. The Old Testament exodus from Egypt was a type and shadow of that redemption.

The disciples do not grasp the significance of the marvelous event that is taking place before their eyes. They think Elijah has come to inagurate Messiah's reign, and that the kingdom is soon to be set up on the earth. In each of their hearts is the longing to remain in this atmosphere of glory. They would like to extend the stay of the heavenly visitors, and to make the experience permanent. Peter says to Jesus:

" 'Master, it is delightful and good that we are here. Let us construct three booths or huts: one for You, and one for Moses, and one for Elijah!'—not noticing or knowing what he was saying.

"But even as he was speaking, a cloud came and began to overshadow them. They were seized with alarm and struck with fear as they entered into the cloud" (Lk. 9:33, 34).

This shining cloud composed of light is the visible glory which covers and manifests the divine presence. It is the same as the pillar of cloud and fire in the wilderness, the Shekinah glory which rested upon the ark of the covenant, and the glory cloud that filled the tabernacle and Solomon's temple.

"Then there came a voice out of the cloud, saying, 'This is My Son, My chosen One—My Beloved. Listen to, and yield to, and obey Him!' " (Lk. 9:35).

These words, in which God the Father testifies to Christ's divine Sonship, are similar to those spoken at His baptism. They contain a striking confirmation of Peter's confession.

As the disciples behold the cloud of glory, and hear the voice of God—the same voice which caused Mount Sinai to tremble in Moses' day—they fall on their faces, filled with fear and wonder. In humble adoration, they remain with their faces to the ground, until Jesus comes and touches them.

"Get up," He says to them, "and don't be afraid."

When they raise their eyes, they see that the heavenly glory has passed away. The forms of Moses and Elijah have vanished. They look upon Jesus only . . .

The next morning the four of them descend to the plain. At the foot of the mountain they see that a large crowd is gathered. "As they came down from the mountain, Jesus charged them, saying, 'Tell the VISION to no man, until the Son of man be risen from the dead' " (Matt. 17:9, KJV).

Notice that Jesus called the transfiguration occurrence a

"vision." Whether it was seen in a trance-like state, or as a wakeful reality, has often been discussed. Certainly it consisted of "something seen otherwise than by ordinary sight," to quote the definition of a vision given in the introduction to this book.

What the disciples had beheld was to be pondered in their hearts, not to be published abroad until after Jesus' resurrection. The multitudes would only ridicule it, or be carried away by political enthusiasm. Even the other disciples were not yet in a spiritual state to receive the lesson it taught.

Besides this, if the transfiguration were proclaimed, the credibility of it would be nullified by the shock of Christ's sufferings —which were soon to follow. But after His resurrection, the telling of it would be a great confirmation of His deity and His glory.

So Peter, James, and John kept still. They told no one at that time any of the things they had witnessed.

The transfiguration scene is the only vision in the Bible viewed by more than one person at the same time. In this unique case, three people saw the identical thing simultaneously. They all heard the same words.

Christ's promise that some of His disciples would see the coming of His kingdom in power and great glory was thus visually manifested. The voice of God Himself gave audible testimony and climactic proof that Jesus was the One to whom all Old Testament prophecies pointed, and in whom they were fulfilled.

Zacharias

We find the word "vision" used twice in the gospel of Luke.

It is first recorded in connection with the annunciation of the birth of John the Baptist. For this occasion we go back to the days of Herod the Great, king of Judea. The time is about six months before the angel Gabriel made his visitation to the virgin Mary.

Zacharias, a priest descended from Eleazar the son of Aaron, was serving in the temple at Jerusalem. He was married to a woman named *Elizabeth.* It was perfectly lawful for a priest to marry if the woman was an Israelitess; and the priests took care to marry from the tribe of Levi, the priestly line. Elizabeth was also a descendant of Aaron. In fact, she bore the same name as Aaron's wife (Exod. 6:23).

Both Zacharias and his wife were good pious Jews, strict and faithful to obey all the commandments of God. But they had no children. Elizabeth was barren, and now they were both very old.

One day as Zacharias was going about his work in the temple —his division being on duty that week—the honor fell to him by lot to enter the sanctuary and burn incense before the Lord. To avoid disputes, the various functions were decided by drawing lots. Incense was burned every morning and evening.

The daily sacrifice of the lamb was offered on the great brazen altar outside the temple proper, in front of the porch. Incense was offered inside the sanctuary on the golden altar of incense, which stood before the veil of the holy of holies.

The officiating priest was alone within the holy place while offering the incense. The other priests and the people remained outside, worshiping in the various temple courts. The offering of sweet incense was the highest act of worship and the most solemn part of the day's service. It symbolized Israel's prayers to God, and their acceptance by Him.

Zacharias went into the holy place of the sanctuary, and began burning incense at the altar. *Suddenly an angel appeared, standing to the right of the altar!*

The sight of an angel from the Lord was almost too much for the old priest. He was paralyzed with fear and anxiety. What could this mean?

Remember, no communication of any kind had come from God to His people since the days of the prophet Malachi, four hundred years ago. Now, without any warning, four centuries of silence were about to be broken! At last God was going to speak again to a son of Israel. Small wonder that Zacharias was terrified!

The position of the angel on the right side of the altar was an indication of favor, but he was too shaken to take note of this.

"The angel said to him, Do not be afraid, Zacharias. Your

petition was heard, and your wife Elizabeth will bear you a son. You must call his name John (meaning God is favorable)" (Lk. 1:13).

Zacharias' prayer, while in the holy place, was not for off-spring. Because of their advanced years, he and Elizabeth had long ago given up hope in this regard. His prayer was for the coming of the kingdom of God. The only suitable petition for so solemn an occasion would be for the advent of the Messiah and the salvation that He would bring. It was a maxim of the rabbis that "a prayer in which there is no mention of the kingdom of God is no prayer at all."

Yet the former prayers for a child, and the prayers for the kingdom were both about to be answered.

The mission of Zacharias' son would be to proclaim the coming of the Messiah. His oft-repeated cry to the people of Israel was to be "Repent, for the kingdom of heaven is at hand!"

The angel went on to say that Zacharias' son would be great in the sight of the Lord. Filled with the Holy Ghost from his mother's womb, he was to be set apart as a chosen instrument, turning many Israelites to God. In the spirit and power of Elijah, he would prepare his people for the Lord.

Zacharias was stunned by the splendor of his visitor, and overwhelmed by the prediction he had made. He said to the angel, "But how can I be sure of this? For I am an old man now, and my wife is also well along in years."

We can understand the priest's incredulity about the birth of a child. But the miraculous appearance of the angel ought itself to have been a sufficient sign to Zacharias.

"I am Gabriel," the angel said to him. "I stand in the very presence of God. It was He who sent me to bring you this good news!

"And now because you haven't believed me, you are to be stricken dumb, unable to speak until the child is born. For my words will certainly come true at the proper time!"

Zacharias' unbelief was immediately silenced, and the punishment for his distrust was itself to be the sign he felt he needed. But at the birth of the child, his lips would again be opened.

Over five hundred years before, Gabriel had made known to

Daniel the prophetic period which was to extend to the coming of Christ. The end of that period was near. The same messenger through whom the prophecy was given had come to announce its fulfillment.

Meanwhile the crowds outside were waiting for Zacharias to come out. They wondered why he was taking so long. Because the people always feared that the officiating priest might be struck dead for omitting some formality, it was customary for the priest to finish his ministry as quickly as possible.

Finally Zacharias emerged. His duty was now to pronounce the priestly benediction. But this he could not do.

"When he did come out, he was unable to speak to them. And they (clearly) perceived that he had seen a VISION in the sanctuary. He kept making signs to them, still he remained dumb" (Lk. 1:22).

Zacharias had seen more than a vision. The archangel Gabriel had visited him in person and made a startling announcement. Though he was stricken speechless, the look on his face and his gestures were sufficient evidence to convince the people that he had seen some kind of vision in the temple.

Soon after the birth of the promised child, the father's tongue was loosed. He spoke, praising God. The moment speech was restored to Zacharias, he was filled with the Holy Ghost. He prophesied of the coming Messiah. He said that his own son John would "be called the prophet of the Highest", the destined forerunner of the Lord Jesus Christ.

On The Road To Emmaus

The second mention of the word "vision" is found in the 24th chapter of Luke's gospel. This is the scripture which tells the beautiful story of the resurrected Christ's appearance to two disciples on the way to Emmaus.

Late in the afternoon on the very day of the resurrection, two disciples were walking from Jerusalem to Emmaus, a little town about seven miles away. They had come to the city to keep the Passover, and now they were returning home. One of them was named *Cleopas.*

They were deeply engrossed in conversation about the events

that had taken place in Jerusalem during the last few days. Their journey was not far advanced when they were joined by a stranger. It was Jesus Himself, but they didn't recognize Him, for God kept them from doing so. "Living Gospels" records the narrative like this:

"You seem to be in a deep discussion about something," Jesus said. "What are you concerned about?" They stopped short, sadness written across their faces.

One of them, Cleopas, replied, "You must be the only person in all Jerusalem who hasn't heard about the terrible things that happened there last week."

"What things?" Jesus asked.

"The things that happened to Jesus, the Man from Nazareth," they said. "He was a prophet who did incredible miracles and was a mighty teacher, highly regarded by both God and man.

"But the chief priests and our religious leaders arrested Him and handed Him over to the Roman government to be condemned to death, and they crucified Him. We had thought He was the glorious Messiah, and that He had come to rescue Israel."

Turning now to the Amplified Bible, we read that Cleopas added these words: "Yes, and besides all this, it is now the third day since these things occurred.

"And moreover, some women of our company astounded us and drove us out of our senses. They were at the tomb early (in the morning), but did not find His body. And they returned saying that they had (even) seen a VISION of angels who said that He was alive!" (Lk. 24:21-23).

So unbelievable was the testimony of the women after they returned from the sepulchre, that the apostles who heard it considered their experience an illusion. The appearance of angels seemed to them a fanciful vision, not a reality.

Even when some of the apostles went to the tomb and saw for themselves that it was empty, they were still inclined to discount the women's report. For they saw no angels, and certainly they did not see a risen Lord.

Jesus said to Cleopas and his companion, "You are such foolish, foolish people! You find it so hard to believe all that the prophets wrote in the scriptures! Wasn't it clearly predicted by the prophets that the Messiah would have to suffer these things before entering His time of glory?"

Then Jesus quoted passage after passage from the writings of the prophets. Beginning with Moses and going right on through all the prophets, He explained what the passages meant, and what they said about the Christ.

By this time they were nearing Emmaus and the end of their journey. Jesus would have gone farther, but they begged Him to stay the night with them, as it was getting late. He consented to go home with them.

When they sat down to eat the evening meal, the Stranger put forth His hands to bless the food. Then He broke the bread and passed it to them. Suddenly both of the disciples were stricken with astonishment. This was exactly the way Jesus had blessed and then broken the loaves at the feeding of the five thousand! (Cleopas and his friend probably had not been present in the upper room when the Lord's supper was instituted, but they had been there when the multitude was fed.)

They looked more closely at those hands, and lo—there were the prints of the nails! Instantly their eyes were opened, and they recognized the Stranger. *It was Jesus, their Lord!*

At once they knew that He had truly risen from the dead. They remembered the women who said they had seen angels at the tomb, and these angels had told them Jesus was alive. But now these two disciples were seeing the living Lord Himself!

No one could tell them that this was a vision, as they had attributed the angelic appearance. Jesus had walked miles with them, questioned them, expounded the scriptures to them, yielded to their entreaties to abide with them, and had sat down to eat with them. At this very moment He was breaking bread and giving it to them. All this could not possibly be a vision. It was a reality, and they knew it!

They rose to cast themselves at His feet and worship Him. But immediately He vanished out of their sight.

The two of them began recalling how their hearts had felt strangely warm as He talked with them, opening up the scriptures during their walk down the road. "We must go back at once and tell the others that we have seen the Lord, and what He said to us!" Hurriedly they left, setting out again along the same path by which they had come.

Back in Jerusalem, they found the disciples gathered together with other Christians. All of them were excited over the news that the Lord had appeared to certain of their company. Mary Magdalene had seen Him first, then the women returning from the tomb had met Him. Later in the day He had appeared to Peter.

The two from Emmaus told what had happened to them. Just as they finished speaking, behold—*there was Jesus Himself standing in the midst of them!*

"Peace be unto you," He said.

It was such a sudden and miraculous appearance that it terrified the disciples, and they took Him for a ghost. Jesus assured them that His body was the same one they had seen before His death. He showed them His hands and feet, suggesting that they touch Him to prove He was not a spirit.

Then He asked for something to eat. When they gave Him a piece of broiled fish and a honeycomb, He ate it before them.

After this He opened their minds to understand the many prophetic scriptures that concerned Himself. Faith and joy took the place of unbelief. With feelings which no words could express, they acknowledged their risen Saviour . . .

CHAPTER SEVEN

Some Startling Encounters

During the forty days after His resurrection, the Lord Jesus made a number of personal, bodily, visible appearances to His followers. Can you recall *how many* appearances there were? Do you know *to whom* they came?

Let's reconstruct the order of events on the morning of Christ's resurrection . . .

Just before dawn, we find the tomb still shrouded in darkness. The great stone is in place, its seal unbroken; the Roman guards are keeping their watch. Suddenly there is a tremendous earthquake!

In a flash of brilliant light, an angel of the Lord descends from heaven. His countenance is like lightning, and his raiment white as snow. The angel rolls back the huge stone as if it were a mere pebble, and then he seats himself upon it.

At the sight of this glorious being, the soldiers shake with fear and become as dead men. Looking into the open tomb, they see that it is empty—its occupant gone! In terror they flee into the city. Locating the chief priests and elders, they breathlessly report all that they have witnessed.

True to the wickedness of their characters, Israel's Christ-rejecting leaders display a further act of treachery. Offering a large sum of money to the soldiers, they tell them to change their story and say instead that Jesus' disciples came by night and stole the body while they (the guard) slept.

"If the governor hears about it," the council assures the soldiers, "we will protect you from any punishment."

The Roman soldiers accept the bribe. With the lie on their tongues, they leave to do as they have been told.

Meanwhile *Mary Magdalene,* and some *other women* who were devoted to Jesus, make their way to the sepulchre. They are bringing spices to anoint the body of their Lord. Mary arrives first. To her astonishment she beholds the stone rolled away, and the tomb empty! Quickly she goes back to get Peter and John.

When the rest of the women—Mary, the mother of James the less; Salome, the mother of James and John; Joanna, and the others—reach the scene, they too discover the open grave. Venturing to look inside, they see that the body is not within. They become aware of the angel in shining garments sitting by the tomb.

"Don't be frightened," the angel says to the women. "I know you are looking for Jesus, who was crucified. But He isn't here! He has risen from the dead, just as He said He would. Come and see where His body was lying. Then go and tell His disciples that He is alive and will meet them in Galilee as He promised."

Hurriedly the women depart to inform the disciples of the wondrous news.

By this time Mary has found Peter and John. In great distress she tells them, "They have taken the Lord's body out of the tomb, and I don't know where they have put Him!"

Peter and John run to the burial place to see for themselves. After viewing the empty sepulchre and the undisturbed graveclothes, now bereft of their precious body, they return home. Mary remains there alone, weeping.

Presently she looks inside the tomb. There are two angels—one sitting at the head, and the other at the foot of where the body of Jesus had lain. They ask her why she weeps. She tells them it is because they have taken away her Lord.

Even while she is talking with the angels, Christ Himself appears at the door of the sepulchre. As Mary turns around, she sees Him—but does not know that it is He. In the early morning dimness, and blinded by tears, she supposes Him to be the gardener. "Sir," she says, "if you have taken Him away, tell me where you have put Him and I will go and get Him."

At that moment Jesus makes Himself known to her. He speaks her name—"Mary." Instantly she recognizes Him. "My dear

Master!" she joyfully exclaims, reaching out her arms to embrace Him.

"You must not hold on to Me," cautions Jesus, "for I have not yet ascended to My Father. Go and tell the good tidings to My brethren . . ."

Thus the honor of being the first to see the risen Lord was bestowed upon Mary Magdalene, the woman from whom Jesus had once expelled seven demons.

The second witnesses of the resurrected Christ were the women who left the tomb. As they were on their way to give the angel's message to the disciples, Jesus met them and spoke a word of greeting. The women fell to the ground before Him, clasping His feet, and worshiping Him.

The Lord said to them, "Tell My brethren to go into Galilee and there they will see Me."

Did you notice that in both of these appearances the risen Christ called His disciples "My brethren"? Though they had shamefully deserted Him in His suffering, even denied Him, still He gave them the endearing title "My brethren." Such forgiveness! And what a loving and kind way of letting them know that He would not reproach them for their past cowardice and unbelief.

Have you ever wondered why the Lord Jesus selected Galilee —about eighty miles from Jerusalem—as the appointed meeting place after His resurrection?

The Bible does not tell us His reason, but it may have been at least two-fold. In thoughtfulness for those followers living in Galilee who possibly could not come to Jerusalem—and also in consideration of the frightened disciples within the holy city, who were hiding because they feared what the Jewish leaders might do to them—the Lord chose the safer, more distant region of Galilee.

Jesus next appeared to Simon Peter. No details regarding this personal visitation are given. His fourth appearance was to two of His followers *on the way to Emmaus.* We have already dealt with this in the previous chapter.

Later that same evening He came and stood in the midst of the disciples and the others gathered with them *in the upper room in Jerusalem.* On this occasion He showed them His hands and side to convince them of the truth of His resurrection. As they watched, He ate a piece of broiled fish.

Then Jesus said to them, "When I was with you before, don't you remember My telling you that everything written about Me by Moses and the prophets and in the Psalms must all come true?" He opened their minds to understand the scriptures.

Again He spoke to them and said, "As the Father has sent Me, even so I am sending you." Commissioning them to be His agents upon the earth, He breathed on them and said, "Receive the Holy Spirit."

A week passed. In the evening of *the second Sunday after the resurrection,* Jesus appeared once more to the disciples. This time Thomas was with them, for he had been absent the week before. The Lord bade doubting Thomas to put his fingers into the nail wounds, that he might no longer be faithless but believing.

We aren't told whether Thomas actually put the reality of Jesus' body to the test. We do know that he answered with a profound confession of faith—"My Lord and my God!" This marked Christ's sixth appearance.

His seventh appearance took place not in Jerusalem, but in Galilee *at the sea of Tiberias.* The disciples and many of the brethren had obeyed the instructions to go into Galilee, for Jesus had promised to meet them there. It was on the seashore where He first was seen in Galilee . . .

Seven of the disciples were returning from an all-night fishing trip, in which they had caught nothing. As they neared the land, they saw a man standing on the beach. He told them to cast their nets on the right side of the boat and they would get some fish. To their amazement the catch was so great they were not able to haul it in.

At this point John recognized the man. "It is the Lord!" he exclaimed. Immediately Peter sprang into the sea to meet Him. By the time the other disciples landed the boat, Jesus had made a fire of coals. Fish was laid thereon, and bread. Jesus served the morning meal to them.

All the disciples were present when He next appeared *in*

Galilee. This was on the mountain which Jesus had previously designated as the meeting place. After this the risen Lord was seen of about *five hundred brethren at once*, probably on the same mountain in Galilee. It was here that Christ delivered the Great Commission (Matt. 28: 16–20).

Then He appeared to *James*, His half-brother. Although James apparently did not believe on Christ until after the resurrection, yet Jesus granted him a special visitation. James became a leading member, if not the head, of the Jewish Christian church in Jerusalem. But he was never classed as an apostle.

Following this, Jesus was seen by all the apostles on *the mount of Olives* at the time of His ascension into heaven.

All told, the Lord made *eleven* separate, visible, bodily appearances during the forty days after His resurrection. Possibly there was one more, depending on how we interpret Paul's reference in I Corinthians 15:5 to Christ appearing to "the twelve." If Paul used it as an official term to include Matthias, the apostle chosen by lot to take the place of Judas Iscariot, then Jesus may have made twelve appearances.

Subsequent to His ascension, the scriptures record that the glorified Christ appeared—not bodily, but in vision form—to four individuals. These manifestations were granted to *Stephen*, to *Paul*, to *Ananias*, and to *John* on the isle of Patmos.

Stephen

Soon after the early church began its witness to the Jewish nation in Jerusalem, seven men were appointed by the disciples for a special ministry. They had to be men of good character and reputation, filled with the Spirit and with wisdom. Their responsibility was to look after the distribution of assistance to the widows of the church. This would free the apostles for purely spiritual tasks.

One of the seven men chosen was Stephen. A deacon in the church, he was a well-educated, bright young man, zealous for the Lord, and excelling in everything good. The Bible describes him as: "a man of faith (that is, of a strong and welcome belief that Jesus is the Messiah) and full of and controlled by the Holy Spirit" (Acts 6:5).

The same chapter also tells us that: "Stephen, full of grace—divine blessing and favor—worked great wonders and signs (miracles) among the people" (Acts 6:8). Stephen did more than the particular work assigned to him. He performed spectacular miracles, and preached the gospel in power and eloquence.

His witness to the Jewish leaders, however, was rebuffed and violently opposed. Some of them undertook to debate and dispute with him. Stephen spoke in the wisdom and under the inspiration of the Holy Spirit, and the Jews could neither support their own arguments nor answer his. They proved to be no match for him.

So they resorted to other tactics. Hiring men to swear that they heard Stephen curse Moses, and even God, they incensed the people to fury against him. He was arrested and brought before the Sanhedrin.

The lying witnesses testified that Stephen was constantly speaking against the temple and against the law of Moses. They declared: "We have heard him say that this Jesus the Nazarene will tear down and destroy this place, and will alter the institutions and usages which Moses transmitted to us" (Acts 6:14).

The entire council turned toward Stephen to hear his reply to these charges. As they gazed intently at him, every one of them observed his face. Undisturbed serenity and undaunted courage were written across his features. Radiating from his countenance was an ethereal mixture of mildness and majesty.

The Bible says simply: "His face (had the appearance of) the face of an angel" (Acts 6:15).

God permitted His radiant glory to shine through Stephen for a definite purpose. He was the chosen instrument to deliver the Lord's final testimony to the Jewish nation. As such, God honored His faithful witness by causing a supernatural splendor and brightness to illumine his countenance. His face appeared angelic in order to convince the people that what he said was the truth. Possibly they might be brought to repentance, and thereby avert the terrible judgment that otherwise must fall on them.

The high priest asked Stephen, "Are these accusations true?"

In his defense, Stephen did not deny that he had said certain things they charged him with saying. But he clearly showed that his accusers were the ones who were breaking the law, and dishonoring God and the temple worship.

Stephen's speech to the Sanhedrin is recorded in great length, attesting to the importance the writer (Luke) attached to it.

Beginning with Abraham, Stephen related Israel's history through Isaac, Jacob and Joseph. He pointed out that it was Joseph's own brethren who, through jealousy, sold him into slavery. Even Moses was rejected by his brethren when he first attempted to deliver Israel from Egyptian bondage. "Who made you a ruler and judge over us?" they demanded of the man sent by God to be their redeemer.

Going on with the story, Stephen recounted Israel's miraculous deliverance. He quoted the prophecy made by Moses: "God will raise up for you a Prophet from among your brethren as He raised me up." Yet the people refused to listen to Moses, or obey him. They wanted to return to Egypt. Their forty years in the wilderness were filled with rebellion, lawlessness, and apostasy.

Stephen cited the nation's idolatry from the time they made the golden calf in the wilderness, until God gave them up to the worship of their heathen gods and sent them into Babylonian captivity.

As for the temple, he reminded them of what King Solomon had said. God doesn't live in temples made by human hands. Heaven and earth cannot contain Him, how then could a house built by men?

Rebuking the Jews for continuing to show contempt for divine revelation, just as their ancestors had, Stephen concluded his discourse by boldly stating: "You stubborn and stiff-necked people, still heathenish and uncircumcised in heart and ears, you are always actively resisting the Holy Spirit. As your forefathers (were), so you (are and so you do)!

"Which of the prophets did your forefathers not persecute? And they slew those who proclaimed beforehand the coming of the Righteous One, whom you now have betrayed and murdered

. . . you who received the Law as it was ordained and set in order and delivered by angels, and (yet) you did not obey it!" (Acts 7:51–53).

This direct accusation of killing their Messiah stung the Jewish leaders to fury. They ground their teeth in rage.

"But Stephen, full of the Holy Spirit and controlled by (Him), gazed into heaven and saw the glory—the splendor and majesty —of God, and Jesus standing at God's right hand;

"And he said, Look! I see the heavens opened, and the Son of man standing at God's right hand!" (Acts 7:55, 56).

Through the power of the Holy Ghost, Stephen was given this supernal vision. *For one magnificent moment he saw heaven opened, the glory of God, and Jesus Christ standing on the right hand of God the Father.* What a sight!

At this point the Jews raised a great shout, drowning out Stephen's voice. They put their hands over their ears so they could hear no more. Then they rushed upon Stephen as beasts upon their prey. Dragging him out of the city, they began to stone him.

The official witnesses—the executioners—took off their coats and laid them at the feet of a young man watching the procedure. He was from Tarsus, and his name was Saul. It was he who held the garments of the murderers while they set about their gruesome business.

"As they were stoning Stephen, he prayed, Lord Jesus, receive and accept and welcome my spirit!

"And falling on his knees, he cried out loudly, Lord fix not this sin upon them—lay it not to their charge! And when he had said this, he fell asleep (in death)" (Acts 7:59, 60).

What a way to take leave of this world! To die on your knees, committing your soul into Christ's keeping, without a trace of malice toward your murderers—in fact praying for their forgiveness with your very last breath! An extraordinary man indeed was Stephen, the first martyr of the church!

Some of the devoted Christians gathered up the poor crushed and broken remains of Stephen's body and gave it a solemn burial. They sorrowed greatly over him, not ashamed to show their esteem for this faithful servant of Jesus Christ, and for the cause for which he suffered. Neither were they afraid of the wrath of those who were enemies to it.

Beginning that day a wave of persecution swept over the church in Jerusalem. Most of the Christians fled into Judea and Samaria. Saul—the young man who watched approvingly as Stephen was stoned to death—laid waste the church, diligently searching for believers. He even entered private homes and dragged out men and women alike, committing them to prison.

But the believers who had left Jerusalem went everywhere preaching the Good News about Jesus!

A year or so after Stephen's martyrdom, the glorified Christ again appeared in a vision. (It had now been three or four years since the ascension.) The person to whom the revelation came was none other than the enemy and persecutor of the church— *Saul of Tarsus.*

This happened on the road to Damascus. Later Paul was to see the Lord Jesus on two more occasions—both times in the temple at Jerusalem. Since all three of these appearances were in vision form, we will examine them in detail in this chapter.

Saul's Conversion

Paul did not class himself with the other apostles, who had been eyewitnesses of Jesus from the beginning of His ministry. He said of himself that he was "born out of due time." By this he meant that he was born out of the season when the twelve disciples were chosen and trained. Paul always considered that he was the least of them, and not worthy to be called an apostle because of his past persecution of the church. But through the grace of God, he was given equal rank and authority with the others.

This great preacher and missionary to the Gentiles was born a Roman citizen, the son of wealthy Jewish parents. His Hebrew name was Saul. He lived in *Tarsus,* the capital city of Cilicia. Considerably north of Palestine, Tarsus was located in what today is the country of Turkey.

In Saul's day Tarsus was a bustling metropolis, with a university matching those in Athens and Alexandria. Saul, however, was sent to Jerusalem to be educated by the noted rabbi *Ga-*

maliel. His training was according to strict Jewish faith and traditions. All boys in his country were taught a trade, so Saul learned how to make tents. Later he supported himself by working at his tent-making trade while he preached in various towns.

Have you ever tried to imagine what this great preacher and organizer of the early Christian church looked like? Do you picture Paul as tall and ruggedly handsome, with a commanding air about him, possessing a most impressive personality, and a powerful and eloquent way of speaking?

The scriptures suggest quite a different image. In I Corinthians 2:3 he says of himself: "I was with you in weakness, and in fear, and in much trembling."

In 2 Corinthians 10:10 he tells us that some people said of him: "His letters are weighty and impressive and forceful and telling. But his personality and bodily presence are weak. His speech and delivery are utterly contemptible—of no account."

One of the apocryphal books of the New Testament, "Acts of Paul and Thecla," gives this vivid description of him: "A man of little stature, thin-haired upon the head, crooked in the legs, of good state of body, with eyebrows joining, and nose somewhat hooked. He was full of grace, for sometimes he appeared like a man, and sometimes he had the face of an angel."

So, instead of being tall and handsome, Paul was short, balding, bow-legged, with a hooked nose and eyebrows that grew together! Yet despite all this, he was so filled with grace that at times his countenance was described as angelic.

Saul was of the tribe of Benjamin. He became a zealous Pharisee and a member of the high council at Jerusalem. In their persistent and vicious efforts to suppress Christianity, Saul was a most effective agent.

The Sanhedrin was allowed by the Romans to exercise civil and criminal jurisdiction over the whole Jewish community, even outside Palestine. Thus it was that Saul went to the high priest in Jerusalem requesting a letter addressed to synagogues in Damascus, requiring their cooperation in the persecution of any Christians found there. He intended to bring them back in chains to Jerusalem to be punished.

As he was journeying to Damascus on this mission, suddenly

about noon a brilliant light from heaven shone down upon him. He fell to the ground. He heard a voice saying to him in Hebrew, "Saul! Saul! Why are you persecuting me?"

This very personal, gentle reproof must have stunned Saul as much as did the glory of the light. Until now he had thought he was persecuting a company of weak, fanatical heretics. He never dreamed that all the while it was One in heaven whom he was injuring.

"Who are you, Lord?" Saul asked.

The voice replied, "I am Jesus of Nazareth whom you are persecuting."

The name of Jesus was well-known to Saul. How often he had blasphemed it! His enmity and rage had been directed toward obliterating that name from the religious scene. *And now the very One whom he had insulted was standing before him in light so bright it outshone the noonday sun!*

Those who were with Saul saw the light and fell to the earth with him. They heard the sound of the voice, but they could not distinguish the words.

"What shall I do, Lord?" questioned Saul.

Convicted instantaneously of the righteousness of Christ, and of how wrong he had been, Saul repented of his sin. He desired to know how he might find pardon. In humble surrender to the Ruler of all heaven and earth, he was ready to make atonement for the harm he had done.

Jesus replied, "Arise and go into Damascus. There you will be told what you are to do."

Here we have further evidence that God does not reveal everything to His servants all at once. He leads us by degrees, teaching us to walk by faith and not by sight.

As Saul got up from the ground, he discovered that he was blind. He had to be led by the hand into the city. There he remained for three days. Stricken with physical blindness, and grieved in his soul for his past sins against the Lord, Saul could take neither food nor drink all that time.

Yet he was filled with wonder. He remembered that within that intensely bright light, he had seen Jesus in His ascended and glorified body. This was indeed a "heavenly vision," as Paul himself was later to term it when giving an account of his conversion to King Agrippa (Acts 26:19).

Ananias

Two more visions followed closely on the heels of the first. One was given to a certain devout disciple in Damascus named Ananias. Possibly he was one of the heads of the Christian body in that city.

"Now there was in Damascus a disciple named Ananias. The Lord said to him in a VISION, Ananias. And he answered, (Here am) I, Lord.

"And the Lord said to him, Get up and go to the street called Straight. Ask at the house of Judas for a man of Tarsus named Saul, for behold, he is praying there" (Acts 9:10, 11).

In this vision Ananias not only saw the Lord, but he heard His voice and had conversation with Him. This certainly proves that God-given visions are not mere ideas in the mind. They are real pictures to the eyes, and real experiences in the recipient's life.

This particular vision was a two-party affair, for Saul also was given a vision of Ananias. Jesus revealed this as He continued speaking to Ananias:

"And he (Saul) has seen in a VISION a man named Ananias enter and lay his hands on him so that he might regain his sight" (Acts 9:12).

Here is an interesting example of an individual actually viewing ahead of time what was about to happen in his own life. Saul had already seen Ananias coming into the house in which he was praying. He saw him lay hands on him so that his sight might be restored. It was after this that the Lord appeared to Ananias and instructed him regarding his part in fulfilling the vision given to Saul.

Ananias could hardly believe his ears when Jesus told him to go to this man, Saul of Tarsus. He protested to the Lord about the many terrible things he had heard concerning what Saul had done to the believers in Jerusalem. Furthermore, he knew that Saul was intending to arrest every Christian in Damascus. But the Lord admonished Ananias to do as he was told. He said of Saul, *"This man is a chosen instrument of Mine to bear My name before the Gentiles, and kings, and the descendants of Israel"* (Acts 9:15).

Jesus added that He would forewarn Saul how much he must suffer for His name's sake. Instead of spending the rest of his life in persecuting others, as he had done in the past, henceforth he must spend it in being persecuted—for the very preaching he once violently opposed!

Ananias went immediately to the house where Saul was staying. He laid hands on him and said, "Brother Saul, the Lord Jesus who appeared to you along the way . . . has sent me that you may recover your sight and be filled with the Holy Spirit" (Acts 9:17).

Instantly something like scales fell from Saul's eyes. He could see! Then he arose and was baptized. Afterward he ate some food and was strengthened. He remained with the believers in Damascus a few days, and during that time he went into the synagogues proclaiming Jesus as the Son of God.

All who heard him were amazed. "Isn't this the same man who bitterly persecuted Jesus' followers in Jerusalem?" they asked. Saul was fervent in his preaching, and adept in his comparison of the life and works of Christ with the prophets. He clearly proved to the overwhelmed Jews that Jesus was the Messiah.

After this Saul retired into the desert regions of Arabia. There he spent much time in prayer. It is believed that during this period of three years, he received more visions and revelations of the Lord.

When he returned to Damascus, the Jews determined to kill him. Saul learned that they were planning to murder him as he passed through the gates of the city. So, during the night, some of his converts let him down in a basket through an opening in the city wall. He escaped safely and made his way to Jerusalem.

His ministry there lasted scarcely two weeks, for again the Jews sought to kill him. To avoid them, Saul returned to Tarsus, the city of his birth. He spent there a silent period of some ten years.

At the end of that time, *Barnabas,* who had met Saul in Jerusalem, requested him to come to Antioch to help in a flourishing Gentile mission there. After a year of notable blessing, Saul and Barnabas were sent by the Antioch church on an evangelistic tour. They embarked upon their travels about A.D. 46.

Do you know how and when Saul's name became Paul?

Most people are under the impression that it happened at the time of his conversion, but the Bible does not support this. More than fourteen years after his encounter with Christ on the Damascus road, the apostle is still called "Saul" in the scriptures.

It was while he and Barnabas were on the island of Cyprus, during their first missionary journey, that Saul is for the first time called Paul. Saul was his Hebrew name. As a Roman citizen, his name was Paul. Now that he is sent forth among the Gentiles, he is appropriately called by his Roman name.

In order to complete the visions of Paul, we will depart from strict Biblical sequence, which at this point takes up visions connected with the apostle Peter. These we will investigate, after dealing with all scriptural references pertaining to Paul and his visions.

Paul's Call To Europe

The next time we read of a vision being given to Paul, we find that many years have elapsed since his miraculous conversion. Paul is on the second of his three great missionary journeys. He has a new companion, *Silas,* with him on this tour. At a stop in Lystra, young *Timothy* joins them.

Forbidden by the Holy Spirit to evangelize westward at that time, they travel north through Galatia, coming to Troas, the chief port of Mysia. Today this is part of the country of Turkey, the extreme western portion. Apparently it is here that the physician *Luke* is added to the group. And it is at Troas that Paul is given a very important vision.

We read in Acts 16:9: "(There) a VISION appeared to Paul in the night. A man from Macedonia stood pleading with him and saying, Come over to Macedonia and help us!"

The man was recognized as Macedonian by his speech or by his dress. The province of Macedonia lay considerably northwest of Troas across the Aegean Sea. It encompassed the northern part of modern Greece. How fitting that the introduction of Christianity into the continent where it was destined to win its greatest triumphs, was prepared for by a special revelation!

"When he had seen the VISION, we (Luke is writing) at once endeavored to go on into Macedonia, confidently inferring that God had called us to proclaim the glad tidings (gospel) to them" (Acts 16:10).

Paul's vision of a man of Macedonia initiates a distinct development in his methods of evangelism. At *Philippi* for the first time he took advantage of his high civil station. Philippi, a leading city, was one of six Roman colonies included in Macedonia. Here Paul enjoyed support in the cultured circles to which he naturally belonged. This was in sharp contrast to their hostility at earlier points in his route.

On the first missionary journey, high-ranking women who worshiped with the Jews, together with the prominent men of Antioch, had caused the apostles to be expelled from the city. And at Iconium, where they had gone from Antioch, they fared no better with the cultivated element. The Jewish religious leaders stirred up the Gentile rulers against them. An attempt was made to accuse Paul and Barnabas of sedition, a crime punishable by stoning. They were forced to flee Iconium.

The apostles then went to Lystra, where there were few if any Jews. The inhabitants were mainly idolaters. After Paul healed a man crippled from birth, these pagans took the apostles for gods. Their local priest brought garlands of flowers, and the people prepared to sacrifice oxen in heathen rites at the city gates.

Though Paul and Barnabas vehemently refused this kind of worship, they could scarcely restrain the crowds from sacrificing to them. Yet these same people were soon persuaded by some Jews, just arrived from Antioch and Iconium, to stone Paul! What a demonstration of the changeableness of human nature!

Having brutally stoned Paul, they dragged him out of the city and left him for dead. But as the believers stood around him, he got to his feet. The next day he and Barnabas departed for Derbe.

Of these experiences, Paul afterward said: "At Antioch, at

Iconium, at Lystra—what persecutions I endured! But out of them all the Lord delivered me" (2 Tim. 3:11, KJV).

Now, on his second missionary tour several years later, Paul has come to Philippi. The number of Jews is very small here, and the apostles are not likely to be pursued or driven out of this city.

It was in Philippi that Paul made his first European convert.

One sabbath day Paul, Silas, Luke and Timothy went out of the city gates to the bank of the river where there was a place of prayer and worship. This was a spacious, uncovered amphitheater, one of many such places on seasides or near rivers. Where the Jews were too few to build a synagogue, they assembled in these open-air places beside a body of water for convenience of purification.

As the people were gathering together to begin worship services, Paul's group sat down and spoke to some of the women. One of them was a businesswoman named *Lydia,* a dealer in fabrics dyed in purple. She was a long way from home, having come from the city of Thyatira in the district of Lydia (from whence she got her name).

Thyatira lay across the Aegean Sea in Asia. Lydia must have been the overseas agent of a Thyatiran manufacturer, and was probably arranging the sale of dyed woolen goods in Philippi. Lydian purple dye, in which she traded, was renowned. Being a proselyte to Judaism, she came on the sabbath day to worship with the local Jewish congregation.

Lydia was a woman of some wealth and position. She was either a widow or unmarried, for she was the head of her household. The Bible tells us that the Lord opened her heart, and she accepted all that Paul said to her. Lydia became the first convert in Europe. She and all her household were baptized. Afterward her home was used as a meeting place for Christian assembly.

Paul's second group of converts in Philippi was very different from the first. This group consisted of *a jailer and his household.* But in this case, it took an earthquake to bring the jailer to repentance and consequent salvation and baptism!

From Philippi, the apostles went to *Thessalonica.* Here Paul's preaching of Jesus as the Messiah caused a number of devout

Greeks and leading citizens to believe. Another Christian mission was founded. But Jewish opposition was strong. They incited a riot, charging the apostles with treason. Forced to leave the city by night, the missionaries came to *Berea*.

The Berean Jews were more open-minded than those in Thessalonica, and were not consumed with jealousy. They gladly listened to the apostles' message, searching the scriptures to authenticate it. Many of them became believers, along with numerous prominent Greeks.

It wasn't long, however, before some Thessalonican Jews came to Berea and stirred up trouble. Paul left immediately for southern Greece; Silas and Timothy remained behind.

In *Athens* Paul delivered his immortal address on Mars Hill. From there he went to *Corinth*, where still another church was established. Now there were Christian assemblies in Philippi, Thessalonica, Berea, and Corinth.

Certainly in Macedonia Paul proved himself as an independent missionary leader. Ever afterward he was to look back upon that area with profound affection, and he was always eager to return. The Macedonians were willing donors to Paul's Jerusalem fund, and several of their number were added to his regular retinue of assistants.

Thus was the evangelization of Greece set in motion. And it all began with the vision of a man from Macedonia beckoning to Paul to come and help them.

*   *   *

Corinth, one of the most wicked cities of the ancient world, was the scene of another vision bestowed upon Paul.

At this time Corinth was the capital of Greece. It was the seat of the Roman proconsul, as Athens was its center of learning. Located forty-six miles west of Athens, Corinth was a seaport, filled with false religions and Oriental immorality.

About A.D. 50 Paul came alone (so far as we are told) to Corinth. He was anything but confident, as we learn from the opening verses in the second chapter of his first letter to the Corinthians.

Paul stayed with a Jewish couple, *Aquila* and *Priscilla*. Their occupation—that of tentmaking—was the same as his. They were probably already Christians. Recently they had been deported from Rome, in accordance with the edict of the emperor expelling all Jews from that city. The reason for this was because of tumults arising in the Jewish quarter when the faith of Christ was preached there.

Every sabbath Paul went into the synagogue in Corinth, trying by his arguments and discourses to convince Jews and Greeks alike. After Silas and Timothy arrived from Macedonia, Paul spent his full time preaching and testifying to the Jews that Jesus is the Messiah. This enraged his listeners. The hostility provoked by his message culminated in a breach between him and the synagogue.

When the Jews blasphemed and hurled abuse at Jesus, Paul shook off the dust from his robe. He said to them, "Your blood be upon your (own) heads! I am innocent (of it). From now on I will go to the Gentiles" (Acts 18:6).

Paul's ministry to the Jews was so violently rejected that he left them to perish in their unbelief and blasphemy. Turning to the Gentiles in Corinth, he went to the house of a man named *Titus Justus.* Though not a Jew, Titus worshiped God. He lived next door to the synagogue.

While Paul was preaching in this Gentile's house, he made a very important Jewish convert—*Crispus,* the leader of the synagogue. Crispus presided over all Jewish assemblies, interpreted the scriptures, decided what was lawful and unlawful, punished and executed the rebellious, solemnized marriages, and issued divorces. He and all his household believed in the Lord Jesus and were baptized—as were many others in Corinth.

To have the chief ruler of their synagogue converted to Christ was unbearably galling to the Jews. Their opposition to Paul reached the point where his very life was in danger. Should he leave vice-ridden Corinth just when his message was beginning to be received?

His mind was in a state of acute distress. It was then that the Lord spoke to him in a vision.

"One night the Lord said to Paul in a VISION, Have no fear, but speak and do not keep silent. For I am with you, and no man shall assault you to harm you. I have many people in this city" (Acts 18:9, 10).

This assurance that the divine Presence was with him to protect and deliver him encouraged and comforted Paul, and prevented him from leaving Corinth. The Lord had made clear that His will was for Paul to stay there.

And so he continued in Corinth a year and a half, teaching the word of God. The *Thessalonian* epistles, earliest of Paul's writings, were penned during this time.

Christ Appears To Paul In Jerusalem

Paul's next recorded vision of the Lord Jesus occurred in the temple at Jerusalem.

Several years had passed since Paul departed from Corinth. From there he stopped briefly at Ephesus, the commercial metropolis of Asia. Here he left Aquila and Priscilla. After a quick trip to Jerusalem to observe the Passover feast, he returned to Antioch in Syria. This completed his second missionary journey.

Following a time of sojourn in Antioch, Paul moved his base of operation westard to Ephesus. He spent several years there. In many ways this was the most important period of his life. The province of Asia was evangelized, and the Christian outposts in Greece secured.

During those years he wrote the *Corinthian* letters and *Romans—Galatians* having previously been written. In the providence of God, all of Paul's epistles were to constitute holy and authoritative scripture.

For the apostle this was a time of triumph and defeat, of gospel proclamation and threatening heresies, of joy and frustration, of activity and prison meditation. The risen Christ used all these things to mould Paul into His image, and to speak His word through him to the church.

Ephesus was one of the largest and most cosmopolitan cities in the Roman empire. Noted for its luxury and licentiousness, it was also the worship center of the goddess Diana (whose Greek name was Artemis).

The magnificent temple of Diana was one of the seven wonders of the ancient world. Built of white marble about 400 B.C., one hundred massive pillars sixty-five feet high supported the structure. The interior of the temple was extravagantly decorated with sculptures, paintings, and gold ornamentation. The discovery a century ago of this long-buried temple was an epic in archaeological research.

Ephesian craftsmen and silversmiths carried on a flourishing business by selling images of Diana to the worshipers. These statues made of gold and silver, and some of bronze and ivory, were offered on the altar as a gift to the goddess. Miniature silver shrines were purchased by those who came from afar to pay their devotions to Diana in her temple.

Paul's preaching of the gospel at Ephesus was a threat to the craftsmen. Many of his enthusiastic converts publicly burned their books on black magic and threw away their silver idols. Because of this, Demetrius—a prosperous silversmith—succeeded in arousing the people to mob action against Paul and the other apostles.

After the uproar had ceased, Paul departed from Ephesus and set forth on a tour of Macedonia and Greece. This was part of his third missionary journey.

On his return trip Paul sailed on past Ephesus. His ship was brought into port at Miletus, some distance southward. Here he called together the Ephesian elders to bid them *a final farewell*.

In his speech he told them that he was determined to go to Jerusalem. Drawn there irresistibly by the Holy Spirit, he was well aware that he faced imprisonment and suffering. "But none of these things move me," declared Paul. "Neither do I esteem my life dear to myself. If only I may finish my course with joy, and the ministry which I have obtained (entrusted to me by) the Lord Jesus, faithfully to attest the good news (gospel) of God's grace" (Acts 20:24).

Paul admonished the elders to feed and shepherd Christ's flock, the church purchased with His own blood. "For the Holy Spirit is holding you responsible as overseers," he told them.

After he left, Paul said that false teachers would come in like vicious wolves. Even from among themselves, some would distort the truth in order to draw a following. "Therefore be always alert and on your guard," he cautioned. Then he touch-ingly committed his brethren to God's protection and care.

"And I commend you to the Word of His grace," Paul said. "It is able to build you up, and to give you your rightful in-heritance among the Lord's set-apart ones—those consecrated, purified, and transformed of soul" (Acts 20:32).

His final words were a reminder that he had never sought worldly wealth, but had always worked hard for a living, shar-ing what he had with the needy. So also ought they to do. He closed with a quote from the Lord Jesus not found anywhere else in the New Testament: "It is more blessed to give than to receive."

Having spoken thus, he knelt down with them all and prayed.

"And they all wept freely and threw their arms around Paul's neck and kissed him fervently and repeatedly, being especially distressed and sorrowful because he had stated that they were about to see his face no more.

"And they accompanied him to the ship" (Acts 20:37, 38).

Despite the warnings from the Holy Spirit regarding what would befall him if he went to *Jerusalem,* after some stops along the way Paul arrived in the city at Pentecost. Jewish pilgrims from Asia recognized the apostle to the Gentiles. They accused him of heretical teaching, and of violating the temple. He was charged with bringing Greeks into the inner court, which was forbidden to Gentiles.

This incited the crowds to riot.

Paul was dragged outside the temple gates and was being beaten. Roman soldiers appeared and arrested him. Bound in chains, he was taken to the fortress Antonia adjoining the temple.

The mob shouted, "Away with him! Kill him!" Paul asked for, and was granted, permission to address the people.

Standing on the stairs of the armory, he motioned to the crowd to be quiet. Soon a deep silence enveloped them, and Paul began to speak to them in Hebrew. In his defense he answered their allegations against him. He said that he was a Jew by birth, trained by Gamaliel, and so zealous for the Law that he had been a persecutor of the Christian faith.

He told them how his conversion to Christianity had come about, that it was the result of a direct divine revelation made at Damascus. This vision was confirmed by a subsequent revelation to Ananias, also in vision form.

Paul said that even after his conversion he continued to honor the temple and to worship there. In fact, it was in that very temple where he received another vision of the Lord. Listen to his own words:

"Then when I had come back to Jerusalem and was praying in the temple enclosure, I fell into a trance—an ecstasy.

"And I saw Him as He said to me, Hurry, get quickly out of Jerusalem, because they will not receive your testimony about Me" (Acts 22:17, 18). Apparently Paul heeded this vision and went back to Tarsus (Acts 9:30).

Note that in this trance-vision Paul said he "saw" the Lord. There is no question but that Paul visibly looked upon Jesus. Ananias is quoted as saying, "The Lord Jesus who *appeared* to you . . ." In another account Ananias said to Paul: "The God of our forefathers has destined and appointed you to . . . *see* the Righteous One, Jesus Christ the Messiah, and to hear a voice from His own mouth and a message from His own lips" (Acts 22:14).

Barnabas, in bringing Paul to the apostles in Jerusalem, declared to them that Paul "had *seen* the Lord in the way, and that He had spoken to him." In his first letter to the Corinthians, Paul asked: "Am I not an apostle? Have I not *seen* Jesus Christ our Lord?" In the same letter he also wrote: "And last of all He (Jesus) was *seen* of me . . ."

Returning to his speech to the mob, Paul continued the story of the temple vision in which he again saw the Lord. He told them he made the following reply to the suggestion that he leave Jerusalem:

"Lord, they themselves well know that throughout all the synagogues I cast into prison and flogged those who believed . . . on You.

"And when the blood of Your (martyr) witness Stephen was shed, I also was personally standing by, consenting and approving, and guarding the garments of those who slew him" (Acts 22:19, 20).

Paul reasoned that if the Jews were reminded of what he had been before his conversion, they would have to ascribe so great a change in him to the power of divine grace. But Christ knew better. Having already told Paul that they would reject the gospel, the Lord Jesus now simply commanded him to depart from Jerusalem and go and preach to the Gentiles.

"The Lord said to me, Go, for I will send you far away unto the Gentiles" (Acts 22:21).

The Jews listened until Paul came to that word "Gentiles." This outraged them. It was an intolerable offense to have Paul imply that Gentiles were equal to Jews, and were included in God's grace. Irritating enough was his teaching that the Messiah of the Jews was a crucified malefactor.

With one voice the mob shouted, "Away with such a fellow! He is not fit to live!"

The commandant brought Paul inside the barracks and ordered him lashed with whips to make him confess what his crime was. Paul was spared this scourging by claiming his rights as a Roman citizen. The next day he was brought before the supreme Jewish court in an attempt to get evidence against him. But Paul's testimony to the Sanhedrin was broken up by the clever way the apostle set the Pharisees and Sadducees at variance one with another.

In the ensuing uproar, soldiers were ordered to rescue Paul and conduct him back to the barracks.

That night as he lay on his bunk, Paul had good reason to be disheartened. He wondered if he would be put to death before he could realize his long-time desire to witness for Christ in Rome. *Just then Jesus Himself again visited Paul in a vision.*

"That same night the Lord stood beside Paul and said, Take courage, Paul. For as you have borne faithful witness concerning Me at Jerusalem, so you must also bear witness at Rome" (Acts 23:11).

This visual appearance of Christ was given Paul to assure him that he had not yet finished his work. His life would not be cut short before the fulfillment of his dream to go to Rome and preach the gospel.

All the events that took place from the evening of this vision until the departure of Paul for Rome make fascinating reading. But for our purposes, they must be briefly summarized . . .

Paul was removed to Caesarea to prevent his being lynched in Jerusalem. There he was arraigned and tried before *Felix, the Roman governor of Judea.* The charges against him were these: stirring up sedition among all Jews throughout the world, being "a pestilence," a ringleader of heresy, and a defiler of the Jewish temple.

After hearing Paul's defense, Felix was convinced that he had done nothing worthy of imprisonment or death. But the Roman procurator did not have the honesty or courage to release him. Therefore Paul had to languish in the Caesarean prison for two years.

When *Festus, Felix's successor,* became the new governor, the Jews sought to have Paul brought back to Jerusalem. They planned to kill him on the way. Festus asked Paul if he was willing to go to Jerusalem and clear himself there. The apostle requested instead that his case be heard by the emperor in Rome. He knew full well what would happen to him in Jerusalem, so he made appeal to Caesar.

It was granted him. Before he was sent to Rome, he was given a hearing in the presence of the governor's guests, *King Agrippa* and *Bernice.* In Paul's testimony to them he again related the story of his conversion. When he came to the part where Jesus appointed him to be an apostle to the Gentiles, he stated:

"Wherefore, O King Agrippa, I was not disobedient unto the heavenly VISION,

"But made known openly first of all to those at Damascus— then at Jerusalem and throughout the whole land of Judea, and also among the Gentiles—that they should repent and turn to God, and do works and live lives consistent with and worthy of their repentance" (Acts 26:19, 20).

Paul's case was now out of the hands of the governor of Judea. Arrangements were made to send him under guard to Rome. So it was that—a quarter of a century after his conversion on the way to Damascus—the great missionary and evangelist embarked upon another journey, this time as a prisoner in chains.

An Angel In The Storm

Paul's sea voyage was a stormy one.

As they sailed along the southern coast of Turkey, the winds became increasingly strong. It was only with great difficulty that they made port at Fair Havens, a small bay on the south coast of Crete. There they stayed for several days. The late autumn weather was becoming dangerous for long voyages. Paul warned the ship's officers that trouble lay ahead if they continued the journey.

"Sirs," he said to them, "I perceive (after careful observation) that this voyage will be attended with disaster and much heavy loss, not only of the cargo and the ship, but of our lives also" (Acts 27:10).

His advice to remain at Fair Havens went unheeded. The centurion in charge of the prisoners paid more attention to the pilot and to the owner of the ship than to what Paul said. Most of the crew suggested they try to go farther up the coast to Phoenix, in order to winter there. Fair Havens was an exposed harbor—a poor place to spend the cold months. Phoenix would provide more favorable shelter.

So when a light wind began blowing from the south, they pulled up anchor and sailed along close to shore.

But soon afterward the weather changed abruptly. A typhoon ("a northeaster," they called it) caught the ship and blew it out to sea. It was impossible to get back to shore. Giving up, they simply let the ship drift with the gale.

The next day as the seas grew higher, the crew began throwing the cargo overboard. The terrible storm raged unabated. On the third day, they threw out the ship's furniture. At last all hope was gone.

No one had eaten for some time when Paul called the crew together. First he reproved them for not taking his advice and staying at Fair Havens. Had they listened to him, they would have avoided all this injury and loss. But then he was quick to comfort them with an assurance of personal safety. This is what he said:

"(Even) now I beg you to be in good spirits and take heart. There will be no loss of life among you, but only of the ship" (Acts 27:22).

Paul told them that the basis he had for this confidence was a divine revelation. "For this (very) night there stood by my side an angel of the God to whom I belong and whom I serve and worship" (Acts 27:23).

This appearance of an angel to Paul in the night was a vision, not a tangible bodily manifestation. Calling Paul by name, the angel told him not to be frightened. He said that the apostle would surely stand trial before Caesar in Rome. And more than that, God promised for his sake to save the lives of all those sailing with him. On board were about two hundred seventy-six men.

"So cheer up," Paul encouraged the crew. "I have faith in God that things will turn out as it was told me. But," he added, "we will be shipwrecked on an island."

And this is exactly what happened.

About midnight on the fourteenth night of the storm, they were driven near a coastline. When it was daylight, they tried to land. But the ship hit a sandbar and ran aground. All who could swim jumped overboard and made for shore. The rest reached there with the help of heavy planks and debris from the broken ship. Everyone escaped safely to land—which turned out to be the island of Malta . . .

Thus another prophetic vision in the life of St. Paul was fulfilled.

*   *   *

It was spring of the next year before they at last reached Rome.

For two years Paul dwelt in this city, which at that time was the largest in the world. Under house arrest, Paul spent his time writing his prison epistles—*Philemon, Colossians, Ephesians,* and *Philippians.*

Many people came to the home in which Paul was confined to hear him expound the scriptures. He taught openly about the Lord Jesus Christ, and preached with all boldness both to Jews and Gentiles.

One of the apocryphal books indicates that Paul was released in A.D. 63. He visited Spain and the Aegean area where he wrote *1 Timothy* and *Titus*. He was rearrested, taken back to Rome, and put in a dungeon. Here, in the closing years of his life, Paul wrote *2 Timothy*.

About A.D. 67, during the persecution of Christians which took place under Nero, Paul died a martyr's death. He was not yet sixty years old. The apostle was beheaded, and his body buried along the Ostian Way where a church was later built—St. Paul's Outside-the-Walls.

There is one last reference regarding Paul's visions. It is found in the first verses of 2 Corinthians 12. In commending himself as a servant of the Lord, Paul mentioned a sublime vision he had experienced fourteen years before. His purpose was to defend his ministry against false workers.

"True, there is nothing to be gained by it; but (as I am obliged) to boast, I will go on to VISIONS and revelations of the Lord.

"I know a man in Christ, who fourteen years ago—whether in the body or out of the body I do not know, God knows—was caught up to the third heaven . . ."

Of course this man is none other than St. Paul himself. Verse 7 makes this clear: "To keep *me* from being puffed up by these revelations . . ."

The apostle was in a trance, or ecstatic state, in which consciousness of the outer world was for the time suspended. Earthly sight, hearing, feeling were gone. He was lost in contemplation of the glory of God that was being revealed to him.

"I know that this man was caught up into Paradise." Here the word "Paradise" is used as a synonym for the third heaven, or highest state of bliss. "And he heard utterances beyond the power of man to put into words, which man is not permitted to utter."

Lest Paul be uplifted by spiritual pride as a result of these visions, "a thorn in the flesh"—the very work of Satan—was inflicted upon him. Three times he earnestly prayed to have it removed. But the Lord did not take it away. Instead He replied, "My grace is sufficient for thee; for My strength is made perfect in weakness."

Certainly if anyone ever knew the grace of God in all its fulness, it was the apostle Paul. He knew that experiences of testing and chastening must come to the Lord's servants, as well as experiences of glory. Suffering, though caused by satanic power, is permitted by God for the purpose of teaching two things. First, that *divine grace is completely sufficient to meet every trial.* And secondly, that *only in human weakness is divine strength fully realized.*

Therefore Paul gloried in his infirmities. The power and strength of Christ rested upon him like a tabernacle. To the end he fought the good fight, finished the course, and kept the faith.

When Paul's time of departure was at hand, he knew it, and he was ready to go. His last words, so far as we have any record, were written to Timothy, his son in the faith. Paul charged him to preach the Word, be strong in Christ, endure suffering and hardship as a good soldier, and strive lawfully for the crown that is laid up in heaven for those who prove true.

Paul's life was a marvelous example of all that he preached. What a victor's crown of righteousness awaits him!

Peter

The apostle Peter had a most significant vision. We turn now to him and to some of his colorful experiences.

Peter's Hebrew name was *Simon.* His home as a child was in Bethsaida, a town on the northeast shore of Lake Gennesaret. This body of water is more often referred to in the New Testament as the Sea of Galilee. The apostle *Andrew,* Simon's brother, and the apostle *Philip* also came from the same village.

After Simon was married, he settled in Capernaum, a city on the northwest shore of the Sea of Galilee. There he and his wife lived with her mother. Their home was at the lakeside, and Simon was a successful fisherman. Though untrained in the

Law, he maintained the piety and outlook of his Jewish people.

His brother Andrew was a disciple of John the Baptist. It was John's testimony about Jesus that caused Andrew to turn from him to Christ. After spending one day with the Person whom John the Baptist called "The Lamb of God," Andrew told Simon, "We have found the Messiah!" Andrew introduced Simon to Jesus. This was before the Lord had begun His public ministry.

At their very first interview, Jesus read Simon's character and gave him the Aramaic name *"Cephas,"* which translated in Greek is *Peter*—meaning "rock" or "stone." Jesus recognized Peter to be as firm and strong in soul as a rock, and as hard and unyielding in purpose as a stone.

Peter was one of the first disciples that Jesus called. He was also one of the three who formed an inner circle around the Master. His impulsive devotion is frequently portrayed in the scriptures, and he seemed to be spokesman of the twelve. Jesus singled out Peter on several occasions for special consideration.

He sat in Peter's boat to preach to the multitude on the shores of Lake Gennesaret. When Jesus walked upon the Sea of Galilee, He called to Peter to come to Him across the water. He chose Peter to stay with Him in the garden of Gethsemane the night before the crucifixion.

The angel who appeared to the women at Christ's tomb on the morning of the resurrection gave a personal message for Peter. Of all the disciples, Peter was the only one to whom the risen Lord appeared in an individual visit on the day of the resurrection. Later, at a breakfast meeting with seven of the apostles at the sea of Tiberias, Jesus gave particular orders to Peter: *"Feed My sheep."*

Peter's failings were many. Boasting, cowardice, frequent changes of mind, false judgments and unwise action, the blurting out of statements which he later regretted, his angry denial of even knowing Jesus at the time of His trial—these were some of his weaknesses. But his great love for Christ, and his enthusiastic faith in Him as the Son of God, more than made up for his failings.

After the ascension Peter began his ministry, and he did not falter in it until his death. He preached first in Jerusalem, then in various cities of Palestine, making many converts. He helped start the first church, baptized thousands, worked miracles— even raised a woman from the dead.

Philip the evangelist took the gospel into Samaria. Shortly afterward, both Peter and John were sent there to minister further to these racially and religiously mixed people.

But Peter alone was the first apostle to be associated with the mission to the Gentiles. This had to come about by divine inter- vention, for the Jews considered all Gentiles "unclean." They had shut them out from religious privilege as "dogs."

Here again it was a vision that God chose as the means of making known His will and purposes. In fact, in this case, there were four visions involved. One was given to Cornelius, and the subsequent vision to Peter was repeated three times. Let's look at the details of the story . . .

Cornelius

About eight years have passed since Pentecost. During this time the gospel has been preached mainly to Jews. The church was founded by Jews for Jews. But the Lord was preparing a drastic change in the gospel program.

"Now living at Caesarea there was a man whose name was Cornelius, a centurion of what was known as the Italian regi- ment.

"He was a devout man who venerated God and treated Him with reverential obedience, as did all his household. He gave much alms to the people, and prayed continually to God" (Acts 10:1, 2).

Caesarea at this time was the capital of the Roman province of Judea, and the residence of the governor. While Pontius Pilate was procurator, he had occupied the governor's palace in Caesarea. The city was magnificent. Built by Herod the Great, it was located on the Mediterranean shore about sixty-five miles northwest of Jerusalem.

The great caravan route between Tyre and Egypt ran through Caesarea, making it a busy commercial center. The city was lavishly adorned with palaces, public buildings, and an enormous amphitheater. A huge temple dedicated to Caesar contained numerous statues of the emperor. The population was mixed, and clashes between the Jews and other elements of the populace (particularly the Greeks) were frequent.

This, then, was the city in which the centurion Cornelius—a semi-proselyte to Judaism—lived.

He was one of the class of Gentiles known as *"God-fearers"* because of their attachment to Jewish religious practices, such as almsgiving, fasting, and prayer. The Italian band, of which Cornelius was captain, was an auxiliary cohort of Roman citizens who had been recruited in Italy.

"About the ninth hour (three o'clock) of the day he saw clearly in a VISION an angel of God entering and saying to him, Cornelius!" (Acts 10:3).

Because the ninth hour of the day was the time of offering the evening sacrifice in the temple, it was made an hour of prayer by devout people. Cornelius was praying when an angel of God appeared to him. Evidently he saw him with his physical eyes, not as in a dream, but in a clear vision presented to his sight.

The angel called him by name, "Cornelius!" Here we have further proof that God knows personally and individually those who truly love Him.

"He (Cornelius) gazing intently at him became frightened, and said, What is it, Lord? The angel said to him, Your prayers and your (generous) gifts to the poor have come up (as a sacrifice) to God, and have been remembered by Him" (Acts 10:4).

This statement seems to indicate that acts of genuine piety cause God to remember us for good. Cornelius, by using well the grace already manifest in his life, was considered worthy to receive greater grace.

The angel of God continued speaking to Cornelius in the vision:

"And now send men to Joppa. Have them call for and invite here one Simon, whose surname is Peter. He is lodging with Simon a tanner, whose house is by the seaside" (Acts 10:5, 6).

From these instructions, we note two points of particular interest. First, *although Cornelius has an angel from heaven talking to him, yet he cannot receive the gospel of Christ from an angelic being.* It must come to him by means of a human agent. Peter is to have the honor of imparting what an angel could not do.

In addition, we see that the Lord knows where to find His own. Peter was not at home. He was out-of-town, staying with a friend in Joppa. But the angel called the friend by name, mentioned his occupation, and gave the location of his house. How comforting to realize that we are never out of sight to God, no matter where we are!

Joppa was a distance of about forty miles from Caesarea. It was the only seaport for Jerusalem, which was about thirty-five miles away from Joppa. Today tourists visiting Palestine can see a mosque purporting to mark the site of the house of Simon the tanner. A minaret embellishes a corner of the flat rooftop. This rooftop is to play an important part in the story.

Since tanning was a malodorous task, it was usually undertaken on the outskirts of town near abundant water. A person who dealt in hides, whether of clean or unclean animals, was held in contempt by the Jews. Peter's visit to Simon the tanner illustrates that he had already overcome some of his scruples against contact with what was ceremonially unclean.

Also it showed that the apostle was not staying with "the better class" of Joppa, but was willing to live outside the city in the humble abode of a lowly tanner. Peter had been there for considerable time teaching and preaching Christ.

As soon as the angel in Cornelius' vision was gone, the centurion called two of his household servants and a godly soldier, one of his personal bodyguard. After telling them what had happened, he sent them to Joppa.

Peter's Vision of Unclean Animals

The next day, as the messengers were nearing the city, Peter went up on the flat roof of the tanner's house to pray. This was the place in Oriental houses which was used for prayer, meditation, recreation, and sleeping.

It was noon, and Peter was hungry. After he had finished praying, while he waited for lunch to be prepared, he fell into a trance.

A trance, ecstasy, or waking vision is one of the modes of divine revelation. It is a state in which one is insensible to his surroundings, conscious only of the subject of the vision. By this means, a special disclosure is about to be made to the chief of the apostles.

Cornelius had received positive orders from heaven telling him to send for Peter. But Peter had to be dealt with to make him willing to go to an uncircumcised Gentile. Therefore, while the messengers were on their way, the Lord began to prepare Peter to accept the invitation sent by Cornelius.

"And he (Peter) saw the sky opened. Something like a great sheet, lowered by the four corners, descended to the earth.

"It contained all kinds of quadrupeds and wild beasts, and creeping things of the earth, and birds of the air" (Acts 10:11, 12).

Then there came a voice in the vision saying, *"Rise up, Peter, kill and eat."* Now many of the creatures in this sheet were "unclean," according to Jewish designation. For a Jew to eat unclean or defiled meat was forbidden by Mosaic law. Peter was shocked.

"By no means, Lord!" he protested. "I have never eaten anything that is common and unhallowed or ceremonially unclean."

The voice came to him again a second time. "What God has cleansed and pronounced clean, do not you defile and profane by regarding and calling common and unhallowed or unclean" (Acts 10:15).

This same vision was repeated three times to confirm and establish the lesson taught by it. Then the sheet was pulled up again to heaven.

"Now Peter was still inwardly perplexed, and doubted as to what the VISION which he had seen could mean. (Just then) the messengers that were sent by Cornelius, who had made inquiry for Simon's house, stopped and stood before the gate.

"They called out to inquire whether Simon who was surnamed Peter was staying there" (Acts 10:17, 18).

Peter was having difficulty comprehending the meaning of this strange vision. Long ago Jesus had taught that it was not what entered into a person from without that defiled him. It was the evil which came from within, out of the heart. But Peter had not understood this truth. He still held on to the old Jewish tradition regarding the distinction of meats.

"While Peter was earnestly revolving the VISION in his mind and meditating on it, the (Holy) Spirit said to him, Behold, three men are looking for you!

"Get up and go below. Accompany them without any doubt (about its legality), or any discrimination or hesitation, for I have sent them" (Acts 10:19, 20).

The Holy Spirit settled the matter with dispatch. Peter was ordered to go along with the messengers, doubting nothing, *"for I have sent them."*

At once Peter went down and informed the men that he was the person they were looking for. He asked what they wanted. They told him about Cornelius, the Roman officer—how he was well thought of by the Jews, and how an angel had instructed him to send for Peter to come and tell him what God wanted him to do.

Peter invited them in. Though they were Gentiles, he lodged them overnight. The vision had made him ready to comply fully with the purposes of God. The next morning he went with the messengers, accompanied by some other believers from Joppa.

They arrived in Caesarea the following day. Cornelius was waiting for him. He had called together his relatives and close friends to meet Peter.

As the apostle entered his home, Cornelius fell to the floor before him in worship. Having been brought up a pagan, Cornelius was accustomed from boyhood to seeing divine honors rendered to heroes. No doubt he thought Peter was a heavenly personage, since an angel of God had bidden Cornelius send for him. It was not strange that he would bow to Peter.

But Peter said, "Get up. I'm not a god; I'm just a man."

They talked together for awhile, then went in where the others were assembled. Peter said to them:

"You yourselves are aware how it is not lawful or permissible for a Jew to keep company with, or to visit, or (even) to come near, or to speak first to any one of another nationality. But

God has shown and taught me by words that I should not call any human being common or unhallowed or (ceremonially) unclean" (Acts 10:28).

Peter now understood why he had received the vision at Joppa. The designation of "unclean" meats was abrogated by God, so that henceforth Jew and Gentile could associate and eat together on terms of equality. As long as the meat distinction was observed, both the church and the Jews were cut off from social communication with Gentiles, who placed "unclean" food on their tables.

Cornelius told Peter all the details of his vision four days ago, and his prompt obedience to the angel's instructions. He expressed appreciation for Peter's courtesy in coming.

"We are here," Cornelius concluded, "waiting before the Lord, anxious to hear what He has told you to tell us!"

Peter opened his mouth and said: "Most certainly and thoroughly I now perceive and understand that God shows no partiality and is no respecter of persons.

"But in every nation he who venerates and has a reverential fear for God, treating Him with worshipful obedience and living uprightly, is acceptable to Him and sure of being received and welcomed (by Him)" (Acts 10:34, 35).

Then he preached the gospel of the Lord Jesus Christ to them. His theme was salvation by faith. While he was still speaking, the Holy Ghost fell upon all those listening. The Jews who came with Peter were amazed that the gift of the Holy Spirit would be given to Gentiles too. But there could be no doubt about it, for they heard them speaking in tongues and praising God.

Peter asked, "Can anyone object to their being baptized, now that they have received the Holy Spirit just as we did?" So he ordered that they be baptized in the name of Jesus the Messiah. Afterward Cornelius begged him to stay with them for several days, that they might be further instructed.

The story of Cornelius is of far reaching importance, and that is why Luke relates it in great detail.

Cornelius is considered to be the first Gentile convert to Christianity. Actually, his was not the first Gentile baptism. Previous to this, *an Ethiopian eunuch* was baptized by Philip on the road from Jerusalem to Gaza. But the latter was a private affair, while the baptism of Cornelius was the first such baptism to be publicly recognized.

Cornelius and his house are also regarded as the first Gentiles to hear the gospel since Pentecost. Until then it did not occur to the church that anyone *could* be saved unless he was circumcised and kept the law of Moses.

To prevent this fallacy from continuing, God intervened. By means of a four-fold vision, He convinced Peter—and through him, the other apostles—that salvation and the gift of the Holy Spirit are available to everyone who exercises faith in Jesus as Saviour.

The high wall of religious difference between Jew and Gentile had to be broken down. Christ was building a church, and He wanted both Jews and Gentiles to be the living stones of which it is formed. The conversion of Saul of Tarsus had recently taken place, and it too was in preparation for this extension of the gospel to Gentiles, and "unto the uttermost part of the earth."

When Peter arrived back in Jerusalem, several of the Jewish believers argued with him. The news that Gentiles were being converted was not too welcome to the brethren.

"You fellowshipped with Gentiles and even ate with them!" they accused Peter.

They could not attack the baptism of Gentiles, for the Lord's command to baptize all nations was too definite to be questioned. They attacked, therefore, Peter's undoubted breach of Jewish law and custom. What they apparently desired was that if uncircumcised Gentiles were baptized, they should be regarded as an inferior class, and not allowed to eat at the same table with their Jewish superiors.

Peter did not discuss the general principle. Rather, he defended himself on the ground that he had received a special revelation authorizing—and indeed commanding—him to act as he did in this particular case. He began by saying:

"I was in the town of Joppa praying. (Falling) into a trance, I saw a VISION of something coming down from heaven, like a huge sheet lowered by the four corners. And it descended until it came to me" (Acts 11:5).

Then Peter recounted the entire experience. When the Jews heard it all, they made no further objection. They praised God for granting to the Gentiles, as well as to them, the privilege of turning to Him and receiving eternal life.

The church at Jerusalem unanimously endorsed Peter's action. Doubtless they did so because the case was an exceptional one, and was not likely to become a precedent. When Paul made a regular practice of doing what Peter had only done as a rare exception, the controversy was revived. But that is another story.

Peter's Jail "Vision"

There is one more reference to a vision in connection with the apostle Peter.

About the year A.D. 44, *Herod Agrippa*—the son of Aristobulus, and the grandson of Herod the Great—began a cruel persecution of the church at Jerusalem. At this time *James,* the brother of John, was killed with a sword. Thus one of the three disciples who had been closest to Jesus, became the first martyr among the apostles.

When Herod saw how much the death of James pleased the Jewish leaders, he arrested Peter during the Passover celebration and imprisoned him. Herod intended to deliver Peter to the Jews for execution after the Passover. But fervent prayer by the church was going up to God for his safety all the time he was in prison.

The night before he was to be executed, Peter was asleep—double-chained between two soldiers. Two more soldiers stood guard in front of the prison gate. Suddenly a brilliant light shone in the cell, and an angel of the Lord appeared beside Peter! The angel slapped him on the side to awaken him.

"Get up quickly!" he ordered. The handcuffs fell off Peter's wrists. "Now get dressed," said the angel, "and follow me."

This marked the second time Peter was liberated from prison by an angel. Both of these occasions were actual physical appearances of angelic messengers, not visions.

"And (Peter) went out following him. He was not conscious that what was apparently being done by the angel was real, but thought he was seeing a VISION" (Acts 12:9).

They passed the first and second cell blocks and came to the iron gate leading to the street. To Peter's amazement, the gate opened to them of its own accord! They went through and walked along together for a block. Then the angel left him. Peter finally realized that this was no dream or vision.

"It's really true!" he said to himself. "The Lord has sent His angel and saved me from Herod, and from what the Jews were hoping to do to me!"

As a finishing touch to the account, the scripture includes an additional episode . . .

When Herod found out that Peter had escaped, he had all sixteen of the guards (four soldiers for each of the four watches) court-martialed and sentenced to death. Then he left for Caesarea. Shortly after his arrival there, the king arrayed himself in his royal robes. Taking his seat upon the throne, he delivered an oration to the assembled crowd.

At its conclusion the people gave him a great ovation. They shouted, "It is the voice of a god and not of a man!"

Herod did not rebuke this excessive flattery and undue praise. Instead he was very willing that he should be thought a god and have divine honors paid him. Instantly an angel of the Lord struck him with a sickness, so that he was filled with maggots and died!

Accepting the people's worship—taking glory that belonged to God—was the final act that filled Herod's cup of iniquity to the brim. Persecution of the church of Christ, the murder of James, imprisonment of Peter with the intention of putting him to death, plus all the other evils he had done, were culminated in this display of pride and self-aggrandizment.

And so, at the age of fifty-four, Herod's life came to a sudden and mortifying end. His body was eaten up by worms.

Peter's dreaded enemy was dead. Now he could go about again

in Herod's territory without fear. For at least twenty more years Peter continued his missionary work in many parts of Palestine, in Asia Minor, and other of the Mediterranean countries. He faithfully preached the gospel of the Lord Jesus Christ in supernatural power, and with signs and wonders.

About A.D. 67 he met a martyr's death during the persecution of Christians by the emperor Nero. This is said to have taken place in the Neronian gardens in Rome. According to tradition, the apostle was crucified head downward at his own request. He considered himself unworthy to even resemble his Lord in death.

As he had done in life, so Peter also glorified God in the manner of his death.

Peter's name has been revered down through the centuries. The record of his deeds, as well as two of his epistles, are preserved forever in God's Holy Bible. The largest and most famous Christian church in the world was built over his tomb. His name is prominently inscribed in the Lamb's Book of Life. And he himself has returned in glory to the Shepherd and Bishop of his soul.

Nero, the emperor who put him to death, is remembered by later generations only for his ruthlessness and cruelty. The year after Peter was crucified, Nero was declared a public enemy by the Senate. He fled from Rome, but was overtaken and killed himself. So hated was he by the people that after his suicide all records of his name, his statues, and his buildings were destroyed.

Truly "the way of the wicked is as deep darkness . . . But the path of the righteous is like the light of dawn, that shines more and more until it reaches its full strength and glory in the perfect day" (Pr. 4:18, 19).

CHAPTER EIGHT

How It All Will End

Genesis, the first book in the Bible, tells us how all things began. Revelation, the last book, tells us how all things will end. The word "revelation" means: *"the unveiling of something hidden, so that it may be seen and understood for what it is."*

What a wonderful God we have! To think that the Almighty Creator would go to great lengths to disclose to us His plan of the ages, His will and His ways with man, His power and glory, His nature and character—in short, Himself—in order that we might know Him!

And what a culmination to our study of dreams and visions in the Bible! For Revelation is one gigantic vision of the future.

The consummation of God's plan and purposes for time and eternity is revealed within its pages. In prophetic sequence it unfolds the greatest event in human history—*the return of the Lord Jesus Christ to this earth.* All the background surrounding this climactic occurrence is dramatically pictured in scene after scene. Finally the story of earth is concluded, and the destiny of God's people and of the world is made fully known.

The author of the "Book of Endings" is the apostle John.

He was the son of Zebedee, and the brother of James. His mother was Salome, a devout follower of the Lord. She was one of the women who went to the tomb on resurrection morning. Salome is usually regarded as the sister of Mary, the mother of Jesus. If this identification is correct, John was a cousin of Jesus on his mother's side.

His parents appear to have been well-to-do. His father, a fisherman, had hired servants; and Salome was one of the women who "provided for Jesus out of their means."

Five times in his gospel John calls himself "the disciple whom Jesus loved." Christ nicknamed him and his brother James "the sons of thunder." This was because they were both high-spirited impetuous men, whose zeal was undisciplined and sometimes misdirected. They were among the first disciples called by the Lord.

John—along with Peter and James—was chosen to be present with Jesus at such important times as the Transfiguration, and the Garden of Gethsemane. It was John who leaned on Jesus' bosom at the Last Supper. He was the only disciple who remained faithful to Christ during His crucifixion. As the Lord was hanging on the cross, He entrusted the care of His mother to John.

On the morning of the resurrection, John ran with Peter to the tomb and was the first to glimpse the undisturbed grave-clothes without the Lord's body inside them. He was present when the risen Christ revealed Himself to seven of the disciples by the sea of Tiberias.

After Christ ascended into heaven, John and Peter boldly preached the lordship and the messiahship of Jesus to the Jews in Jerusalem. John was with Peter when the first miracle of healing after Pentecost took place. A man, lame from birth, asked alms of the two apostles as they were entering the temple. Instead of giving him money, Peter said to him, "In the name of Jesus Christ of Nazareth rise up and walk!" The man leaped to his feet and walked.

The people who saw what happened were stirred by this miracle, and many believed in Jesus because of it. The Jewish religious leaders could not deny the healing, for the man was standing right there beside them. Nevertheless, they arrested and imprisoned Peter and John.

Finding no way to punish them, the Sanhedrin could only threaten dire consequences if they spoke or taught in the name of Jesus again. The apostles were then released. Undaunted, they resumed their evangelistic endeavors.

A second time the Sadducees had them thrown in jail, but an angel of the Lord opened the prison doors. They were arrested a third time, and beaten. Still they continued to teach and preach Jesus Christ . . .

John helped Peter to establish the Christian church in Jerusalem. After his brother James was slain by Herod Agrippa about A.D. 44, John left Palestine. Tradition tells us that he traveled to Asia Minor in missionary work. For some time he resided in Ephesus, becoming the pastor of the church there. During this period he wrote his gospel and his three epistles, somewhere around A.D. 90.

Under the reign of the cruel Roman emperor *Domitian*— Nero's successor—the elderly John was banished to Patmos for preaching the Word of God and for testifying of Jesus Christ.

It was common for the Romans to send exiles and criminals to the most desolate islands. The isle of Patmos, off the coast of Turkey in the Aegean Sea, was a rocky and barren place. It was here that John was given his stupendous vision of the future of all mankind, which comprises the Book of Revelation. He wrote it about A.D. 95.

Afterward he returned to Ephesus and lived in that city to an extreme old age—some say one hundred years. He was the sole member of the twelve apostles to die a natural death.

Revelation is the only book of prophecy in the New Testament, and the only book to contain Christ's message after His ascension—His last words to the church. It opens with these important sentences:

"(This is) the revelation of Jesus Christ—His unveiling of the divine mysteries. God gave it to Him to disclose and make known to His bond servants certain things which must shortly and speedily come to pass in their entirety. And He sent and communicated it through His angel (messenger) to His bond servant John,

"Who has testified to and vouched for all that he saw (in his VISIONS), the Word of God and the testimony of Jesus Christ" (Rev. 1:1, 2).

This tells us that God Himself gave the revelation to Christ. Jesus conveyed its message by signs and symbols to John through an angel. John received it in a series of visions, which the angel explained to him. The setting for some of the visions was heaven. For others, the scene was earth. The complete revelation was to be delivered to God's servants, the church. While seven specific churches are addressed, they represent the whole body of Christ during the entire church age.

A blessing is promised to all who read the words of Revelation, to those who hear it, and to those who keep the things written in the book. Its closing verses warn that if any man adds to the book, God will add to him the plagues described therein. And if anyone takes away from it, God will take away his part out of the Book of Life, out of the holy city, and out of the blessings written in the Revelation.

So we see that its contents are not to be ignored, tampered with, or taken lightly.

Revelation's theme is Christ's second advent. This is made clear at the very beginning:

"Lo, He is coming with the clouds, and every eye will see Him, even those who pierced Him. And all the tribes of the earth shall gaze upon Him, and beat their breasts and mourn and lament over Him. Even so (must it be). Amen—so be it" (Rev. 1:7).

Confirmation of this declaration is immediately given by the Lord Jesus Himself: "I am the Alpha and the Omega, the Beginning and the End, says the Lord God, He who is and who was and who is to come, the Almighty—the Ruler of all" (Rev. 1:8).

When Christ comes back, it will not be as His first coming. Then He came as the Son of man, whose earthly life had a beginning and an ending. His first advent was as Saviour and Redeemer. His return will be as Almighty God, Judge of the world, Ruler of all—the eternal Christ who had no beginning, and of whose kingdom there shall be no end.

The Exalted Christ

The first vision begins one "Lord's day." John is "in the Spirit," meaning a trance-like state in which he is in perfect union with the Holy Spirit and wholly yielded to Him. Suddenly John hears behind him a great voice like a trumpet.

The voice says: "I am the Alpha and the Omega, the First and the Last. Write promptly what you see (your VISION) in a

book, and send it to the seven churches which are in Asia . . ."
(Rev. 1:11).

When John turns to see the voice, he beholds seven golden
candlesticks, or lampstands. In the midst of these candlesticks
stands a glorious Being. John describes Him as One who looks
like Jesus, the Son of man . . .

He is clothed with a robe which reaches to His feet, and He
has a girdle of gold about His breast. This is the attire of a
priest. His hair is as white as snow, signifying profound wisdom.
His eyes flash like a flame of fire, denoting omniscient insight.
His feet glow like fine brass, bespeaking judicial firmness. His
voice is as the sound of many waters, symbolizing the awe-inspiring pronouncement of the Judge of the Universe.

In His right hand are seven stars; their meaning is later explained. Out of His mouth proceeds a sharp two-edged sword.
This is the sword of judgment and justice based on the Word
of God. His countenance is like the brightness of the sun,
showing forth His eternal glory.

This description of the glorified Christ vividly reminds us of
the Messiah as viewed by the prophet Daniel in his fourth vision.
And the effect of the two visions is the same. Both Daniel and
John fall at Christ's feet as dead, so powerful is the transcendent
glory of each appearance.

Remember that in John's case he is looking at the same Person
whom he had known on earth, who had walked and talked with
him, upon whose bosom he had lain. He is seeing again the One
in whose company he had been for three years, and whom he
once beheld brilliantly transfigured, talking with Moses and
Elijah on a mountain. Yet so changed is Jesus in His exalted
state, and particularly in this appearance as the Omnipotent
Christ of the future, that John is prostrated at the sight of Him.

Jesus lays His right hand on John and tells him not to be
afraid. He goes on to say:

"I am the Ever-living One—I am living in the eternity of the
eternities. I died, but see, I am alive for evermore. And I
possess the keys of Death and Hades (the realm of the dead)"
(Rev. 1:18).

What words of comfort and assurance! Jesus, having conquered death, is alive forevermore. The ultimate victory of good over evil is certain, for Christ holds the keys that unlock the grave. He has dominion over hell itself.

"Write therefore the things which thou hast seen," Jesus instructs John, "and the things which are, and the things which shall be hereafter" (Rev. 1:19, KJV).

At the beginning of the vision Christ commanded John to write in a book what he was *about to see*. Now he is told to write what he has *just witnessed*. Also he is to record the things concerning *the churches,* as well as the things which *will be shown* to him regarding the hereafter.

"The seven stars which you saw in my hand," explains Jesus, "are the angels of the churches. The seven candlesticks are the churches." Whether these angels refer to human leaders of the church or to angelic messengers, we do not know.

There follow *seven messages* spoken by Jesus in the first person to the various churches. The Lord chose them to represent His church as a whole. In addressing them, Jesus is speaking to the entire church and to all individual believers from that day until His return to earth. Judgment of the church must take place before judgment of the world, for "judgment begins at the house of God."

The messages are given as an essential part of the vision, but we cannot go into them in detail. These "letters," as they are called, merit a study in themselves. They are Christ's personal warnings to Christians, and they are filled with such repeated phrases as:

"I know your works . . . I have this against you . . . Repent, or else . . . Behold, I am coming quickly . . . Hold fast until I come."

Jesus knows all about every church and every one who calls himself a Christian. He promises eternal rewards to those who are truly born again, who live a sanctified life, who are ready, watching, and waiting for their Lord's return. He also promises that they will not have to pass through the terrible time of suffering. "The hour of testing which is coming on the whole world, to try those who dwell upon the earth," is the way He refers to it (Rev. 3:10).

Those who are Christ's will be glorified and taken to heaven before the tribulation begins. But what about the multitudes of professing Christians—those who are not living faithful, consecrated lives, who love the things of this world—whose real spiritual condition is lukewarm?

There are so many Christians whose churches are man-made institutional systems, or social cubs in which the preaching is an evasion, distortion, or denial of Jesus Christ as Lord and personal Saviour through His sacrificial death on the cross. What will happen to them?

To all of these people, Christ declares that this kind of "Christianity" nauseates Him. All such churches and individual believers will be rejected when He comes.

At the conclusion of these messages of warning to Christendom of all ages, John's vision of *"the things which are"* ends.

God's Throne of Judgment

With the second vision, the great revelation of *"the things which shall be"* commences to unfold. John looks, and lo—a door is standing open in heaven! The same trumpet-like voice of Christ that he heard in the first vision speaks to him again:

"Come up here, and I will show you what must take place in the future" (Rev. 4:1).

Under the power of the Holy Spirit, John is caught up to heaven. There he views a spectacular panorama. The center of attention is a throne, and seated on it is Someone beyond human description. John can only say that the Personage appeared like brilliant flashes of light as from a glittering diamond—and like the brightness of fire, as from a shining ruby. Encircling the throne is a rainbow, glowing like an emerald.

Here again we are reminded of another vision given to one of the Old Testament prophets. In Ezekiel's first vision of the glory of the Lord, he too saw the throne of God, with its Occupant seated thereon. And he described the scene in much the same way. Incidentally, this throne is not the throne of grace, on which Jesus is seated at the right hand of the Majesty on high. This is the throne of judgment.

Surrounding the throne are twenty-four smaller thrones, with twenty-four elders sitting on them. All are clothed in white, with golden crowns upon their heads. These elders are redeemed saints engaged in priestly services.

Lightning and thunder issue from the throne in awe-inspiring grandeur and power. Voices are heard in the thunder. Directly in front of the throne are seven lamps burning with fire, signifying the fulness and power of the Holy Spirit. Spread out beneath the throne is a shining crystal sea, as clear as transparent glass.

Four living beings, with eyes in front and back, stand at the throne's four sides. Each of these creatures has six wings. Day and night they say: *"Holy, holy, holy is the Lord God Almighty, who was and who is and who is to come"* (Rev. 4:8).

This, of course, recalls to us the vision of Isaiah in the temple. He too saw the seraphim performing a ministry of holiness around the throne of God. And we remember also the cherubim who appeared in several visions of Ezekiel.

These living creatures are angelic beings, a blending of cherubim and seraphim. They are guardians of God's holiness, and agents of His power. Together with the twenty-four elders, they worship the One sitting on the throne, giving glory and honor and thanks to Him. The elders fall prostrate before the Eternal. Casting their crowns at His feet, they sing praises to His holy name.

John continues with the vision:

"I saw lying on the open hand of Him who was seated on the throne a book (scroll), written within and on the back. It was closed, and sealed with seven seals.

"And I saw a strong angel announcing in a loud voice, Who is worthy to open the scroll? Who is entitled and deserves and is morally fit to break its seals?" (Rev. 5:1, 2).

This book, resting on the outstretched hand of God, is believed by some to contain the title deed to the universe. They interpret it as being a legal document recording the inheritance that was lost with Adam's fall in the garden of Eden. It decrees the dispossession of Satan and all evil from the earth. At the same time, it guarantees Christ's full possession of what has been purchased.

According to this interpretation, the book holds the assurance of finished redemption for the whole creation, which has long groaned and toiled to be delivered from the curse imposed upon it.

Others are of the opinion that the book contains the revelation of judgments that must befall the earth before full redemption and deliverance can be realized. Also within its covers, they believe, is included the disclosure of God's purposes for the future.

Still another interpretation is that this book is the same one Daniel was told to seal up until the time of the end.

Whatever its contents, the book is closed and sealed with seven seals. This signifies that the knowledge is completely hidden from angels and men. No created being in all heaven or earth, or from among the dead, is found fit to open it or to inspect it. John weeps bitterly because of this.

Then one of the twenty-four elders tells him to stop weeping, for One has been found. The Lion of the tribe of Judah, the Root of David, has conquered and proved Himself worthy to open the book and to break its seven seals!

When John looks up, he sees a Lamb standing between the throne and the four living beings, and in the midst of the elders. On the Lamb are wounds that once had caused His death. He has seven horns and seven eyes . . .

We readily identify the Lamb as the Lord Jesus Christ, but why should He be depicted with horns and so many eyes?

In the scriptures the number seven always denotes completion, fulfillment, and perfection. Horns symbolize power. Eyes represent insight. Thus the Lamb is pictured as having the full power and perfect discernment of the Holy Spirit upon Him for judicial administration over the earth.

By His sacrificial death on the cross, and the perfection of the redemptive work that He accompished, Christ has won victory. He has overcome the world and the devil. God's purposes for man, which depended on the atonement, can now be carried out.

The Lamb steps forward and takes the scroll from the right hand of the One sitting upon the throne. As He does so, the living creatures and the elders fall down before Him. Each of them has a harp, the instrument of praise. They also have golden bowls of incense, representing the prayers of the saints. They begin singing a new song, saying:

"You are worthy to take the scroll and to break the seals that are on it. For You were slain (sacrificed), and with Your blood You purchased men unto God from every tribe and language and people and nation.

"You have made them a kingdom (royal race) and priests to our God. And they shall reign (as kings) over the earth!" (Rev. 5:9, 10).

In the vision John hears the singing of millions of angels surrounding the throne, as they join the chorus of praise to the conquering Lamb. Then *every creature in heaven, on earth, under the earth, and in the sea* echoes, "Blessing and honor and glory and power be unto Him that sitteth upon the throne, and unto the Lamb for ever and ever!"

Many of us have thrilled when a tremendous choir with full symphony orchestra presents "The Hallelujah Chorus." But that is only a hint of what this great song will be like. Oh the splendor and majesty and wonder of the scene! Imagine the sound of all heaven and earth uniting their voices in worship, and in proclaiming the worthiness of the Lamb!

This event is really Christ's coronation. It marks the time when He receives His kingdom. All judgment and power is given to Him from the hand of God. Although the Father is over all, He commits the future to His Son.

This is what the prophet Daniel saw in his first vision given almost seven hundred years before John's vision. Daniel witnessed the Ancient of Days seated on His judgment throne. He beheld the Son of man coming in glory on the clouds of heaven, and brought before the Most High.

Both Daniel and John saw in vision form the second advent of Christ the Messiah. They each viewed the presentation to Him of His everlasting kingdom, over which He will have dominion throughout eternity.

Thus God confirms in the Old and in the New Testament, and to both Jews and Christians, this magnificient prophecy that is yet to be fufilled.

The Seven Seals

The setting of John's vision shifts now from heaven to earth. As the seven seals are broken by Christ the Lamb, one at a time, the contents of each seal are revealed pictorially.

The opening of the seals ushers in *Daniel's seventieth week,* the final seven years of terrible trouble which is to engulf the earth. Those who belong to Christ escape this *period of tribulation.* Just before it begins, they will be caught up in the clouds to meet the Lord in the air when He comes for His own. This is called "the rapture of the church."

Jesus will personally, bodily descend from heaven with a shout, with the voice of the archangel, and the trumpet of God. The dead in Christ are to rise first. They will be resurrected, and those living who are Christ's will be translated. Together the saints are to be transported to heaven (I Thess. 4:16, 17).

But on the earth there will ensue seven years of oppression, persecution, and suffering. During this period God permits sin to work out its tragic results. Human ambition, lust, hatred, and cruelty are allowed free course. As God's hand is lifted from man and beast, the earth will be filled with violence, corruption, war, hunger, famine and pestilence.

"Then I saw as the Lamb broke open one of the seven seals. And as if in a voice of thunder, I heard one of the four living creatures call out, Come!" (Rev. 6:1).

When the first seal is opened, judgment is called forth upon those who have rejected the Son of God. The command, "Come!" is repeated three more times as the second, third, and fourth seals are broken. Each of the four living creatures uses the command to summon one of four horsemen. Literature has made famous these "Four Horsemen of the Apocalypse." They symbolize the forces God will use for purposes of judgment.

The first horse is white. Its rider carries a bow. A crown is given him, and he rides out to conquer in many battles. The white horse and crown signify conquest and victory.

The second horse is red. Its rider is given a long sword and the authority to banish peace and bring anarchy to the earth. War and killing break out everywhere.

The third horse is black. In this rider's hand is a pair of scales. A voice from among the four living beings says: "A loaf of bread for a whole day's wages, or three pounds of barley flour. But the oil and wine are not to be hurt."

Black is the color of famine, which results from the conquest and wars of the first two seals. Bread by measure and weight denotes scarcity of food. Although oil and wine are not injured, these luxuries prove unsatisfying when daily bread is withheld from the people by its high cost.

The fourth horse is a pale horse. Its rider's name is Death. Hell follows with him. They are given control of one-fourth of the earth, to kill with war and famine and disease and wild animals. Great pestilence follows the wars and famine of the first three seals. Where the dead bodies are fallen, there the beasts are gathered to eat them.

It is believed by many that while there are four horses in the vision, there is only one horseman. The rider is the same on all of the horses. He is, of course, Antichrist—"that man of sin, the son of perdition" who will oppose God and exalt himself above all that is called God, or that is worshiped.

This future world leader will gain power over the entire territory of the old Roman empire. He enters the scene at the beginning of the tribulation period "riding a white horse," imitating and claiming to be Christ. The bow he carries depicts his evil designs and conquests. The crown given him comes from Satan. War, famine, pestilence, death and hell are the result of his reign.

The focus of John's vision moves back to heaven at the opening of the fifth seal. He tells us: "When the Lamb broke open the fifth seal, I saw at the foot of the altar the souls of those whose lives had been sacrificed for (adhering to) the word of God and for the testimony they had borne" (Rev. 6:9).

The opening of this seal reveals the death of many saints. They were saved after the rapture of the church, and were killed in the first half of the tribulation. The sacrifice of their lives is represented as having been offered on a heavenly altar. At the foot of it, their blood has been poured out.

"They cried in a loud voice, O (Sovereign) Lord, holy and true, how long now before You will sit in judgment and avenge our blood upon those who dwell on the earth?" (Rev. 6:10).

These martyrs are calling out for the punishment of their murderers. God is not unheeding, but judgment must wait until the full number of their brethren is complete. Meanwhile they are given white robes of victory, and told to rest for a little while in heaven. After their fellow servants arc killed on earth, and have joined them, recompense will be meted out upon those who put them to death.

With the opening of the sixth seal, the wrath of God begins. This ushers in the latter half of the tribulation, the second three and onc-half years. Jesus called it "the great tribulation." The prophet Jeremiah spoke of it as "the time of Jacob's trouble."

"When He (the Lamb) broke open the sixth seal, I looked, and there was a great earthquake. The sun grew black as sackcloth of hair. (The full disc of) the moon became like blood" (Rev. 6:12).

Following the vast quake, the sun is darkened and the moon becomes blood-red. The stars of the sky drop to earth. The heavens are rolled up as a scroll. Every mountain and island is dislodged from its place.

As this happens, humanity at last realizes that God's wrath has begun.

Kings, world leaders, high-ranking military officers, the rich as well as the poor, hide themselves in the caves and among the rocks of the mountains. Apparently at this point heaven is opened for a moment—long enough for these people to see the throne of God.

They call to the mountains and the rocks to fall on them—in order to hide them from the face of Him who sits on the throne, and from the wrath of the Lamb! Unbelievers cannot bear the sight of God and His Son. In terrible fear, they recognize that the day of retribution has come, and who is able to stand before it?

Between the sixth and seventh seals *two brief visions are interposed.*

Their purpose is to explain certain things which occur along with the main events of the period, but which are not in the contents of the seals. In these "parenthetical visions" John sees two specially protected groups. They are the saved of the tribulation period.

The first group is comprised of one hundred forty-four thousand Jews living on earth who have been converted to Christ during the first part of the tribulation. They are sealed upon their foreheads by an angel who carries the seal of the living God. The name of the Father is written upon them, marking them as His. That they are all Israelites is clear from the fact that there are twelve thousand from each of the twelve tribes of Israel.

The angel with the seal ascends from the east. "And with a loud voice he called out to the four angels who had been given authority and power to injure earth and sea,

"Saying, Harm neither the earth nor the sea nor the trees, until we have sealed the bond servants of our God upon their foreheads" (Rev. 7:2, 3).

John is then given a glimpse of another group. This "great multitude" is made up of Gentiles who have been saved during the tribulation. These are not seen on earth, but in heaven. They have been killed, and death has brought them to glory.

"After this I looked and a vast host appeared which no one could count, (gathered out) of every nation, from all tribes and peoples and languages. These stood before the throne and before the Lamb. They were attired in white robes, with palm branches in their hands" (Rev. 7:9).

All of them are loudly proclaiming, "Our salvation is due to our God who is seated on the throne, and to the Lamb. To Them we owe our deliverance!" One of the twenty-four elders around the throne informs John that these have come out of great tribulation.

The elder goes on to say that this company serves God in His temple day and night. He adds that they will never hunger or thirst any more, nor will any heat scorch them. For the Lamb who is in the midst of the throne is their Shepherd. He will feed them, and give them to drink from everlasting fountains of life. The elder closes with these beautiful words: "And God will wipe every tear away from their eyes" (Rev. 7:17).

When the seventh seal is opened, a very dramatic thing happens. *There is absolute silence in heaven for half an hour.*

Among all the seraphim, cherubim, angelic hosts, and the company of the redeemed—there is not a sound. Everything is still. There is just a waiting in hushed awe, as though God and His ministering angels shrink from what is about to fall upon the earth. This is the only time we read of silence in heaven . . .

The contents of the seven seals having been made known, we are now going to hear the successive blowing of seven trumpets. Their individual disclosures are unveiled in the next division of our study.

The Seven Trumpets

In attempting to understand the book of Revelation, it is helpful for us to remember that it pictures three series of judgments. The first series is that of the seven *seals.* The second series is that of the seven *trumpets.* The last series depicts the judgments of the seven *vials,* or bowls of wrath.

After the seventh seal is opened, and the half hour of silence in heaven has ended, John says: "Then I saw the seven angels who stand before God. To them were given seven trumpets" (Rev. 8:2).

In the great government and plan of God there is perfect organization. These seven angels who stand in the presence of the Lord are to blow their trumpets consecutively between the seals and the vials. They signal a succession of disasters which befall the earth as punishment for the wickedness of men. Palestine is to be the center of these judgments, but the entire earth will feel the effects.

As John watches, another angel with a golden censer comes and stands at the altar before the throne. A large quantity of incense is given him. This is presented, with the prayers of God's people, as an offering upon the golden altar. The perfume of the incense, combined with the prayers, ascends upward from the angel's hand. The prayers of the saints reach God, and the judgment about to fall upon the earth is His answer.

The angel then fills the censer with fire from the altar. He throws it down upon the earth. Thunder crashes and rumbles, lightning flashes, and there is a terrible earthquake.

"The first angel blew (his) trumpet. There was a storm of hail and fire mingled with blood cast upon the earth. A third part of the earth was burned up. A third of the trees was burned up, and all the green grass was burned up" (Rev. 8:7).

At the sounding of the second trumpet, what appears to be a huge burning mountain is thrown into the sea. It causes a third part of the ocean to become blood. A third of the fish therein die, and a third of all the ships are destroyed. Under the seals the moon became "like blood," but here part of the sea actually "becomes blood."

The third trumpet blows. A great flaming star falls from heaven upon a third of the rivers and springs. The name of the star is "Wormwood," meaning bitterness. A third part of the waters become so bitter that they cause the death of many people.

The judgments are intensifying. Under the seals, *one fourth* of the earth was affected; but under the trumpets it is *one third.*

When the fourth trumpet sounds, immediately a third of the sun is darkened, and a third of the moon and the stars. Daylight is dimmed, and the nighttime darkness deepens.

John continues with the vision. "Then I (looked and I) saw a solitary eagle flying in midheaven. And as it flew, I heard it crying with a loud voice, Woe, woe, woe to those who dwell on the earth, because of the rest of the trumpet blasts which the three angels are about to sound!" (Rev. 8:13).

An eagle, whose swoop upon the prey is another symbol of judgment, announces *three woes* upon idolatrous and ungodly mankind. *Each of the last three trumpets heralds one of these woes.*

The fifth trumpet is blown. An angel descends from heaven with the key to the shaft of the bottomless pit. This abyss is the abode of evil spirits or demons. There is a long shaft leading to it. At the opening of this, smoke like that from a huge furnace pours forth, darkening the sun and the air. Out of the smoke issue evil spirits with the appearance of locusts.

They come in a multitude. Power is given them to sting like scorpions. However, they are commanded not to hurt green things, and only to afflict those persons who do not have the seal of God in their foreheads. This means all men except the one hundred forty-four thousand "sealed" Jews. The demons torment human beings with agony like the pain of scorpion stings. But they are not permitted to kill them. And the time of their attack is limited to five months.

"In those days people will seek death and will not find it, and they will yearn to die. But death evades and flees from them" (Rev. 9:6).

John then describes these locust-demons. Their bodies are like horses equipped for battle. On their heads are something like crowns of gold. Their faces resemble the faces of people. They have hair like women, teeth like lions, breastplates of iron, wings with which to fly, and tails like scorpions.

Over them as king they have the angel of the abyss. In Hebrew his name is *Abaddon*. In Greek he is called *Apollyon*, which means "Destroyer."

With the conclusion of this loosing of demons for five months, the first woe is past.

"Then the sixth angel blew (his) trumpet. From the four horns of the altar of gold which stands before God, I heard a solitary voice saying to the sixth angel who had the trumpet, Liberate the four angels who are bound at the great river Euphrates" (Rev. 9:13, 14).

The four angels bound at the Euphrates are fallen ones. Good angels are never bound. These evil angels are the leaders of a cavalry of two hundred million demons. They have been in readiness for that hour, which comes at the exact time foreordained by God. They are liberated to slay one third of mankind.

Whether this means a third of the population in those countries surrounding the Euphrates river, or whether a third of the whole earth is meant, we are not told.

"And in (my) VISION the horses and their riders appeared to me like this . . . The riders wore breastplates the color of fiery red, sapphire blue, and sulphur (brimstone) yellow. The heads of the horses looked like lions' heads. From their mouths poured fire and smoke and sulphur (brimstone)" (Rev. 9:17).

By these three means—fire, smoke, and flaming sulphur pouring out of the horses' mouths—a third of mankind is killed. Also by means of the serpent-like tails of these animals, many people are fatally wounded.

Yet—incredible as it seems—those who are not killed by this infernal army still refuse to repent! They continue to worship idols, commit murder, fornication, theft, and practice sorceries, which includes the using of drugs. Such is the stubbornness, rebellion and depravity inherent in man, and the control that demons have over him when he yields himself to their influence.

Under these last two trumpets, all hell is let loose. Unprecedented demonic activity sweeps across the earth. Sin is allowed full sway, and Satan releases his maximum power to accomplish his objectives.

With the conclusion of the loosing of the two hundred million demon cavalrymen on the earth, the second woe is past.

Between the sixth and seventh trumpets—as between the sixth and seventh seals, and also between the sixth and seventh vials—is another parenthetical episode.

The vision between the trumpets begins this way:

John says, "Then I saw another mighty angel coming down from heaven, robed in a cloud, with a (halo like a) rainbow over his head. His face was like the sun. His feet (legs) were like columns of fire." (Rev. 10:1).

Who is this "mighty angel"?

Many believe it is *Christ Himself*. This majestic personage is clothed in a cloud. His head is encircled with a rainbow. His face shines like the sun, and his feet flash with fire. Others interpret the mighty one as being *an angel who represents Christ,* reflects His glory, and bears the insignia attributed to Him.

In the angel's hand is a little book, open. Is this the same book that Christ took from the hand of God, the seven seals of which He broke? Here again is a difference of opinion. Some think that it is. Others distinguish it from the seven-sealed book.

There are those who believe it is the book of prophecy that Daniel was told to seal up until the time of the end (Dan. 12:9).

Whichever it is, the little book is open—unsealed—and it is in the hand of the mighty angel. Setting his right foot on the sea, and his left foot on the land, the angel shouts with a loud voice like the roaring of a lion.

Seven thunders crash a reply. John is about to write down the words they sounded when a voice from heaven calls: "Seal up what the seven thunders have said! Do not write it down!" (Rev. 10:4).

Then the mighty angel raises his right hand to heaven and swears by Him who lives forever, the Creator of the universe, that "there should be time no longer." In other words, there shall be no more delay. Christ has full authority over the earth, the world He created and redeemed. Now He is preparing to claim what belongs to Him.

What a vivid reminder this is to us of the final vision given to the prophet Daniel! In that vision Christ stood upon the waters of the river. He lifted both hands to heaven, and swore by Him who lives forever that there would be a certain length of time until the end. In Daniel's case the book was sealed up "until the time of the end." In John's visions the book has been unsealed, for the time of the end has come.

The angel vows that when the seventh angel begins to sound his trumpet, then God's mystery is to be finished.

What is "the mystery of God"?

It is Christ as incarnate Redeemer of the earth. The secret design, the hidden purpose of God is centered and unfolded in the Lord Jesus Christ. God has declared the truth of Christ's redemption, kingdom, and eternal glory through His servants the prophets. Now the full revelation is to be made manifest to all mankind. The return of Christ to the earth is imminent.

John goes on to tell us: "Then the voice that I heard from heaven spoke again to me saying, Go and take the little book (scroll) which is open on the hand of the angel who is standing on the sea and on the land" (Rev. 10:8).

John approaches the angel and asks for the little book. It is given to him, and he is told to eat it. "It will embitter your stomach," the angel states, "though in your mouth it will be sweet as honey."

This is exactly the effect it has on John. Truth is always sweet when it is received by revelation from God. But it becomes bitter when the contents are digested and found to be wrath and judgment upon one's own people. Such is the little book's message for Israel during the great tribulation—the latter half of that period. The bright promises of deliverance are preluded by terrible suffering and judgment.

As a result of the assimilation of the little book, John is told by the mighty angel that he must prophesy again. *"You are to make a fresh prediction concerning many peoples, nations, languages and kings."* A measuring rod is given to John and he is told: "Rise up and measure the sanctuary of God and the altar (of incense), and (number) those who worship there.

"But leave out of your measuring the court outside the sanctuary of God. Omit that, for it is given over to the Gentiles (the nations). They will trample the holy city under foot for forty-two months (three and one-half years)" (Rev. 11:1, 2).

John is to measure the sanctuary and altar of the temple in Jerusalem, counting the worshipers there. But the outer court of the Gentiles is not to be measured. It has already been given over, with the rest of the city, to the nations. "Jacob's trouble" has begun.

Antichrist breaks his seven-year covenant with Israel in the middle of it, takes over the temple, and sets up his own image in the most holy place. The people are commanded to worship him as God. This the faithful remnant of practicing Jews refuses to do.

At this point the Lord sends *"two witnesses."* These are prophets who are given power to speak forth the word of God for the last half of the tribulation period. They are dressed in sackcloth, a symbol of mourning. By this they call attention to the sin and wickedness of the people, and the repentance they should be experiencing.

The angel who is talking to John says: "These (witnesses) are the two olive trees and the two lampstands which stand before the Lord of the earth" (Rev. 11:4).

We remember that in one of the prophet Zechariah's visions he beheld two olive trees, one on either side of the golden lampstand. They were explained to him as being two anointed ones standing by the Lord. Since the church, represented in John's initial vision by the seven candlesticks, has been taken up into heaven, the two "olive trees" or witnesses are now the light-bearers of the Lord on earth.

"Anyone trying to harm these two witnesses," the angel goes on to say, "will be killed by bursts of fire shooting from their mouths. They have power to shut up the sky so that no rain will fall during the three and one-half years they prophesy. They also have power to turn rivers and oceans to blood, and to send every kind of plague upon the earth as often as they wish."

Instantly we think of two Old Testament prophets—*Elijah* and *Moses*. Elijah had power to shut the heavens, and Moses possessed power to turn the waters into blood and to smite the earth with plagues. Therefore, many people feel that these two witnesses are Moses and Elijah returned to earth.

But there are others who believe them to be *Enoch* and *Elijah*. The latter were the only two human beings who were translated without seeing death. The Bible says that "It is appointed unto man once to die." Since Moses died once, it would seem to exclude him from coming back and dying again.

At the finish of their testimony, both of these witnesses are killed. Their bodies are exposed for three and a half days in the streets of Jerusalem (the city fittingly described as "Sodom" or "Egypt"). No one is allowed to bury them, and people from many nations crowd around to gaze at them.

A world-wide holiday is declared. Everyone rejoices and gives presents to each other. Parties are thrown to celebrate the death of the two preachers who were such a torment by their warnings regarding the wrath to come.

But after the three and a half days, something very startling happens. *The spirit of life from God enters the prophets' dead bodies, and they are resurrected!* Great fear falls upon people everywhere. A voice from heaven is heard saying, "Come up hither!" The two witnesses ascend to heaven in a cloud, in full sight of all their enemies.

That same hour there is a terrible earthquake. It levels a tenth of the city, leaving seven thousand dead. Those still alive, in their terror, give glory to the God of heaven for His power. But they do not turn to Him in repentance.

With the closing of this episode between the sixth and seventh trumpets, John is reminded that two of the woes have passed. There is now one more woe to come.

"The seventh angel then blew his trumpet. There were mighty voices in heaven, shouting, The dominion (kingdom, sovereignty, rule) of the world has now come into the possession and become the kingdom of our Lord and of His Christ, the Messiah. And He shall reign forever and ever—for the eternities of the eternities!" (Rev. 11:15).

The angelic announcement proclaims the victory of the coming kingdom. Instead of silence in heaven, which followed the opening of the seventh seal, John hears a heavenly chorus. They are loudly rejoicing in the culmination of events which the seventh trumpet is to bring.

The twenty-four elders anticipate the gathering of the raging nations at Armageddon, the judgment of the wicked, and the rewarding of the prophets and saints in Christ's millennial kingdom.

The temple of God in heaven is thrown open. In it is seen the ark of the covenant—the true ark, after which the earthly ark made by Moses was patterned. This is a sign that God is about to consummate the covenants made with His people Israel. The Presence of the Lord is going to come back and take residence upon the earth. He will fill it with His glory—as once He filled the tabernacle in the wilderness, and Solomon's temple in Jerusalem.

The seventh trumpet has sounded. Lightning flashes, thunder crashes and roars. There is a great hailstorm, and the world is shaken by a mighty earthquake.

Seven Personages

Before John is given the vision of the seven vials, which contain the consummation of God's wrath, he views two visions interposed between the trumpets and the vials.

The first vision presents seven personages (Rev. 12, 13). Each of these figures plays an important part in the final days before Christ's return. The initial personage is a woman.

"And a great sign (wonder, warning of future events of ominous significance) appeared in heaven: *a woman clothed with the sun,* with the moon under her feet, and with a crownlike garland (tiara) of twelve stars on her head.

"She was pregnant, and she cried out in her birth pangs, in the anguish of her delivery" (Rev. 12:1, 2).

Some teach that this woman is the church. But we must remember that the church was raptured before the tribulation began, and this event occurs midway in the tribulation period. Others teach that the woman is national *Israel.* The same symbol of the sun, moon and stars was given in a dream to Joseph in the Old Testament. There it definitely referred to Israel. The woman's travail seems a fitting picture of Israel's agony during the great tribulation, and her suffering to bring forth a faithful remnant.

"Then another ominous sign (wonder) was seen in heaven. Behold, a huge, *fiery-red dragon,* with seven heads and ten horns, and seven kingly crowns (diadems) upon his heads.

"His tail swept (across the sky) and dragged down a third of the stars, and flung them to the earth. The dragon stationed himself in front of the woman who was about to be delivered, so that he might devour her child as soon as she brought it forth" (Rev. 12:3, 4).

The second personage, portrayed as a great red dragon ready to devour, is *Satan.* He was a murderer from the beginning. His seven crowned heads depict the seven kingdoms which precede the kingdom of Antichrist, and the devil's rule over them. The ten horns correspond to the ten toes of Nebuchadnezzar's image, the final form of Gentile world power.

These ten horns represent the confederacy of nations which will comprise the revised Roman empire, the kingdom ruled by Antichrist. The horns are not crowned, because power over these countries has been given to Antichrist.

The dragon's tail casting a third of the stars of heaven to the earth is a reference to Satan's original downfall. As the angel

Lucifer, he took a host of morning stars, or angels, with him in his rebellion against God. He was not then thrown down *upon* the earth. His fall was into the atmospheric heavens *above* the earth—the heavenlies. There, with the angels he dragged down with him, he began his reign as prince of the power of the air.

As John's vision continues, we are introduced to the third personage—*the man child,* born of the woman (who is godly Israel).

This child is destined to rule all nations with a rod of iron. Satan, the great dragon, seeks to destroy the man child as soon as he is brought forth. But the child escapes the enemy's hand. He is caught up to heaven and to the throne of God.

The question is often discussed among Christians: *"Who is this man child?"*

Again we find differing interpretations. Some believe the child represents Christ. Others say it symbolizes His church, as a whole or in part. But we must remember that the events related in this vision occur long after Christ has ascended into heaven, and three and a half years after the church has been raptured. So that would seem to rule them out as being the man child.

Other Christians are convinced that the man child represents the one hundred forty-four thousand sealed Jews, the servants of God.

At the time of this vision the one hundred forty-four thousand are still on earth, having been protected through the first six trumpets. Following the blowing of the seventh trumpet, the man child is caught up to God's throne. Immediately after that, the one hundred forty-four thousand are discovered in heaven. If we do not identify them as being the man child, then we must answer these questions: "How did the one hundred forty-four thousand get to heaven? When were they raptured, if not as the man child?"

Also we note that when the one hundred forty-four thousand are seen in heaven, they are called "the first fruits unto God and the Lamb."

This would appear to indicate that they were the first Jews saved and raptured from Israel during the tribulation period. Naturally the dragon was full of wrath toward them because of their divine protection and their evangelistic ministry. He sought to destroy them under the seventh trumpet, but God caught them up to His throne.

"The woman (herself) fled into the desert (wilderness), where she has a retreat prepared (for her) by God. Here she is to be fed and kept safe for one thousand two hundred and sixty days (forty-two months; three and one-half years)" (Rev. 12:6).

This period of time is, of course, the last half of the tribulation. Antichrist has broken his seven-year covenant with Israel in the middle of it, placed his own image in their sanctuary at Jerusalem, and commanded the Jews to worship him.

The woman, representing that part of Israel which believes the scriptures, flees into the wilderness. She recognizes this act of Antichrist to be "the abomination of desolation" predicted by Daniel the prophet. It is the beginning of the "great tribulation" referred to by Jesus.

"When you see the appalling sacrilege spoken of by the prophet Daniel, standing in the holy place . . ." Jesus warned when prophesying of the end time . . . "then let those who are in Judea flee to the mountains. For then there will be great tribulation, such as has not been from the beginning of the world until now, no, and never will be again" (Matt. 24:15, 21).

John's vision continues:

"Then war broke out in heaven, Michael and his angels going forth to battle with the dragon. And the dragon and his angels fought; but they were defeated. And there was no room found for them in heaven any longer" (Rev. 12:7, 8).

The fourth personage to play an important role in this latter day drama is the *archangel Michael*. He is the great prince who is the guardian angel of Israel. Michael is sent with his hosts to do battle against Satan and his army of fallen angels. The war in heaven is the struggle between God and Satan over possession of the heavenlies, where Satan has reigned since he fell from heaven itself.

What is the outcome of that war?

Satan—the age-old serpent, who is called the devil, and the deceiver of the whole world—is defeated. He is forced out of the heavenlies, and into the earth. His angels are flung out with him.

"Then I heard a strong voice in heaven, saying, Now it has

come, the salvation and the power and the kingdom (the dominion, the reign) of our God and the power (the sovereignty, the authority) of His Christ, the Messiah. For the accuser of our brethren, he who keeps bringing before our God charges against them day and night, has been cast out!" (Rev. 12:10).

Satan's expulsion is a cause of rejoicing for those who dwell in heaven. It is a prelude to the establishment of Christ's kingdom on earth. Now all the courts of God are closed to Satan. The accuser of the brethren no longer has access to heaven to prosecute the saints.

"And they have overcome (conquered) him by means of the blood of the Lamb, and by the utterance of their testimony. For they did not love and cling to life even when faced with death —holding their lives cheap till they had to die (for their witnessing)" (Rev. 12:11).

The tribulation saints overcome the devil by the blood of the Lamb, by the faithful word of testimony, and by their martyrdom.

Following this glad exultation in heaven, the third woe is announced.

"But woe to you, O earth and sea! For the devil has come down to you in fierce anger (fury), because he knows that he has (only) a short time (left)!" (Rev. 12:12).

Satan is aware that only a little time remains before he is confined to the abyss. The first thing he does is to vent his rage upon the woman (godly Israel) who gave birth to the man child. He motivates Antichrist to send armies in pursuit of those Israelites who fled to the wilderness.

But the earth comes to the rescue of the woman. The ground opens its mouth and swallows up the flood of men sent out to destroy!

God enables fleeing Israel to find refuge in the place specially prepared for them, where they are cared for during the three and one-half years remaining. This place is thought by some to be the rock city of Petra, capital of Edom. It forms a perfect hiding place, safe from attack.

Satan now turns against *the godly remnant of Jews* still in the land to put them to death. This group comprises *the fifth person-*

age in John's vision. They are individual Israelites who do not flee Judea, and therefore do not escape to safety when the great tribulation breaks out. But they obey God's commandments, and they adhere to and bear witness to the testimony of Jesus.

As events unfold, *the sixth personage* is introduced.

John sees "a beast coming up out of the sea." The sea may refer to the area around the Mediterranean. Or perhaps it merely denotes that the beast is a human being arising out of the sea of humanity. The beast has seven heads and ten horns. Upon the heads are blasphemous titles, and on the horns are crowns.

We remember that the dragon, or Satan, was depicted with seven heads and ten horns. Therefore we know immediately that the devil is the dynamic power behind this beast.

While the dragon's *heads* are crowned, it is the *horns* that are crowned on the beast. Since horns represent power, and crowns signify kingdoms, we readily identify the beast as a political figure heading a ten-kingdom empire. He is the last great ruler of Gentile world power, and is none other than *Antichrist* himself.

His empire partakes of all the satanic qualities of the preceding world empires of "the times of the Gentiles." The names of blasphemy upon his heads indicate complete defiance of God.

"One of his heads seemed to have a deadly wound. But his death stroke was healed, and the whole earth went after the beast in amazement and admiration.

"They fell down and did homage to the dragon, because he had bestowed on the beast all his dominion and authority. They also praised and worshiped the beast, exclaiming, Who is a match for the beast, and who can make war against him?" (Rev. 13:3, 4).

The deadly wound that was healed symbolizes one of the empires which appeared to have been destroyed, but has now been revived. It is the old Roman empire, revised under Antichrist. As the ruler of this kingdom, Antichrist is so powerful that the people worship him. In doing this, they are paying homage to Satan, for the beast is his tool.

Actually, Antichrist is the devil's masterpiece. He endows him with great personal magnetism, and supernatural gifts of oratory. He invests in him all human, governmental, and satanic power. He makes him, indeed, a "superman."

God allows Antichrist to speak great things and utter blasphemies for a period of forty-two months. This is the duration of Jacob's trouble. He further permits the beast to wage war on the saints—Jews and Christians—and to overcome them. Multitudes are killed by him. His authority is extended over every tribe and people and tongue and nation. Everyone in the empire, whose name is not recorded in the Lamb's Book of Life, falls down in adoration and pays homage to Antichrist.

"Then (says John) I saw another beast rising up out of the land (itself). He had two horns like a lamb, and he spoke (roared) like a dragon" (Rev. 13:11).

The second beast who appears on the scene is *the seventh and last of the personages* to walk across the stage in these end times.

He too is a human being. But instead of a political figure, this beast is a religious leader. The Bible calls him *"the false prophet"* (Rev. 19:20; 20:10). Outwardly he appears lamblike, but inside he is as cruel as the first beast. Truly he is "a wolf in sheep's clothing." Both he and Antichrist receive their power and authority from Satan. Together they reign over the old Roman empire territory for the last part of the tribulation.

The second beast causes men to deify Antichrist. He performs miracles, even to calling fire down from heaven, counterfeiting God and His works. Because of lying signs and wonders, many are deceived.

The false prophet commands that a statue of Antichrist be made. Then he works his greatest miracle. Through supernatural demon power, he imparts life to the statue so that it speaks. The death penalty is exacted upon anyone who does not worship the image of the beast.

All men in Antichrist's kingdom have to take a mark, or the name of Antichrist, or the number of his name, in the right hand or on the forehead. That number is symbolically designated as 666. No one is allowed to buy or sell who does not have the mark of the beast.

John's second vision interposed between the judgments of the trumpets and the judgments of the vials has to do with heaven, not earth. Its scene is in marked contrast to the reign of terror going on below.

"Then I looked and lo, the Lamb stood on mount Zion. With Him were a hundred and forty-four thousand (men) who had His name and His Father's name inscribed on their foreheads" (Rev. 14:1).

This company is the one hundred forty-four thousand sealed Jews caught up to heaven at the beginning of the latter half of the tribulation. John sees them standing upon the heavenly mount Zion with Christ the Lamb. A tremendous choir is formed by the one hundred forty-four thousand. Accompanied by harps, their song is presented before the throne of God, the four living beings, and the twenty-four elders.

It is a song of redemption that only they know, for they are the first Israelites to become resurrected and glorified followers of Christ.

They proved their obedience and discipleship on earth during the early part of the tribulation, having separated themselves from the wickedness and idolatry around them. By profession and life, they proclaimed God's word when the whole world believed the devil's lie. Now that their earthly mission for Christ is finished, they sing of God's grace and their redemption by the blood of the Lamb.

Then John sees an angel flying through the heavens. *He is carrying the everlasting gospel to preach to those on earth.*

This gospel proclaims mercy in the midst of judgment. Because God is long-suffering and not willing that any should perish, He still pleads with rebellious mankind. If they have not heeded human evangelists—the one hundred forty-four thousand, or the two witnesses—He gives them yet another chance. An angel from heaven, seen and heard by all men, calls upon them to abandon worship of the beast and reverence God, giving Him glory, not the beast.

A second angel flies through the skies. He announces: *"Fallen, fallen is Babylon the great!* She who made all nations drink of the (maddening) wine of her passionate unchastity (idolatry)" (Rev. 14:8).

The "Babylon" named here is a literal city. It will be the capital of Antichrist before he enters Palestine to make the Jewish temple his headquarters during the last years of the age. But Babylon is also the symbol of the entire satanic world system. It consists of all that is false and evil, unregenerate humanity organized under ungodly principles, with Satan as its head.

A third angel follows the other two. This one shouts *a final warning.* Those in the kingdom of Antichrist who take the mark, name or number of the beast and worship him will seal their own doom, and be punished in eternal hell! They will have to drink of the fury of God, mixed undiluted in the cup of His wrath. Unutterable anguish and ceaseless torment await those who will not repent.

Certainly by this time, those who refuse to listen are absolutely without excuse and deserve their fate!

The angel then speaks words of encouragement to God's people. He tells them to endure patiently every trial and persecution, for they are His who keep God's commandments and retain their faith in Jesus.

At this point in the vision, John hears a voice from heaven saying to him: "Write this down: Blessed are those who die in the Lord from now on. Yes, says the Spirit, they shall rest from their labors, and their good deeds will follow them to heaven" (Rev. 14:13).

This is a special blessing pronounced upon those who refuse to take the mark of the beast or to worship him, and who therefore are killed as martyrs during the tribulation.

Then the scene changes. John says: "Again I looked, and lo, (I saw) a white cloud. Sitting on the cloud was One resembling a Son of man, with a crown of gold on His head, and a sharp scythe (sickle) in His hand" (Rev. 14:14).

Here the apostle views Jesus enthroned on a cloud. Its whiteness indicates purity, righteousness, and divine presence. The title "Son of man" is the one under which Christ deals with earth and its people. The golden crown proclaims His kingship. The sickle is the instrument used at harvest time.

An angel comes forth from the temple in heaven. He tells Christ, "Thrust in the sickle, for the time has come for You to reap. The harvest of the earth is ripe." The Lord Jesus casts His sickle down to the earth, and all the remaining saints are gathered in.

After that another angel comes from out of the temple. He also has a sharp sickle. Then the angel of the fire on God's altar, the fire of judgment, calls for the gathering of the wicked for the wine press of God's wrath.

"And (the grapes in) the wine press were trodden outside the city. Blood poured from the wine press, (reaching) as high as horses' bridles, for a distance of about two hundred miles" (Rev. 14:20).

This is a preview of the gathering of the nations at Armageddon. The assembly-point in the apocalyptic scene of the great Day of God Almighty is Armageddon, located north of the city of Jerusalem in the plains of Esdraelon. Here Christ will tread the wine press of the unmitigated wrath of God in the greatest battle of all time. So tremendous is to be the slaughter that blood will flow on this battlefield in a stream up to the horses' bridles for two hundred miles.

The crisis of all John's visions is drawing near. The enemies of Christ and His church—Satan and Antichrist's empire—have been shown in all their power and cruelty. Now there is to be pictured to John the final temporal judgments about to fall on that empire and on the entire world.

These are depicted in the vision of the seven vials or bowls.

The Seven Bowls

"Then I saw another wonder (sign, token, symbol) in heaven, great and marvelous (warning of events of ominous significance). There were seven angels bringing seven plagues (afflictions, calamities), which are the last. For with them, God's wrath (indignation) is completely expressed—reaches its climax and is ended" (Rev. 15:1).

To the seven angels are committed the seven last plagues.

These scourging punishments, when carried out, will bring to an end the venting of God's wrath upon the earth. He has given the people of the world chance after chance. Now there is to be swift judgment upon those who have rejected God's Lamb.

Just before that judgment commences, John is given a glimpse of the safety and blessedness of the people of God . . .

The apostle first beholds what seems to be "a sea of glass mingled with fire." This is the way the floor of the great throne room of the heavenly temple appears to him. It looks like transparent glass. The glory which proceeds out of the throne flashes upon it in a glittering display of brilliant light and color.

Standing beside this sea are all those who have been victorious over the beast Antichrist and his empire. They are holding harps suited to the heavenly worship of God. They are singing the song of Moses, and the song of the Lamb. These are anthems of triumph and victory—of praise to God for His deliverance, His holiness, and for the manifestation of His righteous deeds and sentences.

Then, for the second time, the temple in heaven is opened to John's gaze. *The final judgments* will originate from God's temple, because they are more severe than the earlier judgments which originated from His throne.

From out of the heavenly temple come the seven angels of the plagues. They are clothed in spotless white linen, with golden belts across their chests. One of the four living beings gives to each of these angels a golden vial, or bowl, containing the wrath of God.

"The sanctuary was filled with smoke from the glory (the radiance, the splendor) of God and from His might and power. And no one was able to go into the sanctuary until the seven plagues (afflictions, calamities) of the seven angels were ended" (Rev. 15:8).

The smoke is the result of the fire of God's wrath, for sin is fully ripe and must be judged without mercy. A great voice out of the temple tells the angels to go their ways and pour out the vials of wrath.

The first bowl is emptied upon the earth. All those who worship the beast and his image—and those who have taken his name or mark—break out in horrible, malignant sores.

The second bowl is poured into the sea. The Mediterranean becomes like the blood of a corpse. Every living thing that is in the sea dies.

The third bowl is emptied upon the rivers and springs of water. They turn into blood. As this is done, John hears the angel declare the justice of this plague. "Because these people have poured out the blood of Your people, O Lord—Your saints and Your prophets—now in turn You have given them blood to drink. Such is their due. They deserve it!"

Then a voice from the altar cries out, "Yes, Lord God Almighty, Your punishments are just and true." The altar adds its testimony. The prayers of the martyred saints, whose blood was poured out, now are answered.

The bowl of the fourth angel is emptied upon the sun, causing it to scorch humanity with fierce heat. The people burned by this fiery blast react by cursing the name of God. They do not repent of their sins. They refuse to amend their ways, or to give God glory.

The fifth angel pours out his bowl upon the throne of Antichrist. His kingdom is plunged into darkness. His subjects gnaw their tongues in torment from their pains and sores. But they do not repent of their wicked deeds. Instead they blaspheme God and blame Him for all their anguish.

The sixth angel empties his bowl upon the great river Euphrates, and it dries up. This makes ready a road for "the kings of the east." The latter phrase is a reference to rulers of the nations east of the Euphrates. By this plague, they are enabled to march their armies westward without hindrance. They will come into Palestine to cooperate with Antichrist at Armageddon.

Have you ever wondered what means Satan could use to persuade all the nations of the earth to gather together to fight in one supreme battle against Israel? A brief vision, given to John between the sixth and seventh vials, explains it.

"I saw three loathsome spirits like frogs, (leaping) from the mouth of the dragon, and from the mouth of the beast, and from the mouth of the false prophet.

"For really they are the spirits of demons that perform signs (wonders, miracles). And they go forth to the rulers and leaders all over the world, to gather them together for war on the great day of God the Almighty" (Rev. 16:13, 14).

This makes it clear how the kings of the earth not under Antichrist will be induced to join him. Lying propaganda and the working of miracles by demon power will lure them. *Unclean spirits are going to inspire ambassadors and convince political leaders of other nations that their future depends on world cooperation.*

At this point in the vision John hears Christ Himself interject these words: "Lo, I will come as unexpectedly as a thief! Blessed are those who are waiting for Me, who keep their robes in readiness and will not need to walk naked and ashamed" (Rev. 16:15).

Satan is determined to stop Christ from taking over the earth at His second advent. Therefore he will muster all his forces in the area where he knows the Lord will return. All the armies of the world will be gathered together at a place called in Hebrew or Aramaic "Armageddon." This is an actual spot which may be found on any map of Palestine today.

The word "Armageddon" means "Hill of Megiddo." Megiddo is in the mountains of central Palestine, across the plain of Esdraelon from Nazareth. It is located in Israel, twenty miles southeast of Haifa and the promontory of Mount Carmel.

Many battles were fought here in Bible times, and throughout the ages. In the 1400's B.C. Thutmose III, one of the most brilliant rulers of the ancient Egyptian empire, said, "Megiddo is worth a thousand cities." In 1918 the British under General Allenby defeated the Turks at Armageddon. It lies at the entrance to a pass across the Carmel mountain range.

This is the place where the rulers of the world will gather to fight the last gigantic battle between good and evil, the battle to decide the sovereignty of the earth.

"Then the seventh angel emptied out his bowl into the air. A mighty voice came out of the sanctuary of heaven from the throne (of God), saying, It is done! (It is all over, it is accomplished, it has come!)" (Rev. 16:17).

With the pouring out of the seventh bowl, God declares that *"It is finished!"* An epoch of human history comes to an end.

Thunder crashes and rolls, lightning flashes. There is a tremendous earthquake of unprecedented magnitude. The city of Jerusalem splits into three sections. Cities around the world fall in heaps of rubble. Every island sinks into the sea, and no mountains can be found.

An incredible hailstorm follows, in which hailstones weighing between 50 and 100 pounds each fall from the skies on the people below. They curse God because the torture of that plague is so terrible.

These, then, are the seven last plagues brought by the angels:

1. Grievous sores on those who worship Antichrist.
2. Mediterranean Sea turns to blood.
3. Rivers and springs become blood.
4. Fiery heat from the sun scorches men.
5. Dense darkness upon Antichrist's kingdom.
6. Euphrates River dries up.
7. Enormous earthquake, followed by immense hailstones falling on the people.

At the end of the seventh plague, the wrath of God upon a Christ-rejecting world is complete.

The Seven Dooms

We come now to the next to last vision given to John. The mighty pageant showing things to come is nearing an end. In this vision seven dooms are shown. They are:

1. The doom of religious systems.
2. The doom of commercial systems.
3. The doom of political and military systems.
4. The doom of Antichrist and the false prophet.
5. The doom of the nations.
6. The doom of Satan.
7. The doom of the lost.

"One of the seven angels who had the seven bowls then came and spoke to me, saying, Come with me! I will show you the doom (sentence, judgment) of the great harlot (idolatress) who is seated on many waters:

"(She) with whom the rulers of the earth have joined in prostitution (idolatry), and with the wine of whose immorality (idolatry) the inhabitants of the earth have become intoxicated" (Rev. 17:1, 2).

In the power of the Spirit, John is taken by the angel into a desert wilderness. There he sees a woman seated on a scarlet beast. The beast is covered with blasphemous titles. It has seven heads and ten horns. The woman is robed in purple and scarlet, and bedecked with gold, precious stones and pearls. She holds in her hand a golden goblet full of obscenities.

On her forehead is inscribed a name, a mystery: "BABYLON THE GREAT, THE MOTHER OF HARLOTS AND ABOMINATIONS OF THE EARTH."

The woman is drunk—drunk with the blood of the saints and with the blood of the martyrs who witnessed for Jesus. As John looks at her, he is utterly amazed and horrified.

"Why are you so surprised?" the angel asks. "I'll tell you who she is, and what the animal she is riding represents."

There follows a lengthy explanation. The animal symbolizes the political kingdoms of the world during the times of the Gentiles. Five of these empires have fallen—the Egyptian, Assyrian, Babylonian, Medo-Persian, and Grecian. The sixth, the old Roman empire, also fell; but it will be revived in the end time to become the seventh kingdom. These are the seven heads on the animal.

The beast's ten horns are the ten powers which comprise the empire ruled by Antichrist. The angel informs John that this kingdom ascends from the bottomless pit, and it will go into perdition. But it causes great wonder and deception among all the inhabitants of the earth, those whose names are not recorded in the Book of Life.

The prostitute sitting upon the scarlet beast vividly symbolizes the corrupt religions of these kingdoms. From their inception in ancient Babylon of Nimrod's time, to apostate Christendom of the last days, all of the false religions have been upheld by political systems. That is why the harlot is pictured riding the animal.

She denotes ecclesiastical organizations and institutions which have compromised truth for worldly power. *Instead of teaching salvation, these religions have sought to solve the problems of the world by political, economic, and social action.* The harlot has intoxicated men by doctrines and practices which violate the word of God.

Having great prestige and power, her influence over the nations has been through religion. All kinds of earthly adornments bedeck her, for she has made herself rich by duping men.

The golden goblet full of obscenities which she holds in her hand depicts her gross infidelity to God and His word. She is drunken with the blood of God's people of all ages. In the end time persecution she participates with Antichrist in the wholesale murder of the true followers of Jesus.

The angel goes on to say that the ten-kingdom federation comprising Antichrist's empire has one common purpose. That is why they will deliver their power and strength to Antichrist for the last part of the tribulation.

"They will wage war against the Lamb, and the Lamb will triumph over them. For He is Lord of lords and King of kings. And those with Him and on His side are chosen and called (elected) and loyal and faithful followers" (Rev. 17:14).

The angel further explains that the waters on which John first saw the harlot sitting represent multitudes of races and nations. When those within the ten kingdoms under Antichrist are commanded to worship him, they turn against their own religious systems. In their rejection of the harlot, they burn her great cathedrals and all her royal trappings. *She is to be utterly destroyed* by men whom she long has dominated.

"For God will put a plan into their minds," states the angel, "a plan that will carry out His purposes." Men mutually agree to worship the beast, and thus they themselves execute the judgment of God upon their former religions.

John has seen the doom of man-made religious systems, represented by Mystery Babylon. Next he is to witness the doom of man's commercial systems, symbolized by the literal city of Babylon. It also is pictured as an harlot. And it too is destined for destruction.

"Then I saw another angel descending from heaven, possessing great authority. The earth was illuminated with his radiance and splendor.

"And he shouted with a mighty voice, She is fallen! Mighty Babylon is fallen! She has become a resort and dwelling place for demons, a dungeon haunted by every loathsome spirit, an abode for every filthy and detestable bird" (Rev. 18:1, 2).

Babylon, under Antichrist, will become the center of demon operations. This is the chief cause of her fall. We remember that in one of the visions of Zechariah, a woman representing wickedness was taken in a bushel basket to Babylon (Zech. 5:5–11). We touched then upon the rebuilding of the city as a great religious and commercial metropolis in the last days.

All the nations of the world will join with her in committing idolatry. The businessmen of the earth will become rich with the wealth of her excessive luxury and wantonness. Antichrist is to control the immense riches of the East. Commerce will flourish, and the people will live in material abundance.

But suddenly God is going to say, "Enough!"

John hears a voice from heaven calling: "Come away from her, My people. Do not take part in her sins, or you will be punished with her. For her sins are piled as high as heaven, and the Lord is ready to judge her for her crimes."

God's people are commanded to come out of Babylon, just as Jesus warned them to flee from Jerusalem. The voice goes on to say that Babylon will be given double penalty for all her evil deeds. She brewed many a cup of woe for others. Twice as much will be mixed for her.

To the degree that she glorified herself and reveled in luxury —to that extent will be matched torments and sorrows. In one day she will face death, mourning, famine, and utter destruction by fire. For mighty is the Lord God who judges her.

"The rulers and leaders of the earth, who joined her in her immorality (idolatry) and luxuriated with her, will weep and beat their breasts and lament over her when they see the smoke of her conflagration.

"They will stand a long way off, in terror of her torment. They will cry, Woe and alas! The great city! The mighty city,

Babylon! In one single hour now your doom (judgment) has over-taken you!" (Rev. 18:9, 10).

No wonder earth's businessmen will weep and grieve over her —she bought so much of their goods! She was their biggest cus-tomer for gold and silver, precious stones, pearls, finest linens, purple silks and scarlet. Her purchases included every kind of perfumed wood, ivory goods, expensive wooden carvings, as well as brass, iron and marble. She bought spices, perfumes and incense, ointment and frankincense, wine, olive oil, fine flour and wheat. She trafficked in cattle, sheep, horses, chariots, and slaves—and even the souls of men.

The kings of the earth freely and gladly destroyed Mystery Babylon without shedding a tear. But they will lament bitterly over the destruction of literal Babylon. They did not become rich through religious systems (Mystery Babylon). Rather, such systems became rich through them. Religion can go with no regret. When it comes to the loss of money—that brings much weeping and wailing!

Business tycoons will cry aloud, "Alas, that great city, so beau-tiful! She was like a woman clothed in finest purple and scarlet linens, decked out with gold and precious stones and pearls!" Shipping magnates, who also grew rich from the commercial system, will weep and grieve over the fact that in a single hour all that wealth is made desolate.

But in heaven just the opposite reaction takes place.

The angels, the holy prophets and apostles, and the saints of God all rejoice over the fate of Babylon. At last God has ex-ecuted vengeance upon her. Those in heaven know that God alone is the real destroyer of the satanic world system, both ec-clesiastical and commercial, no matter what instruments He chooses to employ. And so they rejoice.

In the Book of Revelation heaven is told to rejoice three times. Initially, when Satan is cast out of the heavenlies. The second time, when the city of Babylon is destroyed. And thirdly, when the marriage of the Lamb is come and His wife is made ready.

"Then a single powerful angel took up a boulder like a great millstone. He flung it into the sea, crying, With such violence shall Babylon the great city be hurled down to destruction, and shall never again be found" (Rev. 18:21).

John has viewed the doom of Mystery Babylon, man's religious systems. He has witnessed the doom of literal Babylon, man's commercial systems. Next he is to be shown the doom of the political and military systems. The destruction of the latter will take place at the second advent of Christ. This great happening is now going to be revealed in vision form.

The return of the Lord Jesus Christ to this earth—the most stupendous event of all time—is preceded by a few brief scenes in heaven.

First, John hears a vast crowd in heaven shouting "Hallelujah! Salvation and glory and honor and power belong to our God! The wicked city which corrupted the earth and shed the blood of God's servants has been judged. Babylon will never be restored again. Praise the Lord!"

The living beings, and the twenty-four elders, join in the worship saying, "Amen. Hallelujah!" A voice from the throne calls for praise from all God's servants. In reply comes the sound of an immense multitude . . .

Once before John heard universal praise and adoration. It occurred in the vision of the seven seals, when Christ the Lamb stepped forward to take the scroll from the right hand of God. At that time every creature in heaven, on earth, and under the earth proclaimed glory to God and to the Lamb for His worthiness.

This time—like the waves of a hundred oceans crashing on the shore, and as the mighty rolling of great thunder in the sky—all the angels in heaven, and all the redeemed of all ages, speak in magnificent chorus:

"Hallelujah, for the Lord God omnipotent reigneth!"

What a glorious way to announce that which is to come—the marriage of the Lamb. An outward, public consummation of the inner spiritual union between Christ and His church is about to take place. The bride—composed of all those who will live in the holy city, the heavenly new Jerusalem—has made herself ready.

She is dressed in spotless white, robed in purity and righteousness. Her wedding gown has graciously been given to her by the Lord Jesus. The true church, the radiant bride of Christ, is a sharp contrast to the religious systems of man—the harlot arrayed in the red garments of sin.

The herald angel declares: "Blessed are they which are called unto the marriage supper of the Lamb!" He instructs John to write this sentence down, for he adds that God Himself has stated it.

Overcome with wonder and joy, John falls down to worship the angel. But the angel checks him, saying: "You must not do that! I am (only) another servant with you and your brethren who have (accepted and hold) the testimony borne by Jesus.

"Worship God! For the substance (essence) of the truth revealed by Jesus is the spirit of all prophecy—the vital breath, the inspiration of all inspired preaching and interpretation of the divine will and purpose (including both mine and yours)" (Rev. 19:10).

After this John sees heaven opened. Not just a door open, or even the temple in heaven opened—but all heaven opens! The long-awaited moment has arrived! Christ is about to come forth with all His saints and angels to claim His kingship over the earth.

John's attention is riveted on the triumphant figure as He appears seated upon a white horse. Here the Lord Jesus is called *"Faithful and True."* Always faithful to the will of God, never deviating from it, He is coming now to judge the world, and to wage war in holy righteousness.

His eyes are like flames, signifying the omniscient insight of His judgment. On His head are many crowns, showing Him to be King of kings with absolute authority. A name is written on His forehead, and only He knows its meaning.

Christ the Mighty Warrior is clothed with garments dipped in blood. The blood is not His, for that was shed at Calvary. This is the blood of His enemies, spilt at Armageddon when He treads the great wine press of the fierceness and wrath of Almighty God. In that day of His vengeance, there will take place the most colossal destruction that earth has ever seen or ever will see.

The title by which He is called is *"The Word of God."* This proclaims Him as God and Creator, as well as Redeemer.

Following Him are the armies of heaven, dressed in fine linen, clean and white, and riding white horses. In Christ's mouth He holds a sharp sword to strike down the nations. This sword is the omnipotent word of God that spoke the universe into existence. It—the word and the will of God—slays His enemies, not a literal sword. Jesus shall rule the nations peacefully. But those who are rebellious will find that rule a rod of iron, unflinchingly severe against sin.

On Christ's robe and on His thigh is written a third title: "KING OF KINGS AND LORD OF LORDS." What a portrait of indisputable royal sovereignty! Absolute universal dominion is His.

The greatness of the coming victory is foretold by the scene which next meets John's eyes:

"Then I saw a single angel stationed in the sun's light. With a mighty voice he shouted to all the birds that fly across the sky, Come, gather yourselves together for the great supper of God.

"There you may feast on the flesh of rulers, the flesh of generals and captains, the flesh of powerful and mighty men, the flesh of horses and their riders, and the flesh of all humanity, both free and slave, both small and great!" (Rev. 19:17, 18).

This cry to the birds of prey is to eat the flesh of the armies slain at Armageddon. Here we have another startling contrast—the marriage supper of the Lamb in heaven, and the supper of the great God on earth. What a difference! Yet both suppers are prepared by God. Never forget that God who is love, is also God of justice and God of wrath.

All the kings, captains, mighty men and their deluded followers will be slain—killed by the sword that issues from the mouth of Him who is mounted on the white horse. The catastrophe and carnage of Armageddon are the results simply of a word from the lips of the returning Christ! Vultures will gorge themselves on the flesh of the dead bodies of earth's great politicians, their military leaders, and those accompanying them.

This marks the doom of the political and military systems of man.

As for the doom of the beast Antichrist, and the false prophet —John views that also.

In the battle of Armageddon, Antichrist has mobilized all nations of his empire against Israel. It is the final conflict between Satan and Christ, between the forces of evil and the forces of righteousness. Though the combat has long existed, it comes to a speedy end.

In one day there is total defeat of the mighty satanic armies! All except one-sixth of them are destroyed. The multitude of their carcasses provides food for the fowls of the air and the beasts of the field for seven months. That is how long it will take Israel to bury the dead after Armageddon.

"And the beast was seized and overpowered. With him was the false prophet, who in his presence had worked wonders and performed miracles. By these he led astray those who had accepted or permitted to be placed upon them the stamp (mark) of the beast, and those who paid homage and gave divine honors to his statue. Both of the two were hurled alive into the fiery lake that burns and blazes with brimstone" (Rev. 19:20).

Antichrist and his religious leader are the first human beings to be cast into the lake of fire. We recall that in one of Daniel's visions he described seeing this happen to "the little horn that spoke great things." The prophet said, "I beheld even till the beast was slain, and his body destroyed, and given to the burning flame" (Dan. 7:11).

The apostle Paul confirmed that this would be the end of Antichrist—whom he called "that man of sin, the son of perdition, the wicked one." Paul said, "The Lord shall consume him with the spirit of his mouth, and shall destroy him with the brightness of his coming" (2 Thess. 2:3, 8, KJV). "For the Lord Jesus shall be revealed . . . in flaming fire taking vengeance on them that know not God, and that obey not the gospel of our Lord Jesus Christ" (2 Thess. 1:7, 8, KJV).

Jesus Himself will make an end of Antichrist and his prophet.
He will cast them alive into the lake of fire.

Have you ever wondered about this "lake of fire"? Is the
term merely descriptive symbolism of a state of mental anguish,
or is it a real place?

The lake of fire is more than a metaphorical expression. It
refers to eternal hell—a definite, literal place where torment
never ceases, and from whence none return. Another name for it
is *"gehenna."* The Greek and Aramaic word "gehenna" is
translated in the New Testament as *"hell."* Its derivation is
from the Hebrew "ge-hinnom," the valley of Hinnom. The latter
is an actual location just outside Jerusalem.

In the days of the kings of Israel, the ungodly king Ahaz in
the 700's B.C. burned incense in this valley. He also burned
his children in the fire there, practicing the abominations of the
heathen. Child sacrifice was offered to the pagan god Molech.
Manasseh, another wicked king—who was, in fact, the grandson
of Ahaz—caused his children "to pass through the fire" in the
same valley.

The Lord, speaking through the prophet Jeremiah, mentioned
this valley when He said: "The people of Judah have sinned before My very eyes . . . They have built the altar called Topheth
in the valley of Ben-Hinnom, and there they burn to death their
little sons and daughters in the fire as sacrifices to their gods
—a deed so horrible I've never even thought of it, let alone
commanded it to be done!" (Jer. 7:30, 31, LP).

In Jesus' day, the rubbish and garbage of Jerusalem was
dumped in the valley of Hinnom, and perpetual fires were kept
burning there. The flames destroyed all refuse and purified the
air to prevent pestilence. Whenever Jesus spoke of hell, the
place of final punishment, He always used the word "gehenna."
It is an apt comparison.

Many people ridicule the idea that hell is fire and brimstone.
"A loving God would never cast anyone into hell," they say.
"There is nothing to fear in God." How often have you heard
someone make such a pronouncement? Yet the exact opposite of
this is what Jesus taught!

He said that hell is indeed fire—"everlasting fire," a "furnace of fire" He called it. Several times He referred to "hell fire" and "the damnation of hell." Five times in one passage (Mk. 9:43–48) our Lord spoke of hell as "the fire that shall never be quenched." Three of those five times He added that hell is a place "where the worm never dies."

Furthermore, Jesus said that a person's "whole body can be cast into hell (Gehenna)" (Matt. 5:29, 30). As for fear, He warned the multitude that they *should* fear God. "Fear Him who . . . has power to hurl into hell (Gehenna); yes, I say to you, fear Him!" (Lk. 12:5).

There is no question about it—Jesus pictured hell as an actual region of unquenchable or eternal fire. "Hell (everlasting fire) was prepared for the devil and his angels," Christ said. But He Himself will send a great number of human beings there! (Matt. 25:41).

This, then, is the place of the Book of Revelation calls "the lake of fire and brimstone." A fitting end it is for Antichrist and the false prophet—the two beasts who served and were empowered by the devil. Paul said of them: "whose coming is after the workings of Satan, with all power and signs and lying wonders, and with all deceivableness of unrighteousness" (2 Thess. 2:9, 10, KJV).

Four of the seven dooms have been shown to John in this vision. The fifth doom is that of the living nations. The sixth discloses the doom of the devil. Since these dooms are intertwined in the scripture, we will deal with them together.

"Then I saw an angel descending from heaven. He was holding the key of the abyss—the bottomless pit. A great chain was in his hand.

"And he gripped and overpowered the dragon, that old serpent of primeval times, who is the devil and Satan, and (securely) bound him for a thousand years.

"Then he hurled him into the abyss—the bottomless pit. He closed it and sealed it above him, so that he should no longer lead astray and deceive and seduce the nations, until the thousand years were at an end. After that he must be liberated for a short time" (Rev. 20:1–3).

The bottomless pit, the abyss, is located in the lowest depths of the underworld. It is the abode of demons and evil spirits. It is not the same place as Gehenna, hell, or the lake of fire.

The angel from heaven is the agent of God's authority over the underworld. After he subdues Satan, he binds him with a great chain and confines him in a prison. *The abyss is to be sealed over for a thousand years.* Satan will be kept here so that he cannot deceive the nations during that time. Afterward he must be loosed for a little while.

The binding of Satan, and the reign of the saints with Christ on the earth—both for one thousand years—is known as *"the millennium."* It is the last dispensation for man before the final removal of the curse. The millennium is called in scripture: "the world to come," "the kingdom of heaven," "the dispensation of the fulness of times," "the regeneration," and "the times of the restitution of all things."

In John's vision he viewed the millennial saints and their thrones.

"Then I saw thrones, and sitting on them were those to whom authority to act as judges and pass sentence was entrusted.

"Also I saw the souls of those who had been slain with axes, (beheaded) for their witnessing to Jesus and (for preaching and testifying) for the word of God. They had refused to pay homage to the beast or his statue, and had not accepted his mark or permitted it to be stamped on their foreheads or on their hands.

"And they lived again, and ruled with Christ, the Messiah, a thousand years.

"The remainder of the dead were not restored to life again until the thousand years were completed. This is the first resurrection" (Rev. 20:4, 5).

All who have part in the first resurrection are called "blessed and holy." Over them the second death has no power. They will be ministers of God and of Christ, and will reign with Him a thousand years.

It is helpful to recognize that there are stages, or steps, in the first resurrection. As Paul put it: "In Christ shall all be made alive. *But every man in his own order:* Christ the firstfruits; afterward they that are Christ's at his coming" (I Cor. 15:22, 23, KJV).

The first stage was that of Jesus and the many saints who came out of their graves after His resurrection. These risen saints went into the holy city and appeared to many. They were "the firstfruits."

We are not told the exact order to be observed regarding the rest of the redeemed. But they will all be resurrected in their turn—the Old Testament saints, the New Testament saints, and the tribulation martyrs. The rapture of the church occurs at the beginning of the tribulation period. When Jesus comes for His own, and they are caught up to meet Him in the air, everyone in Christ—dead or alive—will be translated and taken to heaven, the dead in Christ rising first.

All the saints will be at the marriage supper of the Lamb. They will all come back with Christ at His second advent, when He returns to earth to set up His kingdom.

The second resurrection takes place one thousand years after the first one. This is the resurrection of the wicked dead of all ages. They are to be judged at the great white throne judgment. We will discuss this at length when we come to the final doom —that of the wicked, the lost.

The Bible clearly teaches that there will be two resurrections, a thousand years apart. The only people who will never be resurrected are those living in the nations at the time of Christ's second advent, and those still living at the end of His millennial reign. They will not be resurrected. Some of them will continue to live as natural people from the tribulation period through the millennium, and then on into the new earth. The others will meet their "doom" either at the beginning of the millennium, or at the end of it.

The doom of the living nations which is decreed at the beginning of that period occurs at the "Judgment of the Nations." This will happen immediately after Christ returns to earth with His saints. The Lord Jesus spoke very plainly of this at the conclusion of His great prophetic discourse on the mount of Olives. He told the disciples:

"When the Son of man comes in His glory (His majesty and splendor), and all the holy angels with Him, then He will sit on the throne of His glory.

"All nations shall be gathered before Him, and He will separate them (the people) from one another as a shepherd separates his sheep from the goats" (Matt. 25: 31, 32).

What is the basis of this judgment of the Gentile nations? Do you know?

The Lord plainly states that His judgment is based on how the people in those nations have treated "My brethren"—Israel, the Jews. The sheep are those individuals who have received the gospel of the kingdom and treated kindly the believing remnant of Jews. The goats are those who have rejected the gospel of the kingdom and have persecuted the Jewish remnant.

What is the outcome of the judgment?

Simply this: the King (Christ) permits the "sheep," the worthy individuals, to enter the millennial kingdom. The "goats," the unworthy ones, are sent into everlasting punishment. This consignment to hell is the first part of the doom of the nations.

In connection with this particular section of scripture from the 25th chapter of Matthew, it is this writer's firm conviction that it is the most misunderstood, misapplied, and wrongly interpreted passage in the entire Bible!

Modernists and liberals of all kinds, including their theologians, and all the false cults and nominal Christians, invariably refer to it. They use it in an attempt to support the idea that humanitarian acts are the measure of a Christian. How they love to quote Jesus' words: "Inasmuch as you have fed the hungry, clothed the naked, housed the stranger, visited prisoners, and cared for the sick, you have done it unto me."

Their glib interpretation of this is that God's terms are fully met, and heaven gained, by deeds of human benevolence. Of course *the true Biblical teaching is that we come to God only by accepting the Lord Jesus Christ as personal Saviour, and having our sins forgiven and cleansed by His atoning blood.*

The modernists, liberals, and metaphysical teachers completely ignore—if indeed they even comprehend—the context of the scripture. It plainly refers to Christ's second coming—

an event which they do not believe in. Christ's opening words positively identify it as the time when He will return in glory, with the angels and saints, and He will sit upon His throne of judgment.

The people He is judging are *not* Christians. All true Christians have already been judged, and have been in heaven with their Lord. Now they have come back to earth with Him. These subjects of judgment are the nations (Gentiles) who are on the earth at that time, and who have been involved with Israel.

In this scripture Jesus is called both "King" and "Lord." These are titles which false teachers do not give Him. Furthermore, in the passage Christ Himself sends the "goats" into everlasting punishment—a place which those who quote His preceding words do not believe exists. The "sheep" go into life eternal.

These humanitarians are not of His sheep, so no wonder they do not hear what the Good Shepherd is really saying. However, it behooves all of us to study carefully the Word of God, rightly interpreting it. Otherwise, our ignorance of the Bible as a whole may cause us to be taken in by those who partially quote scripture, but who in reality deny the vital message, the life-giving truths it teaches.

Getting back to the seven dooms of John's vision . . .

We have seen how man's religious, commercial, and political systems have all been destroyed. The battle of Armageddon is ended, Antichrist and the false prophet have been cast into the lake of fire. Satan has been bound in the bottomless pit, and those who persecuted Israel have been judged and have been sent into eternal hell.

The Lord Jesus Christ is now ready to rule a literal, earthly kingdom.

Many Christians have believed that at the rapture of the church, those who are born-again believers in Christ will be taken to heaven, there to dwell with the Lord forever. It is true that the entire body of Christ is promised a citizenship in heaven. And it is in heaven where the resurrected and glorified saints will be with Christ during the tribulation period. But they will accompany Him back to earth at Armageddon, and will reign on earth with Him in some capacity as kings and priests.

The real residence of the saints will still be the new Jerusalem in heaven. But during the millennium, they will be able to go back and forth between heaven and earth just as Jesus did in the forty days after His resurrection.

Who are the subjects over whom the resurrected saints will rule? They are the generations of naturally born people who are citizens of the millennial kingdom. The children of those won to Christ during the tribulation who survive the persecution enter the millennium with non-resurrected bodies able to reproduce.

In the Old Testament each of the four major prophets, and all but one of the twelve minor prophets, wrote about the coming millennial kingdom. In particular Isaiah, Ezekiel, and Zechariah prophesied at length and in great detail of conditions in Palestine during Christ's one thousand year reign on this earth.

Christ's government will not be a democratic one. It will be theocratic. This means that the multitude of natural people alive on earth at that time, and all during the millennium, will be governed by the immediate direction of God. The resurrected saints, as God's representatives, will be given power over the nations.

David is to reign as king over Israel. The apostles are to rule over one tribe each. Israel will be a saved, united people, and the chief of nations. And Christ will be over all, ruling "with a rod of iron."

Jerusalem is to be the capital of His world-wide kingdom. Every nation will be required to send representatives to the holy city once a year to acknowledge the Lord Jesus. The beautiful future temple at Jerusalem will be His dwelling place, and the place of His throne.

All the former sacrifices, feasts and rituals of temple worship will be continued as an eternal memorial of what they typified before Christ fulfilled them. Priests and Levites will serve in the temple.

Israel is to be given the entire "promised land." The Gentile countries will be located in that part of the earth God originally gave to them. This division was made with the three sons of Noah. There will be universal civil and religious laws for all nations.

One of the most thrilling aspects of the millennium is that the earth will be full of the knowledge of the Lord, as the waters cover the sea. For the glory of God shall be made manifest, and the Holy Spirit will be poured out upon all flesh. There is to be a pure universal religion, with salvation in its fulness available to all.

Peace, prosperity, and healing will also be universal. No more war, poverty, or sickness. No blindness, deafness, or crippling disease will afflict anyone. Everything will be restored the way it was before sin entered the world.

Animal natures are to be tame and gentle, as before the fall. Deserts will blossom again as a rose. Fruitful seasons will be enjoyed without interruption. Material blessings will abound. Waste places of the earth shall be restored to usefulness, and great highways will cover the earth.

A river of life-giving water is going to flow out from under the threshold of the temple in Jerusalem. It will divide at some point south of the city and become two rivers. One river will flow into the Dead Sea and heal it, so that it will be full of fish. The other river will flow into the Mediterranean.

Along the banks of the river will grow evergreen trees. Fruit from the trees is to preserve life and health, and the leaves of the trees are for medicine. Elements in the leaves no doubt will renew the body cells and cause longevity, as well as do away with sickness.

All men are to have their own homes and other property. But the day of mortgages, credits, debts, and other bondages of the present economy will be a thing of the past. Human life is to be prolonged indefinitely, although some may die as youths at the age of one hundred (Isa. 65:20). Children will continue to be born in the normal increase of mankind.

No favoritism will be shown because of family, church, political or financial connections. Perfect justice will be meted out to all alike, for perfect righteousness prevails. Those who do not obey the law will be dealt with according to it.

But when the thousand years of the millennium are ended, Satan is loosed out of his prison, and the picture immediately changes!

Satan brings with him his fallen angels and demons. They go throughout the earth, once more to deceive the nations. Flocking to their banner will be all those who have not liked the reign of Christ and His strict rule of righteousness, but who could do nothing about it until now. They gave external obedience to Him, while inwardly they were filled with rebellion and enmity.

Satan and his hordes muster these people for battle. How many human beings do you think will unite with the demonic forces rebelling against God? Believe it or not—their number is as the sand of the sea!

What a shocking realization!

Remember that these people have been living under ideal conditions for one thousand years. They have not even needed faith to believe in Christ, for every eye has seen Him personally and visibly. Everyone has KNOWN that He is King of kings and Lord of lords. Yet, even then the majority of human beings do not want Him to reign over them!

They don't WANT righteousness and holiness. They don't WANT peace and perfect justice. They prefer the devil to Christ! And as soon as the opportunity comes to align themselves with Satan, they do so.

This vast host from all parts of the earth, and from the underworld, will mobilize in the land north of Palestine. In one last assault on God's people, they are going to descend upon unarmed Jerusalem, surrounding the beloved city on every side.

But suddenly fire from God in heaven will flash down on the attacking armies and totally consume them!

Ironically, Satan's final act will be a service to the Lord. For the devil will gather together every rebel on the face of the earth, and every demon under the earth—making it easy for God to get rid of them all in one huge bonfire!

This completes the doom of the nations.

As for the devil who led them astray, and whom they chose to follow, he will be thrown into the lake of fire and brimstone. There, the Bible says, the beast and the false prophet *"are."* These two were cast into this lake one thousand years before, and they are still there. This proves that hell and eternal torment are realities. If one's soul cannot burn up in a thousand years, it will never do so. The scripture tells us that they will be tormented day and night for ever and ever—throughout the ages of eternity.

And so Satan's doom is the lake of fire, the place of eternal punishment which Jesus said was "prepared for the devil and his angels."

With him are those from the nations who were sent there by Christ at the beginning of the millennium. Also with Satan are those who rebelled against the Lord Jesus at the conclusion of His thousand year reign.

The final doom in John's vision is that of the wicked, the lost. This takes place at the end of the millennium, when the second resurrection occurs.

Jesus spoke very plainly of the two resurrections when He said: "The hour is coming in which all that are in the graves shall hear my voice, and shall come forth; they that have done good, unto the resurrection of life [the first resurrection]; and they that have done evil, unto the resurrection of damnation [the second resurrection]" (John 5:28, 29, KJV).

The prophet Daniel also referred to the two resurrections. He quoted the words of the angel Gabriel: "Many of them that sleep in the dust of the earth shall awake, some to everlasting life, and some to shame and everlasting contempt" (Dan. 12:2, KJV).

John's visions have made it clear that these resurrections are separated by a thousand years. *With the second resurrection comes the last judgment.*

"Then I saw a great white throne, and the One who was seated upon it. From His presence and from the sight of His face earth and sky fled away, and no place was found for them" (Rev. 20:11).

This is a real throne, but it is not the heavenly throne of God which has been glimpsed several times previously. Its whiteness indicates absolute purity and righteousness of judgment. A literal, visible, and personal trial will take place in God's court, with Christ Himself presiding. God the Father has committed all judgment to the Son, and given Him authority to execute it.

The glory and purity of the presence of Christ and the sight of His face is so awesome that earth and the heavens alike tremble and shake as if they were passing away.

"I (also) saw the dead, great and small. They stood before the throne, and the books were opened. Then another book was opened, which is (the Book) of Life. And the dead were judged (sentenced) by what they had done (their whole way of feeling and acting, their aims and endeavors), in accordance with what was recorded in the books" (Rev. 20:12).

This judgment concerns only the wicked dead—the unsaved, the lost, those who were both physically and spiritually dead.

The saved, those "in Christ," have long ago been judged. After the rapture, they appeared before the judgment seat of Christ in heaven to receive reward, or loss of reward, according to the deeds done in the body (2 Cor. 5:10, also Rom. 14:10, 12). Israel was judged during the tribulation. The nations were judged—part of them at the beginning of the millennium when Christ came in glory to set up His kingdom, and the rest of the nations were judged at the end of that reign.

Now the second resurrection—that of the unsaved dead—has taken place. Judgment Day has come for them.

Standing before the throne are all the lost souls, "the small and the great," no matter what their position on earth may have been. Each of them must appear alone before Christ—face to face—to be sentenced according to their works. The purpose of this judgment is to give every man a formal examination before his eternal sentencing, and to mete out the degree of punishment.

"The books were opened . . ."

God keeps more than one book, but He definitely registers all who are born into the human race. The experiences, motivations, and deeds of every man are recorded with divine accuracy. At the judgment, these books are opened.

"Another book was opened, which is the Book of Life." This book is the register of the saved. None of those who stand before the great white throne judgment seat have their names written therein. They did not accept God's salvation in Christ Jesus, and therefore cannot claim forgiveness on any basis.

They are sentenced strictly according to their works. Their guilt or innocence is not the question. All of them are already condemned, for they "did not believe in the name of the only begotten Son of God." The point of this judgment is to determine the degree of their punishment, and to pronounce the sentence.

"The sea delivered up the dead who were in it. Death and Hades (the state of death or disembodied existence) surrendered the dead in them. And all were tried, and their cases determined by what they had done—according to their motives, aims and works.

"Then death and Hades were thrown into the lake of fire. This is the second death, the lake of fire" (Rev. 20:13, 14).

Death in the scripture never means annihilation or extinction of being. Death always means separation from the purpose for which something was created. The spirit and soul of man are indestructible, and will continue in consciousness whether in heaven or hell.

Physical death is only the separation of the spirit and soul from the body. Spiritual death is separation from God because of sin. One can be "dead in trespasses and sins" and still physically alive. But the second death is eternal separation from God. Man chooses this by his rejection of everlasting spiritual life, which is to be found only in Christ Jesus.

And so the last enemy to be destroyed is death. Along with Hades, the realm of the spiritually dead, death is cast into the lake of fire. *Here all evil will be eternally isolated from God and His people.*

"And if anyone's (name) was not found recorded in the Book of Life, he was hurled into the lake of fire" (Rev. 20:15).

The final doom—that of the wicked dead—is ended.

The New Heaven and the New Earth

John's closing vision is the most magnificent and glorious of all the dreams and visions in the Bible. In it he views new heavens and a new earth, for the former ones have passed away.

In 2 Peter 3:7 we read that "the present heavens and earth have been stored up (reserved) for fire, being kept until the day of judgment and destruction of the ungodly people."

Fire will renovate the earth. The heavens shall pass away with a thunderous crash, and the material elements of the universe will be dissolved with fervent heat. The ground and the works of man that are upon it will be burned up.

This does not mean annihilation, any more than death or the lake of fire mean annihilation. It means that the earth will be changed, reconstructed. There will be new heavens and a new earth in which righteousness, freedom from sin, and restored fellowship with God is to abide. Peter tells us (2 Pet. 3:13) that this is according to the promise of God (made through the prophet Isaiah 65:17; 66:22).

John's vision of the new earth includes this interesting comment: "And there was no more sea." Apparently, large oceans will no longer exist in the eternal state of the earth. If so, all that space will be put to better use.

"And I saw the holy city, the new Jerusalem, descending out of heaven from God, arrayed like a bride beautified and adorned for her husband" (Rev. 21:2).

Here John beholds in all its beauty the holy city of the new Jerusalem. It is being moved from heaven to the renewed earth, there to become its capital. The entire city is adorned with jewels, as a bride is on her wedding day.

The city is called "holy" because nothing unclean has ever entered it. Moral and spiritual defilement are unknown within its walls. It is called "new" because of its eternal freshness and newness. It will never lose its luster. No aging, or rust, or weeds, or any other deterioration can mar its splendor. It is the Jerusalem that has been in heaven, not the one on earth. The historical Jerusalem passed away with the first earth.

Later the city is seen in detail by John. But first a voice from heaven declares what it means, and to whom its blissful glories belong.

"Then I heard a mighty voice from the throne. I perceived its distinct words, saying, Behold! The abode of God is with men. He will live (encamp, tent) among them, and they shall be His people. And God shall personally be with them and be their God" (Rev. 21:3).

God's dwelling with men is now possible, because Adam's curse has been removed. Satan has been judged, the wicked have been punished and banished to the lake of fire. All traces of sin are gone forever.

In the past, the presence of God with Israel was symbolized by the Shekinah glory. It overshadowed the mercy seat in the holy of holies in the tabernacle and in Solomon's temple. *In the future, when the final realization of His eternal plan for man is accomplished, God will actually dwell with the redeemed of all races.*

"God will wipe away every tear from their eyes. And death shall be no more. Neither shall there be anguish—sorrow and mourning—nor grief nor pain any more. For the old conditions, and the former order of things, have passed away" (Rev. 21:4).

God will take from man—and keep from him—all sorrow, pain, sickness, and death. These things belonged to earth under the curse.

John sees the One who is seated on the throne, Christ Himself. He hears Him say: "Behold, I make all things new." Then the Lord again instructs John to write down all that he has seen and heard, for what he has been shown is accurate and trustworthy.

"And He (further) said to me, It is done! I am the Alpha and the Omega, the Beginning and the End. To the thirsty I (Myself) will give water without price from the fountain (springs) of the water of Life.

"He who is victorious shall inherit all these things. I will be God to him, and he shall be My son" (Rev. 21:5, 6).

Those who thirst for righteousness shall receive the water of life from Jesus' own hand. Christ goes on to say that the city is not for those who are too cowardly to endure. Nor is it for unbelievers, or for those who practice idolatrous religions. Murderers, sexual perverts, lewd persons, those who by the use of drugs or spiritism have led people away from God, and all liars, will have their part in the lake of fire—which is eternal separation from God.

Then one of the seven angels, who had the seven vials filled with the final plagues, approaches John. He says: "Come with me and I will show you the bride, the Lamb's wife."

"In the Spirit he conveyed me away to a vast and lofty mountain. He exhibited to me the holy (hallowed, consecrated) city of Jerusalem descending out of heaven from God,

"Clothed in God's glory—in all its splendor and radiance. The luster of it resembled a rare and most precious jewel, like jasper, shining clear as crystal" (Rev. 21:10, 11).

The city is called the bride, the Lamb's wife, because it will be the eternal home of the redeemed of all ages. The church of the New Testament will not be the exclusive bride of Christ. The redeemed of the Old Testament will also be a part of the bride.

In the first part of this vision, John saw the wondrous city from a distance. Now it is shown in full view at close range. God's presence in the city causes it to shine with glory. It is bathed in radiance and unveiled majesty.

Great high walls around it denote safety and security for all its inhabitants. There are twelve large gates in the wall—three on each of the four sides of the city. An angel is stationed at every gate. The names of the twelve tribes of Israel are written on the gates. The walls have foundation stones, and on them are inscribed the names of the twelve apostles of the Lamb.

The angel holds in his hand a golden measuring stick. His measurements reveal the city to be 1500 miles in length, width, and height. This could mean it is tiered with several levels. The thickness of the wall is found to be 216 feet across.

The walls are built of jasper. The city itself is of pure gold, as clear and transparent as glass. The foundation stones are inlaid with precious jewels, twelve gems of unusual brillance and color. These are set in layers, one on top of another. Thus the encircling walls of the city give a rainbow or prism effect of magnificent beauty.

The twelve gates are built of pearls, each gate being made from one solid pearl. The main street of the city is of pure, transparent gold.

"I saw no temple in the city, for the Lord God Omnipotent (Himself) and the Lamb (Himself) are its temple.

"The city has no need of the sun nor of the moon to give light to it, for the splendor and radiance (glory) of God illuminate it, and the Lamb is its lamp" (Rev. 21:22, 23).

There is no visible temple in this city. Her spiritual perfection is such that no special sanctuary is necessary. Almighty God and Christ the Lamb dwell in the midst of the redeemed and may be worshiped in all places—not in just one building, as in the earthly temple at Jerusalem.

Neither is there any need for the sun or moon to light the city. The glory of God is the light. The best of everything that ever existed on earth in the way of art and science, music and literature, is found in the city. Its gates are never closed by day, and there is no night there.

All the talents and possibilities of man will have opportunity for development. There will be no hindering circumstances. Nothing can restrain the unfolding and expansion of life to its fullest powers and perfection. Everything unclean is shut out, and the inhabitants are totally free from sin's defilement and presence. The citizenry is composed only of those whose names are recorded in the Lamb's Book of Life.

John is then shown more of what it is like within the city . . .

The environment is perfect, far exceeding the garden of Eden paradise. The river of the water of life, pure and sparkling like crystal, comes out from the throne of God and of the Lamb. It is readily available to all, as it flows down the center of the main street of the city.

There are twelve great broad ways going through the twelve gates into all parts of the land. While there are no more large oceans covering so much of the earth, there will be many small seas, rivers and lakes. Throughout the holy city are innumerable fountains of the water of life.

On either side of the river grow rows of the tree of life. It bears twelve varieties of fruit; and there is a fresh crop monthly, not annually. The leaves of the tree will preserve eternal health for the nations. Naturally born people will live forever, not by virtue of a resurrection and a change from mortality to immortality, but because they will continually eat of the tree of life.

"There shall no longer exist there anything that is accursed—detestable, foul, offensive, impure, hateful or horrible. The throne of God and of the Lamb shall be in it. His servants shall worship Him—pay divine honors to Him and do Him holy service.

"*They shall see His face.* And His name shall be on their foreheads" (Rev. 22:3, 4).

What a promise! All creatures dwelling in the new Jerusalem on the earth will actually be able to look upon God's face and have intimate fellowship with Him. His name will be on their foreheads, identifying them as belonging to Him and as residents of the holy city. They shall reign and help God administer the affairs of the universe forever.

Then the angel attests to John the truth of these great predictions. He declares that the same God who inspired the prophets of old, and told them what the future holds, has sent His angel to reveal these prophecies to His new covenant servants. For they are soon to be fulfilled.

The voice of Christ breaks in to announce: *"Behold, I come quickly!"*

Then the angel repeats the blessing that was promised at the very beginning of the visions. Anyone who reads, hears, and keeps the words of this prophecy, as faithfully recorded by the apostle, will be blessed. John officially authenticates that he not only heard all these things, but saw them as well.

Realizing that his marvelous visions have come to an end, John falls down to worship the angel who showed them to him.

"But he said to me, Refrain!—You must not do that! I am (only) a fellow servant along with yourself and of your brethren the prophets, and of those who are mindful and practice (the truths contained in) the messages of this book. Worship God!

"And he (further) told me, Do not seal up the words of the prophecy of this book. Make no secret of them. For the time when things are brought to a crisis and the period of their fulfillment is near" (Rev. 22:9, 10).

In contrast to the command given the prophet Daniel at the conclusion of his visions to seal up the prophecies, the angel instructs John *not* to seal this prophecy. The reason given is that the approach of the end time is near. This prophecy is for immediate use. Hearing it will strengthen the believer's faith and exalt his hopes. Whatever trials and persecutions may intervene, the triumph of Christ is certain. And the ultimate destiny of the true Christian is glorious beyond imagination.

The angel then speaks about those who will not turn and repent. Because of the revelation which Christ has now completed, they will not—and cannot—have any greater power brought to bear on them before He comes again. There will be no second chance after death, or the Lord's return, to improve the life and character. The unjust person and the filthy person will still be unjust and filthy. The righteous person and the holy person will still be righteous and holy.

Once again Christ's own voice breaks in:

"Behold, I am coming soon. And I shall bring my wages and rewards with Me, to repay and render to each one just what his own actions and his own work merit.

"I am the Alpha and the Omega, the First and the Last (the Before all and at the End of all)" (Rev. 22:12, 13).

Christ, the creator of all things and Christ the finisher of all things, then affirms the happiness of those who are purified by faith in Him, who have washed their robes in His blood. They alone have the right to enter in through the gates of the eternal city, the new Jerusalem, and to eat the fruit from the tree of life. All unsaved people are debarred, and all evil persons are in hell.

"I, Jesus, have sent My messenger (angel) to you to witness and to give you assurance of these things for the churches (assemblies). I am (both) the Root (the Source) and the Offspring of David, the radiant and brilliant Morning Star" (Rev. 22:16).

Here Christ proclaims Himself the root and the offspring of David. As deity, the Lord was the source of David. In his human incarnation as the son of Mary, Jesus was David's descendant. By virtue of these facts, by promise and by prophecy, the crown of Israel is His.

Born "the King of the Jews," He died as "King of the Jews," and He will yet reign as King of the Jews. Indeed, He will be King over all the earth.

The Lord Jesus also calls Himself "the bright and morning star." Do you remember in our chapter "Strange Happenings in the Night" when the prophet Balaam fell into a trance while wide-awake? In one vision he saw the Messiah. As Balaam prophesied of Christ's coming, he called Him "a star out of Jacob" and "a sceptre out of Israel." Now Jesus confirms the title: "I am the bright Morning Star."

The Holy Spirit and the bride corroborate Christ's declaration by bidding Him, "Come!" Jesus then invites everyone who is listening to say, "Come!" To those who feel in their souls a thirst which nothing in this world can quench, Christ says:

"Let every one come who is thirsty (who is painfully conscious of his need of those things by which the soul is refreshed, supported and strengthened). And whoever (earnestly) desires to do it, let him come and take and appropriate (drink) the Water of Life without cost" (Rev. 22:17).

There follows Christ's personal, *solemn warning* which we mentioned at the beginning of our study on Revelation regarding the prophecies in this book. They are not to be added to, or subtracted from. Then Christ Himself voices *the last promise* in the Bible. It concerns His second advent to the earth:

"Surely I am coming soon." (Rev. 22:20).

He has stated it twice, for emphasis, at the close of John's visions. These are His final words to the church. John replies, "Amen. Even so, come, Lord Jesus!"

And the Book of Endings closes with this benediction:

"The grace (blessing and favor) of the Lord Jesus Christ, the Messiah, be with all the saints—God's holy people (those set apart for God, to be, as it were, exclusively His). Amen—so let it be!" (Rev. 22:21).

Conclusion

How can we adequately summarize the far-reaching prophetic unfoldings which have been disclosed to us through these tremendous visions?

We cannot . . .

They must be read and re-read—studied carefully—if one would fully comprehend what God has revealed within them. Through dreams and visions the Lord has painted vivid pictures of what the future holds for this world—for nations and rulers, as well as for people like you and me.

By this means God unveiled the greatest events that are to take place in the history of man. Events that are soon coming to pass, for we of this generation are living in the end times. Yet centuries ago these future happenings were witnessed in dreams and visions given to Daniel, Ezekiel, Isaiah and others of the Old Testament prophets. And in the New Testament the entire Book of Revelation is one long series of visions previewing things to come.

Are those dreams and visions meaningful and relevant for us today?

Indeed they are! God is still God Almighty. He has not changed. He is the same yesterday, today, and forever. His will and His purpose for mankind still stand—unalterable and eternal. In the past He visited others through dreams and visions in order to make known certain truths. And He visits us in the present as we study the account of those communications.

Why do you think God chose dreams as a method of communication? *What was His objective* in bestowing visions? Couldn't He have spoken to an individual who was wide-awake? . . .

Yes, He could—and many times He did. We saw where the

angel of the Lord appeared "in person" to several individuals while they were awake and going about their business. Yet to others, the angel's appearance was by way of a dream during sleep.

We found that on occasion God would manifest Himself in visible presence, speaking audibly to a fully conscious person. The next time He would impart a message to the same person while the latter was in a deep sleep.

What was the reason for this difference?

The answer lies in the fact that the dream-state has certain advantages. In rest or sleep a person is free from the distractions and activities that occupy him while awake. Sense impressions no longer dominate him. But part of his mind remains conscious, and it will accept without deliberation or examination whatever is placed before it. Thus God can clearly instruct a person while he is sleeping, for the Lord has supreme power over all the faculties of the human mind.

As for visions, it is well-known that one picture is worth ten thousand words. What better medium of revelation is there than a picture, or a drama, enacted before one's very eyes? . . .

Dreams and visions, however, are not restricted to sense perception. While the physical body is limited and confined to the physical world, dreams and visions are not. Through them man has access to another realm of reality above and beyond our material world. In dreams and visions divine knowledge can be imparted. Supernatural experiences can be portrayed. No wonder God chose to visit man this way.

Remember that God is absolutely sovereign and can do anything in whatever manner He chooses. Nothing is impossible with God. Had He deemed another method of contact more desirable or effective, He would have used it.

So much for why God chose dreams and visions. What then was His purpose in bestowing them?

Basically it was this: *to make known His will, and to graphically disclose specific information to mankind.* His messages ranged from simple words of immediate guidance and instruction to panoramic and complex pictures of prophetic revelation.

What about those visions so filled with mysterious symbols,

strange images, and obscure representations? If God's purpose was to reveal, why is His meaning hidden and incomprehensible to the average reader? Many of the visions, like many of the dreams, were unintelligible to their recipients, requiring someone else—even an angel—to interpret them. What was God's reason for doing this? . . .

The obvious explanation is that God *intended* those visions and dreams to be hidden and incomprehensible, for a time at least. The Lord knows what He is doing. His timing is perfect, and He always acts according to design. God deliberately hid those truths from natural man's understanding.

Moreover, the Lord knew that a mystery—a puzzle, something veiled—is infinitely more intriguing to human beings than a plain, self-explanatory fact. And a truth, an insight, a meaning that we must search for, pray about, ponder over, and make an earnest effort to gain is much more highly valued.

* * *

Now that we have touched upon the why and the purpose of God in visiting man through dreams and visions, an important question logically follows: *Does God speak to people today in dreams; does He still give visions?*

Certainly He does. However, it is essential that we make this point very clear: NOT ALL DREAMS AND VISIONS ARE FROM GOD. Almost all of those recorded in the Bible had a divine source. But comparatively few dreams and visions of the average person come from God.

Many of them have a purely physical or human cause. Such things as improper eating, worry, illness, or excessive activity can bring foolish and meaningless dreams. As the scripture puts it:

"For a DREAM comes with much business and painful effort . . ."

"In a multitude of DREAMS there is futility and worthlessness . . ." (Eccl. 5:3, 7).

Every dream or vision comes from one of three sources—divine, human, or satanic. We must use much discernment in examining a dream before we attribute its source to God. Not everything "supernatural" comes from the Lord. Satan is able to present many things to the mind of man when he is asleep, as well as when he is awake.

How can we tell whether a dream is from God or from the devil?

To state it as succinctly as possible—a dream or vision from God will always draw us closer to Him. Anything from Satan will not do this.

If the dream or vision is clear, explicit, distinct—exhibiting goodness, virtue and inspiration—it may be considered to have a divine source. But if it is confused, distorted, disconnected— if it does not contribute to a constructive end, either for oneself or for others—the source of that dream or vision may well be satanic.

Beware of a dream or vision that flatters the ego. Also of one that arouses dread, anxiety, or fear. (We are not speaking of reverential awesome fear, such as Daniel experienced in one of his visions; or of the kind of fear Nebuchadnezzar felt in connection with his dream of the great tree. The fear Satan evokes is not fear of God—but fear that has a torment, causing anguish of mind and body.)

Occult matters, superstition, vulgarity, and irreverence are additional hallmarks of the devil. He is clever enough, however, to include some truth and beauty along with falsehood in order to better deceive his victim.

If a dream contains true knowledge or revelation from God, it will carry its own conviction. It will never conflict with God's written Word. Furthermore, the Holy Spirit will witness to the person's spirit of its authenticity. On the other hand, if a dream is from Satan, it will find no confirmation in the Bible, nor in one's own spirit.

Today an onslaught of satanic deception is being poured out upon the earth. False religious teachings abound. Vast numbers of people are giving heed to the "doctrines of demons and seducing spirits." The Holy Spirit expressly forewarned that this would happen in the latter days (I Tim. 4:1).

Through the widespread use of drugs, increased interest in psychic phenomena, and various occult practices, many are tampering with the supernatural—thus opening themselves to abnormal "spiritual" experiences.

As the rapture of the true church draws near, the full workings of evil spirits will be directed upon the living members of the body of Christ. How can we be sure we are not taken in by false prophecy, or by lying signs and wonders?

There is one sure protection—the test of God's Word. The written Word of God is the only channel of revealed truth in the world. But just to be familiar with pieces of scripture here and there is not sufficient. We must understand what the entire Bible teaches. That is the only safeguard against deception.

We want to know—and we *need* to know—what lies ahead. Even the man-on-the-street is asking with a note of desperation in his voice, *"What is happening to our world?"* Yet God has not left us in the dark. He told us beforehand what would transpire at the close of this age. It's all there in His sacred book, the Holy Bible.

"Do you mean to say that those terrible things depicted in the Book of Revelation are actually going to occur on this earth?" some incredulous person asks as he reads of the severe judgments decreed by God.

The scriptures make it very plain, presenting it in vision form . . .

Tribulation, war, anarchy, famine, disease, pestilence, persecution, earthquakes, disasters coming from the atmosphere, unprecedented demonic activity, moral depravity, violence and bloodshed—all this will befall our planet.

Will we ever have real peace and security?

No . . . not until the Prince of Peace, the Lord Jesus Christ, returns to this earth and establishes His kingdom upon it.

The Bible also gives us a picture—again through visions—of Christ's millennial reign of peace, righteousness, and prosperity. At the end of the thousand years will come the final rebellion, and the ensuing great white throne judgment. Following this, the first heavens and the first earth are destined to undergo a change, being renovated by fire.

Everything will be made new, as we saw in the concluding vision given to the apostle John. How wonderful that the curse upon the earth is to be completely removed, and paradise restored to a more perfect state than before the fall! In the eternal earth there will be no possibility of sin. Man will never again be separated from fellowship with the Lord.

Since God Himself gave these prophetic revelations, and sent an angel to make clear their record, the importance of Biblical dreams and visions cannot be overemphasized. They are of special significance to us today. For with every tick of the clock, we are closer to the time when Christ's last words will be fulfilled:

"Surely I am coming soon."

And we reply with John, "Even so, come, Lord Jesus!"